Cover

Helvetia auf der Reise / Helvetia on her Voyage, as created by Bettina Eichin in 1979/80, is not a heroic representation. She is not defending the country, but has decided to journey throughout Switzerland. Perhaps to see first hand what has transpired in the country during the last 150 years, since she received her position as Mother of the Nation in 1848.

Upon her arrival in Basel, she has interrupted her travels, put down her shield and spear and assumed a contemplative pose from her seated position on the Middle Rhine Bridge. Basel and the Rhine provided the ideal location for her to reflect upon her experiences.

Dear Neil.

Hope to be your guide in Basel.

Kind regards,

Shirley

June 2006

American Women's Club of Basel authors and contributors: Cecily Beard, Jeanie Frankel, Shirley L. Kearney, Simone Littlejohn, Beverly Mar, Margaret Ségal.

Without the original contributions of Mary Caluori and Dr. Hannah Katz to the first edition in 1986, the second would not have been possible.

Special honors to Dr. H. Chr. Ackermann, Dr. U. Barth, Dr. A. Riggenbach, Dr. G. Ségal and Norbert Spichtig for their patience.

The Nuns of Klingental essay contributed by: Barbara and Bob Fiedler.

Supported by Willy A. & Hedwig Bachofen-Henn Foundation
       Family T. & I. Beschle-Rosenberg
       Dreyfus Söhne & Cie AG
       Asahiko and Keiko Isobe, (Tokyo, Japan)
       Irma Sarasin-Imfeld
       Margaret & Georges Ségal
       UBS AG
       VIA MAT Management

Masthead

Basel: A Cultural Experience
Concept, principal author and editor: Shirley L. Kearney
Assistant editor: Margaret Ségal, Basel
Technical and research assistant: Kevin J. Kearney, Basel
Principal photographer and initial layout: Klaus Brodhage, Oberwil
Illustrations: Cornelia Ziegler, Basel & Andy Warhol (Maja Sacher-Stehlin)
Bibliography: Dr. Therese Wollmann, Binningen
Reader: John O'Brien, Basel
Publisher: Spalentor Verlag AG, Basel
First Edition, 2005 (expanded from the 1986 publication)
ISBN 10: 3-908142-23-7
ISBN 13: 978-3-908142-23-2
Cover, typography, realization and production: © Spalentor Verlag AG

Shirley L. Kearney, editor

Basel

A Cultural Experience

Basilisk at the City Hall

CONTENTS

Detail from the Flachslanden tapestry, Basel, c. 1468,

Introduction

Our first impression of Basel was not one of love at first sight. This developed slowly. Uncertainty, a sensation of awe, a strangeness, a disbelief, these were the first emotions. It was too daunting, too different and too foreign. How could the senses handle everything: the new and foreign images, smells, foods and sounds? By looking, watching, sampling and listening, and then giving time for everything to find its place in our world, we slowly began to understand and appreciate each other. It did not happen overnight. After recognizing what our new 'partner' had to offer, and what we could give in return, a give-and-take-relationship developed. Naturally there were the normal ups and downs; the questions, the excitement, the uncertainty, all vying for our energy and soul. It was worth the emotional roller coaster ride, and still is.

Basel may not be a big city, but it has a lot to tell. We need to listen to this small geographical area with its generous heart open to the world. Its history is one of adaptation, energy, fortitude, learning and more; of flexibility, bending when needed, as does the Rhine. Basel is a bridge for and to other countries and their cultures.

The selection of topics and personalities represented in this publication reflects our particular interests in Basel. One of the most difficult aspects of this project was to stop writing. There is so much more to tell; definitely too much to include in this publication. Therefore the selection of Basel's cultural experience must be limited in scope. The goal is to offer a sampling of its past and to give examples of what to experience in the present. Consider the book a compendium of our discoveries. Follow our adage: look up, down and around; listen to the buildings trying to tell their stories. Explore and be receptive. Stroll through the parks, attend a concert, participate in a sports event; the possibilities are waiting for you. Our ABCs tell us to Appreciate Basel Completely.

Shirley L. Kearney, Editor

Foreword

Dear Reader,

Basel lies at the point where Germany, France and Switzerland meet in a tri-national area, right in the heart of Europe. For this reason, over-the-border traffic and a cosmopolitan spirit have characterized our city from time immemorial. Basel is a place where people from all over the world meet. The 'Baslers', the people of Basel, enjoy their city, for it offers everything a big city offers, but within a relatively small space. Yet hospitality looms large in Basel. And so I take a very special delight in the fact that this book about our city was written by a person who was not born here.

As author Shirley Kearney mentions, her relationship to Basel was not 'love at first sight'. For her as an American, our city was at first a place where everything was crowded together into a very small space, where the people spoke a language that was incomprehensible (and un-learnable), where a person, though given a friendly welcome, nevertheless had a feeling of being a stranger. Only gradually did she come to realize the advantages of Basel; she discovered its many museums, she strolled through the old town, admiring the many well-preserved buildings and houses, she was impressed by the numerous fountains and statues, and finally she knew that there was more here than she had first imagined. The more she discovered, the more she felt the desire to make these discoveries accessible to others, making it possible for them as well to have this 'cultural experience'.

Basel's high quality of life is very highly regarded far and wide. The historical old town, the great passion for culture and above all the Rhine as a place for living and recreation are only a few of the features that make our city so unique. The Rhine has played a key role in Basel's history and development. It is therefore only logical to begin a book about Basel with the theme of 'Water'. It is precisely this approach 'from the outside' that makes this book interesting not only to tourists but also for the Baslers themselves.

You are about to find out for yourselves how incredibly much Basel has to offer. On this note I wish you, dear reader, lots of enjoyment in discovering Basel and its many attractions!

Basel, November 2005
Dr. Ralph Lewin, Regierungsrat / Executive Councillor

BASEL AND ITS WATERS

Water has been and continues to be a vital element in Basel's character, history and development. When conjuring up an image of the city, the Rhine immediately comes to mind. But there are other rivers, canals and moats, some still visible, some now covered over, as well as the numerous fountains found throughout Basel, all which lend mystery and sparkle to the city.

Basel's drinking water is taken from groundwater sources in Lange Erlen (a forest and meadow with a small zoo between Basel and Riehen), which is fed from the Wiesental / Black Forest. Additionally, water from the Rhine is pumped to Lange Erlen where it is treated by a sand filter, and further by a natural method using the forest underground as a biological filter. The Hardwasser water-production facility in Pratteln is a complementary source. The best springs from the Pelzmühletal, a picturesque little valley in the rolling hills of the nearby Jura, provide water for *Basler Wasser—IWB's* (the Industrial Services Basel) own bottled and carbonated mineral water.

The Alpine Rhine has two principal headwaters: the Vorderrhein flows from Lake Toma near the Oberalp Pass, and the Hinterrhein originates at the Rheinwaldhorn glaciers west of the San Bernardino Pass; they join at Reichenau near Chur. It then continues approximately 820 miles (1320 km) through—or forms the borders of—five other countries (Liechtenstein, Austria, Germany, France and the Netherlands) before emptying into the North Sea.

In Basel it turns sharply north at what is known as the *Rhein-Knie* (knee, bend or elbow of the Rhine), one of the most difficult points to navigate. The Rhine provides a link to the North Atlantic via the North Sea, and, thanks to the Rhine-Rhône canal, which starts in Alsace, a link to southern waters via the Mediterranean. It is one of the busiest waterways in the world. Basel's four ports—St. Johann, Kleinhüningen (with two basins), Birsfelden and Auhafen—handle around nine million tons of cargo per annum, amounting to approx. 15% of Switzerland's foreign trade. Imports are oil, grain, timber, iron ore, a large variety of other goods and container cargo. Exports are primarily heavy machinery and container cargo. Coal was important until the early 1970s, at which time it was replaced by oil. In 2003 the amount of container cargo reached 71,685 TEU (twenty-foot equivalent unit)—a unit of measurement equivalent to one 20-foot shipping container.

Early Rhine Traffic

To the Celts, the Rhine was called *renos* meaning raging flow. They most certainly chose to build settlements in and near the city because of its location on the river, as did the Romans centuries later.

Romans built docks for their navy along the Rhine Valley, creating an economic boom in the surrounding area. As more and more trading vessels took advantage of the Roman infrastructure, sections of the river evolved into successful trade routes. During the Empire various posts for the collection of duties were established. These tolls constituted a major source of income for the region. With the gradual collapse of the Roman Empire, the shipping industry went into decline; it was not until the Carolingian era (9th/10th centuries) that the river once again became a main artery for commerce. The first mention of commercial shipping in Basel is reportedly by a customs officer at Koblenz in 1209. In the Middle Ages Basel developed into an important trading and transshipment center between northern Europe and Italy, as well as between the Danube basin and the interior of France. With the opening of the St. Gotthard route through the Alps, which coincided with the construction of the *Rheinbrücke* (today the *Mittlere Brücke* / Middle Bridge) in 1225, merchants and pilgrims streamed into Basel. The prosperity of the city depended on the traffic in merchandise from the south, and on pilgrims arriving from the north, crossing the Rhine and continuing their pilgrimage to Rome. Merchandise passed through a *Kaufhaus* / a customs and warehouse—an important source of revenue for the city.

B. Mangold's painting (1910) of the old customs house at the main post office

Editor's note: Basel had three such establishments: the first at Gerbergasse; the second at Freie Strasse (1400s); the third on Steinenberg between the Stadtcasino and Barfüsserkirche, demolished 1873.

During the Middle Ages, boats were constructed for transporting goods and facilitating the pilgrims' return voyage. These boats, the *Lauertannen,* were 'one-way boats'. They could navigate only by following the current in a northerly direction, from Basel to Strasbourg or Cologne. At that time the river did not have a defined bed and tributaries spread out in the so-called *Rheinauen.* After each flood tide the course of the river changed, making navigation even more difficult. Goods were brought to market in Strasbourg or Cologne where the *Lauertannen* were sold or used as scrap-wood.

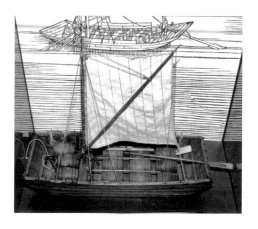

Lauertannen were also used for fishing. Members of the Basel *Zunft zu Fischern* and *Zunft zu Schiffleuten* / guilds of fishermen and sailors, often bought the boats from their colleagues coming from Zurich to Basel. The same 'one-way' problem existed on the Limmat as on the Upper Rhine. Ship building in Basel was more of a craft than an industry—but the *Lauertannen* concept belongs to Basel.

After the discovery of America and the growing importance of the Atlantic ports, the situation changed; the north-to-south direction became more important. Baslers not only lost out on the transshipping revenue from the earlier era, they now had to go to Strasbourg and Cologne to buy goods.

The era of the *Lauertannen* ended in the 18th century.

At the beginning of 19th century, only emigrants with America as their destination used this type of boat in order to reach Rotterdam.

Emigrants departing from Schifflände, 1805

An absolute necessity for all interested in the history of shipping and of the Rhine is a visit to the *Verkehrsdrehscheibe Schweiz und unser Weg zum Meer* / Swiss Shipping Museum. It is a fascinating exhibition space; somewhat off the beaten path, but, on the other hand, ideally situated for its purpose. One can watch the daily work activity, such as moving container cargo, unloading and repacking merchandise, and observe incoming and outgoing ships, before or after a visit to the museum. *See Museums.*

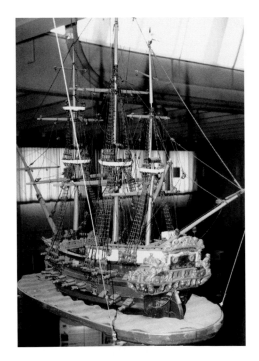

A charming story and exhibit at the museum focuses on a model of the ship, *Dom van Utrecht.* At the age of 14, a Basel citizen Nikolaus von Kilch (1666) went to sea. In 1717, after an absence of 37 years, he returned with a Dutch wife and settled down as a pastry cook.

One year later he approached the city in order to procure citizenship for his wife; his funds were insufficient. He remembered seeing the ship's model at his in-laws' house in Utrecht; he returned, secured it as a gift and promptly offered it to the city in exchange for his wife's citizenship— a happy ending for all.

The Rhine: 19ᵗʰ Century to Today

Numerous toll and tax stations along the Rhine impeded further development of shipping, a common problem along Europe's waterways. In 1815
the Congress of Vienna established the principle of freedom of navigation on
international waterways. The first Convention for Navigation on the Rhine
was signed in 1831 at Mainz by all countries bordering the river. In 1868 the
signatory countries concurred on the *Mannheimer Akte* / Mannheim Accord
(still in force today), which set out the principles for navigation. The accord
is updated periodically to address various issues ranging from the use of
radar to waste disposal and transport of dangerous goods, but without modifications to the basic principles. It is of particular importance to Switzerland as
it allows full rights of passage on the entire Rhine system. Shipping from Basel
is the only fully guaranteed means of international transport. The main points
of the Mannheim Accord, which apply to the entire course of the navigable
Rhine, are:

- All registered ships are granted unimpeded travel.
- All laws and regulations governing policing, safety and operations are
  identical and uniformly applied.
- Any person who erects an obstacle to navigation, such as a power station,
  must provide a bypass free of charge.

An example of the importance of direct waterway access from Basel to the
North Sea, was the selection of the city in 1830 by President Andrew Jackson
of the United States to be the site for the first US representation in Switzerland—the eighth in a foreign country. A commemorative plaque (1961)
placed through the initiative of the American Women's Club of Basel citing
this event, is at Elisabethenstrasse near Bankenplatz.

In 1832 the first steamboat arrived in Basel.

In the last decades of the 19ᵗʰ century
the Rhine was a quietly flowing river.
Occasionally fishing boats floated
by. The lively river traffic of goods,
travelers and pilgrims of the past was
forgotten. With the arrival of the railways in the mid-1800s, the river was
ignored as a primary means of transportation.

Johann Tulla (1770-1828), a German engineer, was working as a colonel in the service of the French in the early 1800s. He raised the idea of modifying the river between Strasbourg and Basel by digging out a defined and much deeper riverbed. This correction, the *Tulla'sche Rheinkorrektion*, was undertaken between 1816 and 1868. At this time the numerous inlets of the Rhine disappeared. Motorized navigation (steamboats) was already in use on parts of the river.

The old Middle Bridge as seen from Rheinsprung, 1858

Thanks to the gifted Basel engineer Rudolf Gelpke, the first major motorized transport between Strasbourg and Basel materialized in 1904 with a steamboat and barge loaded with 300 tons of Ruhr coal. This proved that the waterway between Strasbourg and Basel was suitable for the commercial transport of goods. Each succeeding year witnessed an increase in the number of barges to reach the city.

Today the pioneering feat of Rudolf Gelpke is acknowledged as the beginning of commercial navigation on the *Oberrhein* / Upper Rhine. With the enthusiastic support of Prof. Dr. Paul Speiser, a cantonal and national counselor, the *Verein Schweizerische Rheinschiffahrt* / Society for Swiss Rhine Shipping was founded. Dr. Speiser became president of the new company.

He campaigned tirelessly for an increase in traffic on the river. In 2004 the *Verkehrsdrehscheibe Schweiz und unser Weg zum Meer* / Shipping Museum celebrated the 100th anniversary of Gelpke's and Speiser's notable achievements.

In 1926 Basel celebrated the transshipping of goods from the city to Antwerp and Rotterdam with a festival at the Cathedral, complete with a boat in the middle of the square.

A direct Basel-London cargo service opened in 1936. This successful venture could also be attributed to the construction of the necessary docking facilities, the first built at St. Johann, with others following in rapid succession. As sufficient storage space was not available within the city limits, a decision was taken in 1937 to build another harbor upstream at Birsfelden. An indication of the international status of Basel-Rhine traffic is the number of boats and barges flying foreign flags.

The waterworks and locks at Kembs, France, which include a barrage and

hydraulic power station, went into operation in 1932. During WW II they were damaged, nationalized in 1946 and modernized between 1996 and 1999; Switzerland financed 60% of the cost.

The locks are 'on the far side' of the Basel harbor. The keepers of the locks had the dubious honor of recovering bodies of people and animals who met their fate in the swirling waters of the Rhine. The model for Holbein's painting of the *Dead Christ* in the Kunstmuseum Basel supposedly was 'fished' from the river.

The Rhine was once the most important and largest source of salmon in Europe. Fish was a staple of the Celts' and Romans' diet. Over time, modifications to their habitat, over-fishing and pollution reduced the fish population. When the locks were built, fish ladders were installed to help the fish swim the 12-meter difference between the Rhine and the Grand Canal d'Alsace in order to reach their spawning grounds upstream. Fishing cabins were part of the scene. At Kleinhüningen, a fisherman's house with stable (1764) has been restored.

Fisherman's house at Kleinhüningen before restoration

At various times during WW II shipping came to a standstill. Both the Allies and Germany accused Switzerland of supporting the other side. A comment from Winston Churchill shows his understanding of the situation: "Of all the neutrals Switzerland has the greatest right to distinction. She has been the sole international force linking the hideously sundered nations and ourselves."

The need to establish Swiss maritime law became evident; the provisional Federal Maritime Law went into effect in 1941.

As early as the late-19th century plans were discussed to build a power plant at Birsfelden. It was not until WW II, when electrical energy was scarce, that concrete plans were put forth to build such a facility. The project submitted by Hans Hofmann in 1947 was accepted; it marked a turning point in industrial architecture. The Kraftwerk Birsfelden AG went into production in 1953.

The construction of the Birsfelden hydropower plant and the inauguration of the two locks opened the Rhine to larger vessels and paved the way for the expansion of the Basel-Landschaft ports and their docking facilities. Since their construction, which took place between 1937 and 1940, the Auhafen and Birsfelden ports have been enlarged several times. The transshipping facilities are of key economic importance as they allow access to Switzerland's major transport arteries, as well as to the Rhine.

As previously mentioned, one condition for the construction of a hydropower plant was that the requisite shipping facilities, i.e., locks, be built at the same time. To this day, the Kraftwerk Birsfelden AG is bound to guarantee free passage of Rhine shipping between Basel and Augst as stipulated in the Mannheim Accord.

The plant generates power for households, trade and industry; it is a well-known landmark. Hydropower, which accounts for approx. 55% of the country's total power production, is Switzerland's most important energy source.

There are five major shipping companies operating in Basel and western Switzerland. In 2005, 22 seagoing vessels fly the Swiss flag; approx. 230 Swiss-owned seagoing cargo ships, however, navigate under several other flags. The crews on these ships are mainly Croatians and Filipinos; fewer than 10% are Swiss. With the Rhine as Switzerland's umbilical cord to the sea, it follows that the Swiss Maritime Navigation Office has its headquarters in Basel.

Leisurely Life on the Rhine

Old bathing stations exist at St. Johann and the Breite. Basel children who learned to swim during the 1940s at the former bathing station below the *Münsterpfalz* / Cathedral Terrace remember being lowered into the river on a harness. Following the mores of the time, the men's area was closer to the Middle Bridge, while the women's area was further up towards the Wettstein Bridge.

For centuries men have poled their boats—the Lauertannen—up and floated down the Rhine. It was a method of transporting goods and people; today it is a sport known as *Weidlig-Fahren* and can be observed as participants compete in a tandem course. The same type of boat is shown in Konrad Witz's painting of *St. Christopher with the Christ Child* at the Kunstmuseum Basel.

The *Fähri* / ferryboats provide transportation from one side of the river to the other at four different locations: St. Alban, the Münster, Klingental and St. Johann. By 1854 the town had grown—the one existing bridge could not handle the increased demands. The first *Fähri* appeared. It was an easier, shorter and more exciting way to cross the river; the ferries affectionately became known as the *Fliegende Brücken* / flying bridges. The charming boats, attached to cables stretched high above the river, powered by the flow of the Rhine and directed by a rudder, are part of Basel's uniqueness—and the use of its waters.

The annual summer *Rhyschwimme* / Rhine swim attracts more and more participants every year. Thousands of happy souls enjoy a different view of the city while making their way down the river. A recent innovation, the *Kulturfloss* (a raft moored near the Middle Bridge), presents various cultural events.

Boats leave from Schifflände for various destinations, e.g., Dreiländereck to explore the port and the Shipping Museum, Rheinfelden to relax at the spa, or Augst to visit the excavations and museum at the former Roman city. Meals and other excursions are on offer; special events and outings can be booked; temporary exhibits on ships take place from time to time. International cruise ships dock at St. Johann.

The Basilisk also bicycles

Tours of the hydroelectric facilities and locks at Birsfelden and Kembs are an educational and pleasant way to spend time along the Rhine.

Walking or bicycling along certain stretches of the river is a must. One particularly attractive stretch is the Solitude Park near the Tinguely Museum. Another favorite on a sunny winter's day—or for sunbathing in the heat of summer—is from the Wettsteinbrücke to the Johanniterbrücke. The paths are for our delectation.

A new promenade will be part of the revitalization of the Voltaplatz / St. Johann port area.

The Other Waters

In medieval times fortification moats were a normal part of city planning. Broad streets, squares or parks now stand where the city walls and moats once stood. The word *Graben* translates to moat or ditch (e.g., *Aeschengraben, Petersgraben*). The best remaining example of this planning is in the St. Alban-Tal, where parts of the city wall and moat are visible. *See Architecture.*

Former Spalengraben with deer

St. Alban-Tal today

Models of the city and of the Klingental Convent complex indicating the open waters and moats are on display at the Museum Kleines Klingental; they offer an authentic impression of the fortified medieval city.

One must imagine Basel and the surrounding countryside dotted with moated castles built between the 13th and 15th centuries. Three such castles existed on the Gundeldinger plain. Schloss Binningen had a moat, as did castles in Benken, Pratteln and Therwil. Schloss Wildenstein, situated on a hill above Bubendorf, had a waterless ditch for protection. During droughts, farmers' demands for water rights

Schloss Wildenstein

from the castle owners were generally refused; the moats were too shallow and what water filled the ditches was needed to help stave off any intrusion.

One of most significant moated castles in Switzerland is Schloss Bottmingen, now a historical restaurant. In the Middle Ages it had four towers; one was removed during the 1720 restoration and replaced with an open terrace. Traces of the numerous building periods are visible today.

The rivers Birsig, Birs and Wiese flow into the Rhine. The Birsig is the smallest with its source above Burg in Leimental in the Blauen mountain range; it meanders through parts of France and Basel-Landschaft before emptying into the Rhine at Schifflände. The Birs originates in the Jura and empties into the Rhine at Birsfelden. The Wiese has its source in the Black Forest; it flows through Lörrach and Riehen and empties into the Rhine at Kleinhüningen.

The Birsig River ran openly through a heavily populated area until partially covered over, first at Falknerstrasse in 1899 and later at Heuwaage and Barfüsserplatz in the 1950s and 1960s. There were few mills; household waste was dumped directly into its water, creating a breeding ground for cholera and typhoid epidemics. It comes into the city near the Zoo and then goes underground, running beneath Heuwaage, Barfüsserplatz and Falknerstrasse, before emptying into the Rhine at the Middle Bridge. There are historical references to a hammer and a hemp mill at the Rümelinsplatz powered by the water of the Rümelinbach, before it flowed into the Birsig.

The former open Birsig River, Falknerstrasse

A few other Basel waters are the streams:Aubach, Bettingerbach, Immenbach and the former industrial canals of Albanteich, Riehenteich, Dorenbach and Otterbach. Some of these waters, because of safety—and the need for parking places—are now underground.

Thanks to the plentiful water supply, 15 flour, saw and hammer mills (operating with a hammer-type function) dotted the St.Alban-Tal. Ten of these mills were converted into paper mills; the first established in 1433 by the Cluniac monks at the St.Alban Monastery. This development was undoubtedly a result of the high consumption of expensive parchment used during the Church Council (1431/48). The monks not only operated the mill, but they recorded the Council meetings and paper simplified their task.

One can still get an idea of an earlier Basel near the *Museum für Gegenwartskunst* / Contemporary Art Museum and the Paper Mill Museum where the Albanteich canals were diverted from the Birs River for industrial use. The *Gallizian Mühle* / the Gallician Mill, a flourmill, which until 1428 belonged to the Klingental Convent, was converted into a hammer mill, and in 1453 into a paper mill. In 1788 the manufacturing part of the building was replaced; in 1850 a tobacco firm bought the building. Until its restoration and the installation of the Museum in 1980, it served as a warehouse. The neighboring Stegreif Mill produced paper until 1924. It now houses the administration of the Museum and the Café Papiermühle.

Even more mills—in 1823 they numbered 26—lined the Riehenteich: a system of canals diverted from the Wiese River, which flowed through Kleinbasel emptying twice into the Rhine at the 'Kaserne Klingental area' and powering the mills. In 1923 the open canals were covered over; one runs directly under Teichgässlein. These mills were the genesis of Basel's industries.

Owners of wine cellars in Basel are well aware of the hidden rivers, supplying the necessary dampness and near perfect climate 'under' which to age their wines.

Leisurely Life along the Other Waters

Walking or bicycling along the waters of Basel is a pleasant way to experience their historical and natural importance. Paths are sign-posted. It is possible to go from Basel to Germany along the Wiese; from Basel to France along the small Huningue canal, passing by the waterworks at Kembs and on to the Rhine Canal; along the Birs, which marks the border between *Basel-Stadt* / city and *Basel-Landschaft* / country; and along sections of the Birsig.

Basel and its Bridges

The Middle Rhine Bridge

A significant development for Basel and the Rhine occurred in 1225 when, under the leadership of Bishop Heinrich II von Thun, the *Rheinbrücke*, today's *Mittlere Brücke* / Middle Bridge was constructed. This solidly built bridge facilitated east-west traffic, revived river commerce, and brought additional income to the city in the form of bridge tolls. Basel's status went from 'a city on the banks of the Rhine' to that of being 'mistress of the river'. Kleinbasel originally developed as a stronghold for the bridge; it encompassed the area up to Claraplatz, to the Klingental Convent and to St. Theodore's Church; its courthouse was located at the present-day Café Spitz. It remained under control of the Habsburgs and later passed to the diocese of Constance.

The bridge supports were made of two different materials: wood on the left bank *(Grossbasel)* and stone on the right bank *(Kleinbasel)*; a chapel was built in the middle providing structural support. A plausible reason for the

two materials is that it was only feasible to drive wooden pilings into the deeper riverbed on the city side, and, for defense purposes, wood facilitated its dismantling and reassembling.

The original bridge stood for almost 700 years. Streetcars, introduced in 1895, ran from the main train station over the bridge to the German station. In the early 1900s a competition was held and 28 designs were submitted. The Munich architect, Friedrich von Thiersch, and his Basel associate, Emil Faesch, won the contract. During the construction of the bridge, a temporary wooden structure with tram tracks accommodated the streetcars. The new structure has a cement core with a veneer of granite from Ticino; it is a rendering of the old bridge.

Other Bridges
Other bridges in Basel, beginning at Birsfelden and continuing downstream are:
Eisenbahnbrücke / railroad bridge: built in 1873; rebuilt in 1960/62.
Schwarzwaldbrücke: 10-lane raised motorway built in 1972.
Wettsteinbrücke: original bridge designed in 1877/79 by the architects and engineers Johannes Merian and W. Launer. Enlarged in 1936/37 at which time the four original bronze Basilisks, once decorating pillars on both sides of the bridge, were removed; one has returned; today's bridge was built in 1991/95.

Wettstein Bridge, postcard c.1900

Johanniterbrücke: designed and built in 1879/82 by the same team who built the Wettsteinbrücke; rebuilt in 1964/67.

Dreirosenbrücke: built in 1931/34; completely rebuilt 1999/2004 as a two-level steel and concrete bridge.

Changes to the Environment of the Rhine

The Romans inflicted the first environmental damage to the river by clearing wooded areas along its banks and tributaries to build settlements. This practice continued and intensified during the Middle Ages. Additionally, fishing and hunting increased, and the first mills and dams appeared in the Rhine tributaries. A marked decline of fish and fowl in and along the river, already noted in the 1400s, resulted in the Strasbourg Regulations on Fishing in the Rhine of 1449. This is the first documented evidence of the ongoing struggle between use and abuse of the river.

The never-ending increase in settlements and industries created complex environmental problems. Altering the course of the Rhine throughout the years resulted in an overall shortening of the river by approximately 105 kilometers, augmenting the risks of flooding.

Because of these concerns, in 1950, Switzerland, France, Luxembourg, Germany and the Netherlands created the International Commission for the Protection of the Rhine (ICPR) to serve as a common forum for the protection and management of the river. Its goals, however, were not met. Basel was already the site of companies in the chemical, food, textile and metal-processing industries, all bordering the Rhine; French limestone and salt mines dumped their waste directly into the river.

In 1986 a warehouse full of pesticides at Schweizerhalle caught fire. The water used by the firefighters to extinguish the blaze washed an indeterminable amount of chemicals into the Rhine. The river turned bright red—thousands of fish died; the water became polluted. People who were in Basel at the time remember the sickly-sweet smell similar to that of burning mushrooms.

Public outrage over the Schweizerhalle disaster spurred the ICPR member nations to form the Rhine Action Program setting forth four main objectives: to protect the supply of drinking water; to re-introduce fish species such as salmon, pike, perch and rainbow trout; to purify sediments; and to implement laws safeguarding the ecology of the North Sea. Due to major recovery and sanitation efforts, the river was already on the way to rehabilitation in 1988.

Basel is now sending reasonably clean water to its downstream neighbors. As a direct result, pike, perch, spotted carp and salmon once again populate the river. Through international cooperation, the river is an ecologically sound habitat. People are back swimming in the river, undeterred by the dramatic changes since the Celts and Romans discovered its beauty and value. One can almost hear the refrain of Johann Peter Hebel's, *z'Basel am mim Rhy.*

FOUNTAINS

Some of the more than 170 public *Brunnen* / fountains in Basel, chosen at random, convey a variety of architecture, themes and history—and afford yet another use of Basel's waters. Many of the original figures are in the Historisches Museum Basel. The *Industrielle Werke Basel* / Industrial Services Basel provides the water and maintenance of the fountains—the water is drinkable. Fountains gracing the city were already mentioned by Aeneas Silvius Piccolomini at the time of the Church Council of Basel (1431/48).

Affe: 1867. Andreasplatz, once the location of the domestic animal market. A monkey sits perched on a short column in the fountain. He is sporting a doublet and hat, is eating an orange and holds a bunch of grapes. The theme harks back to a 14th-century sculpture. The stone figure is from a dismantled fountain once near Bankenplatz. (A monkey fountain is also in the courtyard of the Antikenmuseum Basel. It is a copy of the Andreasplatz fountain; however, the monkey is not enjoying the fruits of the market).

Editor's note: The foundation of an 11th-century chapel is outlined in contrasting red brick on the pavement in the square.

Augustiner: 1530. Where Augustinerstrasse, Martinsgasse and Rheinsprung intersect. First mentioned in 1468 as a wooden fountain, it stood in the middle of the street until moved to the side in 1846. A Basilisk clutching Basel's coat of arms with its talons adorns the Corinthian column.

Basilisk: A competition was held in 1884 to design a theme for 'sidewalk fountains'; the Basilisk won. Wilhelm Bubeck (1850-1891) received the commission. Cast in the late 1800s, of the 50 examples made about half still exist. With a revival in the popularity of the Basilisk, more fountains are apt to appear.

***Caritas* / Charity:** 1677. Theodorskirchplatz, in the courtyard of the *Waisenhaus* (former Carthusian monastery and later orphanage). Baroque design with Charity, the good mother, holding and protecting her three children.

Elisabethen: 1862. Elisabethenstrasse / Klosterberg. Neo-Gothic design with two water basins decorated with period motifs. The Saint stands on a pedestal, under which are two bronze swans from whose beaks water flows into the basin. The lower trough fills via two spouts in the form of dolphins. The design by Heinrich Rudolf Meili (1827-1882) of Binningen is likely after the 'St. Sebastian Altarpiece' by Hans Holbein the Younger, which depicts Saints Barbara and Elizabeth von Thüringen, today preserved in the *Alte Pinakothek* / Old Masters Museum in Münich.

***Faule Magd* / Lazy Maiden:** c. 1675. St. Johanns-Vorstadt 34. The figure is contemporary to that of Charity on the Caritas Fountain (1677). The maiden assumes a rather coquettish pose; she originally stood on top of another fountain column at a different location; she arrived at her present site around 1861.

Fischmarkt / **Fish Market:** c.1390. A charming design with angels, prophets, various figures, fruits and vegetables all worked together in a lacy and elegant pattern. The statues of the Virgin Mary, SS. Peter and John the Evangelist are on the three-sided pedestal; St. Agnes with lamb, St. Barbara with tower and St. Catherine with broken wheel are represented on the slender upper columns. The main column is attributed to Johannes Parler and family, stonemasons from Gmünd, Germany; they also planned the reconstruction of the Cathedral choir after the earthquake of 1356. Reworked in 1468/80; re-gilded and cleaned several times, it is considered by specialists to be the most beautiful Gothic fountain in Switzerland.

Flora: In the courtyard of the Music Academy. The lions' heads from which the waters flow, bundles of fruit intertwined with laurel leaves and the Corinthian capital hint of the Renaissance style. Who did the work and whether the column and figure of Flora, the Roman goddess of springtime, were originally meant to be joined together, remains unclear.

Gelpke: 1946. *Kleinhüningen* / the Rhine port. A simple trough filled with a monumental figurehead—a tribute to Rudolf Gelpke who engineered the opening of the Upper Rhine for traffic into Basel. By Willy Hege (1907-1976).

Holbein: c.1550. Spalenvorstadt / Schützenmattstrasse. The lower section of the column replicates the *Bauerntanz* / Peasants' Dance of Hans Holbein the Younger with men and women dressed in period clothing engaged in the

two-step; botanical motifs and bulls' skulls decorate the next section; it culminates with a Corinthian capital and the figure of a bagpiper who appears to be tapping his foot while playing his tune. Inspiration derived from a 1514 engraving by Albrecht Dürer (1471-1528) who spent some time in Basel.

Nische / **Niche:** 1839. Spalenberg / opposite Rosshofgasse. A rectangular recessed fountain supported by two columns is the largest such fountain in Basel. In 1921 the artist Numa Donzé (1885-1952) painted the three walls illustrating the story of John the Baptist.

Pisoni: 1784/85. Münsterplatz. Two previous fountains were at this location. Over time weather took its toll and in 1782 a new fountain was deemed necessary. Paolo Antonio Pisoni (1738-1804) from Ascona won the commission. Water still flows from the original pipes, which protrude from the mouths of whimsical heads, splashing into the classical Louis XVI basin.

Rebhaus: first half 1600s. Riehentorstrasse, Kleinbasel in front of the Honorable Society Rebhaus's Restaurant. A late-Renaissance design of painted red sandstone. The lower portion with four niches contains figures of the musical Muses. This is topped off with decorative motifs and a Corinthian capital, atop which sits a lion holding the coat of arms of the society in its paws.

Samson and Delilah: 1600s, late Renaissance. On a tall pillar at Barfüsserplatz. First made in wood, later in stone, the present group of figures is cast

in plaster. The figures are clothed in the style of the 1600s and Delilah is concentrating on doing a thorough job of trimming Samson's hair while he sleeps. Location has changed several times; in 1875 the two figures were placed in the present basin.

Schmiedenhof: 1650. Accessible from Gerbergasse or Rümelinsplatz. A wall-fountain with the figure of Neptune, offered at the time by the *Zunft zu Schmieden* / Blacksmiths' Guild. A muscular Neptune poses with the tail of a dolphin in his hands, while his left foot pushes down on its head from which water spurts.

Sevogel or Warrior: 1547. Martinskirchplatz, by Hans Dobel. Figure of a warrior referred to as Henman Sevogel, leader of the Basel garrison at Liestal in the 1444 Battle of St. Jakob-on-the-Birs. Originally located at *Kornmarkt*, i.e., Marktplatz. When parts of the Birsig River were covered over in 1899 it was moved into the Historisches Museum Basel where it remained until relocated to its present location.

Stachelschützen / **Crossbow archers:** 1863. Petersplatz / Spalengraben. The 1615 'birds-eye' plan of the city by Matthäus Merian shows a fountain already at this location. Another fountain with the figure of Mars was its replacement in 1676. In 1847 Heinrich Rudolf Meili (1827-1882) received the commission

for a new fountain. Some regard the figure on the column as the personification of William Tell, Switzerland's legendary hero.

Tinguely / *Fasnachtsbrunnen:* 1977. Created by the artist Jean Tinguely who spent much of his life in Basel. This kinetic fountain, located in front of Basel's Theater and the garden of the Kunsthalle Restaurant, is a popular meeting place. During the winter, the fountain turns into an ice sculpture. In the summer, ducks paddle between the moving parts.

Urban: 1448. Blumenrain between the Three Kings Hotel and the Seidenhof. Painted red sandstone Gothic fountain with the figure of Pope Urban I, regarded since the Middle Ages as one of the patron saints of wine growers (another being St. Vincent) and gardeners.

Wettstein: 1953. Between Wettsteinplatz and the Rhine near Theodorskirchplatz. A sculpture of Johann Rudolf Wettstein (1594-1666, statesman) by Alexander Zschokke.

Zschokke: 1941. Located near the Kunstmuseum Basel. A contemporary interpretation derived from Zschokke's interest in Roman art; a monumental composition, reminiscent of a Roman sarcophagus in the round. The three upper figures represent the three ages of man.

Woodcut of Basilisk holding the Basel coat of arms, 1511

A JOURNEY THROUGH THE HISTORY OF BASEL

Our history begins with the Celts, as they are a vital part of Basel's cultural experience.

The Celts

The name *Keltoi* / Celt was first used in the 6th century BC by Greek historians to denote a great barbarian people widespread in transalpine Europe and in the Iberian Peninsula sometime between 800 and 500 BC. In the 4th and 3rd centuries BC the northern tribes expanded into Italy and the Balkans. Around the 2nd century the word *Galli* was used by the Romans to identify these people. The Celts consisted of numerous interrelated tribes, who apparently lived up to the meaning of the word 'barbarian'—energetic, quick-tempered and bellicose.

The power and ability of these peoples – which led to fear and awe from the Greeks (to the Greeks anyone who did not speak Greek was a barbarian) and the Romans—resulted in descriptions and stories, all for our benefit, as the Celts left no written records.

As early as the 6th century BC, they controlled the trade routes along the Rhône, Saône, Rhine and the Danube; they imported Greek luxury items, mainly bronze and pottery vessels for drinking wine, many of which have been found in the chieftains' graves in southwest Germany, parts of Burgundy and Switzerland.

What were these people like? According to ancient sources, the Celtic warrior class was remarkably tall, muscular, and fair-skinned with thick, shaggy hair. Their clothing was made of coarse linen or wool, bright colors were the preference. Decoration and color were important. High-spirited, with a weakness for war and entertainment, they were hospitable and fond of feasting and drinking; music was prized; their aesthetic qualities are visible in their art. Their overriding characteristic is one of immense energy.

Their unique culture and art was the coming together of diverse styles, cultures and decorations. Celtic artistry was both original and exciting. Improving upon the technique of extracting and smelting ore, they were able to cultivate their fields with improved implements, produce finer crafts, and forge better weapons.

Decapitation of their enemies was a normal ritual, as they believed the soul rested in the head; by possessing these heads, they could control that person and their spirit. The 'heads' even became treasured heirlooms.

Offerings made at rivers and springs reflected their belief in reciprocity—if something is gained, something must be given back. After a victory, weapons and offerings were thrown into lakes and rivers.

They lived within an established social structure of workers, warriors, druids and slaves. This arrangement was typical of the late La Tène period. To what degree slaves were engaged is not clear. However, reliable proof shows that slave trade existed.

Before the Romans conquered most of Europe, Celtic settlements were already established in the British Isles, central Europe, northern Italy, western Spain and Turkey.

One could say that the Celtic culture is a primary element in the foundation of European culture.

The Celtic Settlements in Switzerland

La Tène Culture (the Late Iron Age c. 450–20 BC) is the classification given by archaeologists to denote the changing cultural patterns in Europe at that time. It is based on the finds at La Tène near the Lake of Neuchâtel.

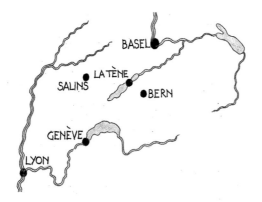

When the course of the nearby river Thiele / Zihl was altered in 1854, the level of Lake Neuchâtel fell by two meters. Remains of wooden bridge supports in their original location, along with numerous other wooden timbers, votive offerings in various materials, skeletons and separate human bones, were exposed on the muddy riverbed.

Editor's note: On the shore, remains of wooden constructions surfaced. At the time a 'romantic' interpretation of Pfahlbauten / dwellings built in the water captured the imagination of the Swiss. The Pfahlbauten, however, are characteristic of the Neolithic and Bronze Ages and they were built along the lakeshore, not in the water.

Excavations were carried out c.1880 and between 1907 and 1918. Over 2,000 Iron Age objects, including swords in their decorated sheaths, spears, tools of all kinds, coins and many more items were recovered. These treasures of remarkable quality belong to an advanced Celtic culture. The area excavated may have been a holy sanctuary or an offering site used to placate the gods. Some researchers are of the opinion that it was a domestic and industrial settlement on dry land, suddenly destroyed by flooding. These treasures are now disbursed in the Swiss National Museum in Zurich, the Latènium Museum in Neuchâtel, the Muscum Schwab in Bienne / Biel and in museums throughout the world.

The Celts in Basel

The *Rauraci* was but one Celtic tribe living on Swiss territory; others had settled in the region and four known tribes were in the Valais. *Helvetii* is the umbrella classification of these various tribes. The Rauraci were previously believed to have occupied the left bank of the Rhine near today's Dreirosenbrücke; whether they were the occupants is no longer certain. Recent research dates the first dwellings at c. 150–80 BC. Archaeologists unearthed this settlement in 1911 when the local gasworks were built; thereafter the site is referred to as the *Basel-Gasfabrik*.

Celtic vase (c.150 BC), Gasfabrik, Basel

In 1988 this Celtic settlement entered into the cultural inventory of the Federation; shortly thereafter, Basel decided to build a highway at this location. Under contract to the city government, the cantonal archaeologists excavated and documented all traces of the settlement. Material evidence has brought to light the evolution of the early Celtic region north of the Alps, to which this site belonged.

Today, the excavation area of the Celtic settlement of 2100 years ago lies in the lower stratum of the Basel highway, the *Nordtangente.* In May 2004 the majority of the excavations closed down; archaeological work continued at the Novartis Campus area.

Using computer-aided design in conjunction with the latest excavation methods, all finds and traces of the settlement can be reconstructed virtually.

The approximately 150,000 m² open settlement some 12 meters above the Rhine needed no further protection. Excavations revealed carefully laid out areas that were accessible through a network of roads. Inside this grid, clusters of simple houses of wood and mud were set in a mixed pattern. The walls were whitewashed and most likely painted. Provisions were stored in earthen cellars; the seeds and corn wintered in giant underground silos. Further pits served as water sources and fountains, or for craft and handiwork purposes. All were held communally and when no longer used were filled with rubble. Occasionally, the dead or sacrificial offerings were buried within. More than 350 *Gruben* / pits of various sizes were discovered by the year 2000.

In addition to bone carvings and pottery workshops, evidence of forges, bronze-casting, minting of coins, glass works, including a considerable amount of glass jewelry in clear and vibrant colors, were unearthed. In some areas, living quarters and workshops were side by side; a ceramic quarter was at the southern section of the settlement.

Luxury goods were imported from the Mediterranean, ceramics from middle Europe and amber from the Baltic Sea. Trade was carried on via the rivers and over land.

The culture of the dead is apparent at the site. Objects for the after-life have been found in burial areas; on the northern side of the settlement, traces of 120 individuals were found buried in a cemetery. Dismembered body parts were found in various locations.

The cantonal archaeologists and other specialists worked fervently to bring to light—and to fit together—pieces of the Celtic puzzle. During the excavations, vestiges of earlier (Bronze Age) and later habitations were uncovered.

In a certain sense, the settlement at the *Basel-Gasfabrik / Nordtangente* marks the beginning of the development of the region, which led to present-day Basel.

It was previously believed that in c.58 BC, the settlement came under pressure from outside forces and the occupants fled. During the recent excavations, however, a date of 80 BC emerged as the latest date of habitation. The settlement was systematically 'closed down'—all the *Gruben* / pits were filled in. There were no signs of a mass destruction, or of any attack. It is unclear what provoked the desertion. Perhaps changes in the economic, political or social structure took place; maybe smaller settlements were more desirable. Presently, all is hypothetical.

The Celtic tribes attempted to move westwards, perhaps in search of more land. In 58 BC they came into contact with Caesar's troops at Bibracte, near today's Autun in France. The Celts were well equipped with shields, spears and body armor, but Roman military strategy proved superior; Caesar ordered them to return home.

The Rauraci territory then legally belonged to the Romans. There are reasons to believe that the settlement and fortification at the Cathedral Square could have been under Roman authority at an earlier date.

It was at this time the Celts built their *oppidum* on the Cathedral Hill. Current opinion is that the date could have been earlier or even marginally later than previously believed. In view of the fact that the Celts did not record their history, and to paraphrase René Teuteberg in his *'Basler Geschichte'*—the *Boden* (earth) must serve as our *Buch* (book).

Editor's note: Excavations in front of the Rollerhof in the Cathedral Square revealed late Celtic and early Roman traces of habitation and burial places.

A moat, as well as a stone and wooden wall some 12-meters wide, protected the oppidum. This was the Celtic fortification—the Murus Gallicus.

The Celts were the architects of Basel's 'first' city wall; a Bronze Age fortification, however, once stood on the Cathedral Hill. A straight 10 meter-wide main Celtic road made of lime mortar followed the line of Rittergasse and Augustinergasse, that is, across the square. It was located two meters below today's street. Traces of this road were discovered during the restoration of the Cathedral in 1974 and further traces continue to surface, the last in 2002/3. Explanation panels and vestiges of the settlement are at Rittergasse 4.

Vercingetorix

Editor's note: The final attempt to contain the Romans in 52 BC at Alesia, near present-day Dijon, was under the leadership of the Celtic chieftain Vercingetorix. After several sieges with brutal consequences, the Gauls (the Celts in France) gave up. Vercingetorix, forced to surrender to the Romans, was sent to Rome where he was imprisoned for five years before being publicly beheaded in 46 BC. A monument by Bartholdi is in Clermont-Ferrand, France; a model of the monument is in the Bartholdi Museum in Colmar (his birthplace).

A new chapter in Basel's early history opens with the Roman occupation and their military fortifications, while at Augst they were building a large city —Augusta Raurica.

The Romans and the Alemanni

An early presence of Roman military in the neighboring area occurred c.58 BC at the time of Julius Caesar's victory in Alsace against the Germanic leader, Ariovistus. Germanic tribes were pushing southwards and the Romans realized that the Rhine formed a useful geographic barrier for offensive as well as defensive purposes. In c.44 BC a colony was founded in the region (Basel or Augst) under the leadership of Lucius Munatius Plancus, Caesar's legate in Gaul. Plancus's Renaissance statue is in the courtyard of the *Rathaus* / City Hall.

About 20 BC Roman soldiers launched a heavy attack towards the Rhine. The Cathedral Hill came under Roman influence and served for the stationing of troops. The Murus Gallicus, no longer used, fell to ruin. This convenient and strategic location was used as a supply center for the advancing Roman troops.

The native Rauraci accepted the presence and strength of the Roman troops and gradually adopted the Roman way of life, learning and adding vernacular Latin to their colloquial speech.

Augusta Raurica is the largest excavated Roman settlement in Switzerland. Due to its position on the Rhine, it was of great strategic and economic importance.

Some 1800 years ago, a fluctuating population of between 10 and 20,000 people lived in Augusta Raurica, a flourishing colony, which at its peak did not have protective walls. Now-

Munatius Plancus, Rathaus

adays the open-air complex offers over 20 areas of historical interest. For example, the best preserved theater north of the Alps—currently being restored after too many attempts at quick restorations—a replica of a Roman house, a Roman animal park, several temples, a walk through 500 years of history. Discovered during excavations in 1997/98, is a bathhouse with an underground well house that had not been entered for 1700 years.

Underground well house, Augst

The museum houses the Kaiseraugst Silver Treasure: coins, cutlery, decorated platters and bowls from the turbulent period 294 to 350 AD. Recovery of these objects occurred during building excavation for a school in 1961/62. Ownership of some items changed hands several times, as evidenced by the number of different names scratched into the silver. The name Marcellianus, a Roman officer, appears on thirteen pieces. The owners of the treasure buried it in a wooden chest inside the fort. In the ensuing confusion, neither the owners nor their helpers recovered the treasure.

Kaiseraugst Silver Treasure

The Alemanni, an amalgamation of Germanic tribes, repeatedly attempted to move into Helvetia and the then Roman territory. Kaiseraugst / Castrum Rauracense was built around 300 AD during the subsequent refortifications of the Rhine border. Constantius II, son of Emperor Constantine the Great, repulsed the Alemanni near Kaiseraugst c.354 AD.

The Alemanni infiltrated again in 357 and were defeated by Emperor Julian Apostata at Strasbourg. In 374 Emperor Valentinian I built 52 Roman watchtowers along the Rhine between Basel and Constance in a final effort to restrain the new wave of 'barbarians'. The only remains of these fortifications in Basel are located in the Fischerstube at Rheingasse 45. The name Basel *(Basilia)* received its first recorded mention at this time by Valentinian's historian, Ammianus Marcellinus.

Editor's note: Other major Roman settlements accessible to the public: Vindonissa / Windisch near Brugg, 40 km from Augst—a Roman military quarters with an amphitheater. Aventicum / Avenches, the Roman capital of the Helvetii— a residential and military settlement with an amphitheater and a theater such as at Augusta Raurica. Octodurus / Martigny, of special importance because of its proximity to the Great St. Bernard Pass—with an amphitheater and an impressive posted archaeological walk. Bern-Engehalbinsel—the smallest amphitheater erected on a previous Helvetian oppidum. Lenzburg—theater discovered in 1964 during the construction of a highway. Noviodunum / Nyon —a museum built on the foundation of a basilica and an amphitheater uncovered in 1996.

One can still walk on stretches of rocky roads trodden by countless Roman legionnaires.

The Migration of the Peoples / *Völkerwanderung* followed the rapid decline of the Roman Empire in the 5th century; nevertheless, Roman resistance continued. The Alemanni crossed the Rhine and took possession of the northern territory, which became German speaking. The Burgundians, who originated on the Danish island of Bornholm, became the rulers of present-day French-speaking Switzerland and the eastern side of the Rhine. Their capital was at Worms near the river. The Franks, originally of northern Germanic extraction, settled in what is now central and western France, hence the German name of *Frankreich*—the realm of the Franks. The eastern Goths took possession of the lower end of the Italian peninsula, while the *Longobards / Lombards* settled further north; the western Goths went on to the Iberian Peninsula.

The Alemanni settled in northern, eastern and western Swiss territories; at one point in time they reached as far south as Bellinzona. Their expansion brought them into conflict with the Franks. In 495 they were conquered by King Clovis and assimilated into the Frankish dominions.

A mid-5th to early-8th century Alemanni burial site excavated at Kleinhüningen interestingly gave no traces of any settlement. The Alemanni remained pagan until about the 8th century.

Development of Christianity

Parallel with this migration was the conversion of Europe to Christianity. With the Edict of Milan in 313, Emperor Constantine the Great, who converted to Christianity, allowed Christians unrestricted freedom to practice their religion. In the year 330 he declared Constantinople his capital. Evidence of early Christianity in the Basel area is a baptistery/chapel at Kaiseraugst (c.346 AD)—a visit to the exhibit and reconstruction makes for a most pleasant and satisfying outing. A Christian community with a bishop and church existed within the Castrum Rauracense. Tombs found at Aeschenvorstadt and Elisabethenstrasse in the 1950s revealed a Roman officer's *fibula* / clasp bearing a Christogram.

Roman officer's clasp with Christogram, 4ᵗʰ/5ᵗʰ century

From around 740 AD bishops took up continuous residence in Basel. Haito (805/23), named bishop by Charlemagne (742–814), built the first cathedral. The Hungarians sacked it in 917. At the end of the 9ᵗʰ century, Basel became part of the Burgundian kingdom.

Medieval Basel

In 1006 the Holy Roman Emperor Heinrich II received the city of Basel as a gift from his uncle King Rudolph III of Burgundy, who was aware of its strategic geographical, political and economic importance. Eventually the city was granted the right to mint coins, levy taxes and administer justice, thereby receiving both temporal and religious powers. This promising situation encouraged commerce and Basel's population increased dramatically with the arrival of artisans, merchants and others aware of the various potential opportunities.

Heinrich II financed the rebuilding of the Basel *Münster* / Cathedral. Aided by his queen consort Kunigunde, valuable church treasures were donated to the city: a one-of-a-kind golden altar frontal mounted on oak board (antependium), and other precious objects. Monstrances, golden crosses, candlesticks, relics and pieces of the True Cross were added to the treasure. A natural consequence was the need to create proper housing for the relics.

Goldsmiths working in Basel produced some of the finest reliquaries of the Middle Ages. Pilgrims traveled to venerate these treasures and 'relic tourism' bolstered the economy.

St. Ursula, 14th century

Editor's Note: Before the Reformation in 1529, the Cathedral Treasury was stored away in a cupboard where it remained for over 300 years. Following the partition of Basel into the two half cantons of Basel-Stadt and Basel-Landschaft in 1833, it was broken up —one-third allocated to the city and two-thirds to the countryside. One of the items in the drawing lot for Basel-Landschaft was the golden antependium. The new half canton was a rural and poor region; it felt obligated to sell these precious objects and an auction was held in Liestal. The golden altar frontal is now at the Museum of Cluny in Paris. Other treasures are scattered from Leningrad to Washington, DC. What is remarkable is its survival. Some of the treasures allocated to the city, in addition to several important pieces purchased by the city through the art trade, e.g., the bust reliquary of St. Ursula, are now on display at the Historisches Museum Basel.

Veneration of Heinrich II continued throughout the Middle Ages. It was his successor, King Konrad II, who united Basel with the Holy Roman Empire, thereby increasing the power of the bishop. The bishop was the center of the political, spiritual and intellectual make-up of the city. At the Cathedral Square, he rendered justice, presided over the ecclesiastic tribunal and issued the rights to sell merchandise. Processions, tournaments and spectacles, both religious and secular took place. Inside the Cathedral the bishop received emperors and kings, as well as itinerant preachers. These official visitors arrived with gifts, including relics, some of which are still in the Cathedral Treasury. When the influence of the bishops began to wane, amassing precious objects became a show of perpetrating strength and power. The Treasury continued to grow until the Reformation.

The bishop also represented the emperor. He accompanied him on his voyages, and at times into battle. When differences arose between the pope and the emperor, the bishop and the city lived with the consequences.

The Basel symbol, a bishop's crosier, supposedly stems from the crosier of Abbot St. Germanus of the Moutier-Grandval Abbey in the Jura, at one time part of the Basel bishopric. During the medieval age, the bishops of Basel carried this crosier of Merovingian origin (seventh to eighth century). It is a unique example of early Christian goldsmiths' work and is at the Museum of Art and History in Delémont.

Under Bishop Burkhard von Fenis (1040-1107), also known as Burkhard von Hasenburg, the first 'real' city wall (1080/1100), that is beyond the Cathedral Hill and now referred to as the inner or *Burkhard'sche* wall, was built. In 1083 the bishop founded St. Alban's Monastery, the first monastery in Basel, which he gave to the monks from Cluny. The monks farmed the land. By diverting water from the river Birs, canals were created which produced power to run grain mills and later paper mills. The construction of St. Leonard's Monastery followed an appeal by artisans in 1133/35 for a parish church.

In 1185 fire damaged the Cathedral. Bishop Henri of Horbourg immediately ordered its reconstruction. Baslers never cease to revere and embellish their Cathedral—in 2003 a new organ was inaugurated.

The new organ in the Cathedral

The population increased. The middle wall, the second (or third if the Celtic and Roman constructions are taken into account) with higher and thicker walls and deeper *Graben* / moats was constructed (1200/50). It ran parallel and close to the Burkhard'sche wall, i.e., slightly removed from the Cathedral Hill, down St. Alban Graben and Steinenberg, to Barfüsserplatz, up to Kohlenberg, Leonhardsgraben and Petersgraben down to the Rhine. Nothing remains of the gates likely constructed (1200/25), that is, after the Burkhard'sche wall and before the new middle wall.

Editor's note: While besieging Basel in 1273, Count Rudolf I of Habsburg (1218-1291) received news that he had been proclaimed German King. One of the king's men replaced Bishop Henri de Neuchâtel (1263-1274). The bishop is quoted as addressing the Almighty: "Sit steady, oh Lord, on Your seat, if You don't want Rudolph to drive You out of Your position."

The Monasteries and the Rhine Bridge

In 1225 Bishop Heinrich von Thun initiated the construction of the *Rhein-brücke,* our *Mittlere Brücke* / Middle Bridge. This linked the two sides of the river, produced income from bridge tolls, advanced the migration of crafts and tradesmen, promoted the growth of the guilds and the development of Kleinbasel. All which gave a remarkable boost to the economy and growth of the city. *See Basel and Its Waters.*

Construction of monasteries and convents continued apace: *St Maria Magdalena* (Dominican, near the Basel Theater) founded in 1230; *Barfüsser* (Franciscan) in 1231; *Prediger* (Dominican, at Totentanz) in 1233; Klingental (Dominican) in 1274; *Augustiner* (Augustine hermits, the Museum of Culture) in 1276; *St.Clara* (the Poor Clares, Franciscan, at Claraplatz) in 1277; *Gnadental* (the Poor Clares, Franciscan, at Spalenvorstadt) founded in 1279/82; and in 1401, the last monastery, the *Kartause* / Charterhouse (Carthusian, near Theodorskirche).

Following the Reformation in 1529, monasteries and convents were closed and their contents dispersed.

Editor's note: Their libraries then became part of the University Library. Some churches have survived and street names now indicate the former monastic locations. The Klingental Convent, now the Museum Kleines Klingental, is the only remaining representation of cloistered life in the city; several rooms of the former Kartause / Charterhouse remain. See Churches and Monasteries.

The medieval scourge of Europe, the Plague, Pest or Black Death, hit Basel in 1348/49, presumably killing some 4,000 people out of an estimated population of 12,000. Arnold Böcklin's painting *The Plague* (1898) depicts the terror.

Another catastrophe struck Basel in 1356 in the form of a devastating earthquake and resulting fire. It destroyed most of the Cathedral and city. The homes were made primarily of wood (timberwork) and the fire spread rapidly. The earthquake severely damaged the city walls; shortly thereafter, a third (or fourth) fortification (the outer wall) was built. The areas previously outside the walls, the *Vorstädte* / suburbs, were enclosed. The fortifications protected citizens as well as refugees, and stood until the late half of the 19th century. Three gates of the original five—St. Albantor, St. Johannstor and Spalentor—still stand; Aeschentor and Steinentor were demolished in the mid-to-late 1800s.

Earthquake (1356) from 'Cosmographia' by Sebastian Münster, 1550

A Brief Summary of the mid-to-late Middle Ages

Perhaps what we should remember about the Middle Ages is that it was a period of tremendous change and growth—the city 'took off'. The presence of Heinrich II led and fed this development. Basel became a destination for pilgrims, artisans and merchants. Trade routes opened. People traveled. It recovered from two catastrophes. Bishops received extraordinary rights and privileges. Many of them gave back to the city all and more of what they received. They built the first cathedral, the first monastery and the first major bridge over the Rhine in Basel, at the time the last bridge before the North Sea. Over time, some took more than they gave back, which helped fuel the disillusionment and eventual revolt of some of the citizens—the Reformation. The development of the city was exciting. Monasteries and churches thrived. It was a city of walled fortifications, towers, turrets and battlements, built from the end of the 11th to end of the 14th century. Waterpower was channeled and managed. Artisans and merchants organized into guilds. The 13th century was a period of transition from mainly ecclesiastic and feudalistic behavior to one of crafts and commerce. With the construction of the bridge, came the collection of tolls; the two sides of the river were linked,

Pintoricchio's fresco (Siena Cathedral) of Piccolomini leaving for the Council of Basel

resulting in the development of Kleinbasel; the arrival of artisans increased the creative spirit of the city. Pilgrims arrived on their journey to Rome. Boat making became an important craft. In the 13th century, the right to elect a mayor and council was granted. One could say that these concessions, coupled with the need to rebuild the cathedral after the earthquake, led to the downfall of the bishops as they extended themselves financially and spiritually. Abuse and neglect eventually took its toll. With the purchase of Kleinbasel around 1392 from Bishop von Blankheim, the bishop's power declined. This atmosphere of increasing independence and stability, together with its geographical position, led to the choice of Basel as the venue for the Church Council (1431/48).

Development of Humanism and the Church Council

By the middle of the 15ᵗʰ century Basel stood in the limelight of European events. The Church Council brought important ecclesiastical and secular leaders to the city; it fostered further advancements, particularly pertaining to paper making and printing. The economy blossomed with the need to feed, house and clothe the participants and their large entourages. Moneylenders and traders arrived, taking advantage of the opportunity provided by the influx of wealthy dignitaries. Transcribing and printing the sessions employed monks and lay people alike. Artists were engaged to paint and carve altarpieces. The primary goals of the council were the religious pacification of Bohemia, i.e., to subdue the Hussites, to establish durable peace between England and France and to reform the church—modest success was achieved with only the first objective.

The plague was an omnipresent cloud hovering over the city and some council attendees succumbed. Days passed deliberating whether to move elsewhere—the threat of the plague being one reason, and geographical convenience for some of the hoped-for participants another. In 1437 it transferred to Ferrara. With the threat of the plague in that city, it moved to Florence in 1439. Some participants stayed on in Basel as a rump council, at which time they elected the antipope Felix V (1440).

Editor's note: A terrifying event for the council participants was the battle of St. Jakob-on-the-Birs on 26 August 1444, fought just outside the city walls. It was an extremely cruel battle against the Armagnacs, fierce French mercenaries from Gascony, who opposed the Burgundians. This event followed by the decisive Battle of Dornach in the Swabian (German) War in 1499 focused the Baslers on the question of remaining an imperial town. The city had served as a buffer state between the Burgundians and the Habsburgs and the socio-political situation was becoming more dangerous.

In 1449 the Papacy ended the council, which in 1448 had moved to Lausanne. This brought to a close the idea of ruling the church through a general council and not solely by the pope.

One particularly learned churchman left his lasting mark on Basel—Aeneas Silvius Piccolomini—later elected Pope Pius II. He mentioned that in his estimation if Basel were not at the very center of Christianity, it was not very far removed. In 1459 he granted the right for Basel to establish a university; it opened the following year, the first and only university on Swiss territory for almost 400 years.

The drawing power of the university, together with a highly developed printing trade, made Basel a center for humanistic learning and Renaissance culture.

There were innumerable printing establishments in the city, all independent from the guilds. Theology was the main discipline at the university and attracted freethinkers and scholars. Translating and printing the Bible into the vernacular made it accessible to the people. New waves of spiritual thought surfaced among all classes; perhaps more so with the peasants.

A sophisticated and questioning generation arrived from all over Europe. Popular literature at the time was *'Brant's Ship of Fools'*, *'Till Eulenspiegel'*, *'Reynard the Fox'* and Erasmus's *'In Praise of Folly'*. Hebrew studies and language remained part of the curriculum at the university, and Hebraic works, although censored, were published.

Sebastian Brant's Ship of Fools, 1494 (note Basel's symbol on cap)

Erasmus of Rotterdam, who translated, edited and annotated the New Testament in Greek and Latin, was a sharp critic of the existing political and social conditions. In Basel he found kindred spirits for his revolutionary conservatism. His dream was a rejuvenation of the Christian idea in all its purity, not a rebellion against the Church. Considered the most learned and respected man of the time, he spent some twelve years in Basel. Hans Holbein the Younger created masterful portraits of the humanist; some were miniatures which circulated freely, much as photos do today.

In 1528 shortly before the Reformation took hold, the bishop's official residence was relocated to Porrentruy. (Since 1828 the seat is in Solothurn).

The Reformation to the18ᵗʰ Century

The Reformation movement in Basel peaked in 1529 with iconoclastic riots at the cathedral and churches. The political and spiritual powers of the bishops, canons and nobility were in decline. Neglect and abuse of the citizens by the clergy and the city fathers continued to increase. In 1528 a group of citizens presented the city council with their requests for both political and religious reform. No action was forthcoming and the first *Bildersturm,* the destruction of religious objects, followed; however, at that time the perpetrators retreated. The Reformation in Basel would be destructive but bloodless.
See Reformation and Iconoclasm.

Most of Europe was in unrest due to this new movement. Basel and other Swiss cities offered asylum to numerous religious refugees.

Meanwhile further dissent was building up among the peasants. Demands for reform, lower taxes and more freedom came from the citizens in the rural areas. In 1585 the city bought its independence from the bishop for 200,000 florins; this emptied its coffers. When in 1591/94 minor taxes were imposed, they were accepted by some villages, but rejected by others—this resulted in the so-called *Rappenkrieg* / 'penny' war. Through the diplomatic skills of Andreas Ryff an explosive conflict was avoided. The city then offered bread, wine and cheese; the rebels disbanded.

Editor's note: A large silver-gilded beaker belonging to Andreas Ryff is at the Historisches Museum Basel.

A later protest concerned the request for cheaper salt, and again more reasonable taxes and reform. This led to rebellions and ultimately the Peasants' War of 1653. Salt was necessary for the peasants' livelihood—the salt deposits at Muttenz had not yet been discovered. The various plagues of the 14ᵗʰ and 15ᵗʰ centuries, coupled with the above-mentioned movements, and subsequently followed by the Thirty Years' War (1618/48)—a period which should be seen within the context of the struggle for European balance of power (1610/90) —resulted in further hardships for the rural residents. During this extended conflict, they were required to pay a tax for military protection. The tax, however, was not used to protect them, but to protect the city. After the war, the tax remained in effect to finance battles against rebel farmers; this was unacceptable. The uprising was modest, but resulted in the execution of the seven principal organizers. All privileges were denied Liestal, and the residents were obliged to pay the entire cost of the war. A monument engraved with the names of the leaders is in the center of Liestal.

The Edict of Nantes issued on 13 April 1598 by Henry IV, while granting the *Huguenots* / French Protestants specific concessions, including a general amnesty and one hundred places where they could live in safety, enshrined Catholicism as the official religion of France; it was revoked by Louis XIV in October 1685. The revocation did not result in a renewal of religious strife within France, but did produce an exodus of skilled and industrious individuals, a number of whom relocated to Basel and other parts of the country. These refugees were instrumental in the development of the watch-making, textile, chemical and banking industries. Bankers and goldsmiths settled in Geneva with the latter eventually starting the jewelry and watch industries in the French-speaking cantons. The silk industry developed chiefly in Zurich. Basel became the center of the silk-ribbon industry—ultimately leading to dye production—which formed the foundation for Basel's chemical industry and today's pharmaceutical giants.

Basel and Napoleon

Napoleon visited Basel many times during the negotiations for the Helvetic Republic; he lodged at the Three Kings Hotel. In 1795 a peace treaty between France, Spain and Prussia was signed at the *Holsteinerhof* in Hebelstrasse. The Austrian Archduke Leopold, another signatory, was a guest at the *Wildt'sche Haus* on Petersplatz.

During the Napoleonic battles Basel was the passageway to France.

Following Napoleon's retreat from Moscow in 1812, Austrian, Prussian and Russian troops quartered in Basel. Francis I, Emperor of Austria and father-in-law of Napoleon, stayed at the *Blaues Haus* on the Rheinsprung near the Cathedral. Czar Alexander I had his quarters at *Segerhof* opposite the Three Kings Hotel. This building no longer exists but its furniture is in the Kirschgarten Museum.

Russian-Orthodox services were held for him at the *Seidenhof,* the mansion on Blumenrain 34 facing the Rhine. King Frederick William III of Prussia stayed at the *Deutschritterhof* on Rittergasse. *See Architecture.*

The middle of the 19ᵗʰ century was marked by a cultural rebirth. One historian maintained that Basel was no better than other cities, but in the field of culture, it differed from the others. Johann Jacob Bachofen (1815-1887) wrote *'Das Mutterrecht'.* Jacob Burckhardt (1818-1897) contributed to the universal fame of his city with his criticisms and philosophical writings on the interaction of history, culture and man. Christoph Merian (1808-1858), the richest man in Switzerland, would become the most generous benefactor to the city.

1833 is a year in Basel's history regarded from strongly divergent points of view. The canton separated into two half cantons: Basel-Stadt and Basel-Landschaft. The latter had been the poorer area whose residents depended on farming and home silk-ribbon production. They felt exploited by the city. Stefan Gutzwiller of Therwil organized meetings at the Restaurant Bad Bubendorf on the cantonal road near Liestal; in 1831 he wrote a manifesto requesting changes to the Constitution of Basel demanding equal rights with the city. In 1833 the Basel troops lost a decisive battle at the Hülftenschanze near Liestal; this led to the partition of Basel into two half cantons. Political efforts to reunite the two are ongoing and it remains an open issue.

The year after the *Sonderbundskrieg /* civil war in 1847, the cantons adopted a Federal constitution granting them all equal rights. Thus, the political history of an independent Basel ended.

The division of the Cathedral Treasury (1833) as depicted by Kelterborn

The Honorable Guilds and Honorable Societies of Basel

Their Origin and Early History

Since the mid-13th century the majority of the adult male citizens in Basel has been organized into fifteen guilds: eleven guilds and eight half guilds. The half guilds united for political reasons. The *Akademische Zunft* / Academic Guild (professors and teachers at the university) was founded in 1836.

Until 1798 the guilds remained the supervisory force over the constitution of Basel and they were the essential power in the political, social, economic, administrative and religious life of the city.

The purpose for founding the guilds was based on the need to protect professional interests, to provide social contacts and to aid in the formation of religious brotherhoods. Formal recognition was given to the guilds by the bishop, political overlord of the town at the time, through signed corroborative certificates. The certificate of the *Kürschner* / furriers' guild dated 1226 is the oldest such document in Switzerland and is kept at the *Staatsarchiv Basel/* Recording Office of the canton. In 1356 during the earthquake and subsequent devastating fire that hit Basel, most of the certificates perished. As a result many of the guilds cannot verify their date of origin.

The formation of the guilds was completed in 1354, with the exception of the Academic Guild. Political power and success were acquired gradually. In 1337 they were accepted in the council and each guild was allowed one delegate; in 1382 the *Zunftmeister* / masters of the guilds were admitted. Following the political turbulence before the Reformation, the councils were comprised solely of guild members. The time of their autocracy had begun.

The political life of Basel was not the only sector dominated by the guilds. In order to defend their economic interests, they created a rather strict protective system, which, at times, proved to be a significant handicap to economic and technical progress. Everyone who wished to become a professional was obliged to join the guild corresponding to his field of activity. Membership in more than one guild was possible.

An executive committee headed each guild: the *Ratsherr* / guild councilor, the *Meister* / master of the guild and die *Sechser* / governing members. The councilors and the masters were delegates to the *Kleiner Rat* / Small Council. Die Sechser served as delegates to the *Grosser Rat* / Big Council. Within the guilds, this committee supervised the protection of the business and its customers by controlling the quality and weights of the manufactured goods. In addition to this regulatory function, the guilds were also responsible for guarding and defending the city, as well as providing the fire-brigade services.

Membership in a guild was acquired through an initiation fee and the taking of an oath. Sons of members could renew their father's membership. Newcomers to the city, who because of professional need required membership in a guild, had to prove their 'personal freedom' and substantiate their formal education. Citizenship of Basel was later declared compulsory for all prospective members. Membership in a guild lasted until death, and one could say beyond, as widows and children were cared for by the guild, as with Hans Holbein the Younger's family *(Zunft zum Himmel)*.

All guilds owned their own houses and *Trinkstuben* / drinking rooms. This was also true of the *Drei Kleinbasler Ehrengesellschaften* / the three Honorable Societies of Kleinbasel, which had public-service functions, e.g., firefighters, police officers, and were represented in the Big Council. The five *Vorstadtgesellschaften* / suburban neighborhood protection societies had no political representation. Their founding, around 1398, followed the completion of the outer city wall. The Citizens' Corporation, the *Bürgerkorporation Kleinhüningen*, was founded with the affranchisement of the village Kleinhüningen to the city of Basel in 1908.

The most significant steps towards the development of Basel were undertaken by the guilds, and a political career was only possible if one belonged to a guild. The guilds elected the councils and therefore ruled the city. The university professors desired more political influence and were granted permission to form their own guild in 1836, thereby permitting their election to parliament. In 1875 when the new cantonal constitution was accepted, all guilds had to give up their protectionist methods, and, at the same time lost their right to the parliament. Independent elections are now held according to the geographical partition of the *Quartiere* / districts. Thus, the guilds lost all political functions and had henceforth to report to the *Bürgergemeinde/ Bürgerrat* / the Community and Citizens' Council of Basel.

The Guilds and Societies Today
The guilds and societies are now active in other ways and assume certain functions for the city. One such event is the yearly organization of the *Jungbürgerfeier*—a coming of age ceremony for all 18-year-old Swiss citizens residing in Basel.

Various decrees control the organization and administration of the guilds. It is still compulsory to be a citizen of Basel. The tradition of excluding women is no longer strictly maintained. Since 1990, and upon full vote of the membership, women practicing the craft or trade of the guild can be admitted. Professional adherence is enforced by some, but not all, guilds. Since 1883, each *Vorstadtgesellschaft* / suburban society consists solely of seven board members.

The guilds now abstain from political activities. Their only legal responsibility is the administration of their property, for which they must present a yearly report to the *Bürgerrat* / Citizens' Council. A portion of the profits from their holdings is donated to various social and cultural institutions of Basel. Some guilds offer financial assistance to students who wish to pursue studies in one of the guild's professions. The *Zunft zu Hausgenossen*, for example, offers grants to qualifying female and male goldsmith students who wish to pursue their advanced studies.

A few of the guilds still own their historical houses; some are restaurants open to the public. *Zunft zum Schlüssel:* Freie Strasse 25 (restaurant); *Zunft zu Hausgenossen:* Freie Strasse 34; *Zunft zu Weinleuten:* Marktplatz 13; *Zunft zu Safran:* Gerbergasse 11 (restaurant); *Zunft zu Webern:* Steinenvorstadt 23; *Vorstadtgesellschaft zur Mägd:* St. Johannsvorstadt 29 (restaurant); *Vorstadtgesellschaft zum Hohen Dolder:* St.Alban-Vorstadt 35 (assembly room available for rent).

The three Honorable Societies of Kleinbasel and the five Suburban Societies

Today the main purpose of the guilds and honorable societies is of a social nature. They preserve traditions and friendships among their members and cherish spiritual and democratic values. As a group they appear relatively seldom in public.

On Ash Wednesday, the guilds *Zum Schlüssel, Zu Hausgenossen, Zu Wein-leuten* and *Zu Safran* visit one another and hold their annual dinner. They are accompanied by their *Spiel*, a group of piccolo players and drummers dressed in traditional garb; the *Spiel* is not a Fasnacht clique! Periodically a 'day of the guilds' is held, but not on a fixed date.

Another yearly event which takes place in January is the *Vogel Gryff*, the festive day of the three Honorable Societies of Kleinbasel. It is an impressive manifestation of how traditions are honored and sustained.

St. George drinking beaker (1600)

Each guild holds individual activities for its members, including a yearly outing and the traditional meal, *Zunft-mahl*. During this gathering, and after enjoying a fine meal, new members are accepted into the guild with a reportedly impressive ritual.

Antique objects pertaining to the history of the guilds, such as standards, arms, materials and important secular goldsmith work, the majority crafted in Basel, are on loan to the Historisches Museum Basel. Of special appeal are the elaborate table decorations and fabulously ornate drinking beakers.

In May 2005, a newly created permanent exhibition space dedicated to the guilds opened at the Historisches Museum Basel.

List of the Honorable Guilds and Honorable Societies of Basel
The guilds are listed in order of rank. The first four being the Herren Zünfte, the others the Handwerker Zünfte, with the exception of the Akademische Zunft. Guilds 8, 9, 13, and 15, a. and b. are half guilds.

A. Corporations

1.	Zunft zum Schlüssel (Kaufleutenzunft)	Merchants and drapers
2.	Zunft zu Hausgenossen (Bärenzunft)	Minters, money changers, goldsmiths, jewelers, bell founders
3.	Zunft zu Weinleuten (Geltenzunft)	Vintners and professions relating to wine distribution
4.	Zunft zu Safran (Krämerzunft)	Grocers, spice traders, iron-silver-and silk traders, pharmacists, plumbers, hat makers, printers, paper millers
5.	Zunft zu Rebleuten	Wine growers, military officers
6.	Zunft zu Brotbecken	Bakers and associated professions
7.	Zunft zu Schmieden	Blacksmiths, weapons (guns, cannons), coppersmiths, watchmakers, wooden shoemakers, millers
8a.	Zunft zu Schumacher	Shoemakers
8b.	Zunft zu Gerbern	Tanners
9a.	Zunft zu Schneidern	Tailors
9b.	Zunft zu Kürschnern	Furriers
10.	Zunft zu Gartnern	Gardeners, rope and basket makers, carriage drivers, cooks and chefs, restaurant owners
11.	Zunft zu Metzgern	Butchers
12.	Zunft zu Spinnwettern	Building artisans, carpenters, stonemasons, brick makers and layers, coopers, sculptors, chimney sweeps, organ makers
13a.	Zunft zum Goldenen Stern	Barbers, barber-surgeons
13b.	Zunft zum Himmel	Painters, glaziers, copperplate engravers, saddlers
14.	Zunft zu Webern	Weavers, dyers, bleachers
15a.	Zunft zu Fischern	Fishermen, fish merchants
15b.	Zunft zu Schiffleuten	Sailors, boatsmen
16.	Akademische Zunft	Professors and teachers at the university

Basel Guilds and the Society of Riflemen (1501–2001)
Andreas Schenk, Scriptorium, Basel

B. Ehrengellschaften / Honorable Societies of Kleinbasel

1. Gesellschaft zum Rebhaus   Represented by the *Leu* / lion
2. Gesellschaft zur Hären   Represented by the *Wilder Mann* / wild man
3. Gesellschaft zum Greifen   Represented by the *Vogel Gryff* / griffin

C. Vorstadtgesellschaften / Suburban Neighborhood Protection Societies
Originally established for defense purposes outside the city walls.

1. Vorstadtgesellschaft zur Mägd at St. Johanns-Vorstadt
2. Vorstadtgesellschaft zur Krähe at Spalenvorstadt
3. Vorstadtgesellschaft zu den drei Eidgenossen at Steinenvorstadt
4. Vorstadtgesellschaft zum Rupf at Aeschenvorstadt
5. Vorstadtgesellschaft zum hohen Dolder at St. Alban-Vorstadt

D. Bürgerkorporation / Citizens' Corporation

Bürgerkorporation Kleinhüningen

Jewish History in Basel

The first recorded evidence of Jews in Basel goes back to the 1200s. How they traveled to Basel is not certain. Perhaps they came up the Rhine, as important communities existed in Köln, Speyer and Worms; or they could have arrived from the west, as there was periodic immigration from Alsace. In any case, the Jewish community in Basel was the first in present-day Switzerland. As was their custom, they formed a well-organized community both culturally and economically. Protection came from the Holy Roman Emperor for which a tax was levied.

The first synagogue in Basel was the focal point for the community. There was no ghetto. Its location was on today's Gerbergasse, in a craft and artisans' area; it was part of St. Leonard's parish, which collected taxes from all its residents and sold houses to Jews. The cemetery of the first community was located in the area near the *Kollegienhaus* (the university building) in the Petersplatz complex; it was in use from about 1220 until 1348.

The Jews integrated into the economic life of Basel, often as moneylenders. One of their debtors was the bishop of Basel, who in 1225 supposedly pawned some of the Cathedral Treasures as collateral in order to pay for the construction of the Rhine Bridge. This loan was to be repaid from the collection of bridge tolls.

Apparently the Basel Jews escaped the persecution at the end of the 13th and beginning of the 14th centuries, during which the Jews of Alsace were less fortunate. In 1345 Basel joined a peace alliance of Alsatian cities directed against their persecution. In 1347/48 the city banned a number of noblemen who had attacked Jews in order to be free of their debts.
Disaster struck in 1348/49. The Black Death took its toll both physically and psychologically. Hysteria with its need for scapegoats triumphed. The persecutions, as now is known, preceded the epidemic by several months. All the Jews that could not escape were rounded up, sent to a tiny island in the Rhine, and burned; an event supported by documentary evidence. Those who opted for baptism in order to survive were later rounded up and accused of poisoning food and the wells; their cemetery was destroyed. It has been questioned if noblemen who were indebted to the Jews and had the power to influence the council in order to write off their debts provoked these actions. Alternatively, was it due to the irrational frenzy found throughout history 'to blame someone' outside the prevailing beliefs? By the end of 1349, the Jewish population was largely exterminated, the cemetery destroyed

and the noblemen's debts were liquidated. Jews were forbidden to live in the city for the next 200 years.

There is evidence, however, that around 1362, they were in Basel at Gerbergasse and the surrounding Rümelinsplatz. A need for funds to rebuild the city after the earthquake of 1356 most likely encouraged their return. The synagogue at that time was in Grünpfahlgässlein.

Very little is known about the cemetery of the second community on the Hirschgässlein within the city walls and mentioned in a 1394 document. On Sebastian Münster's map of Basel (1538), the cemetery is indicated as the *Garden of Eden*. Jews now came under the jurisdiction of the city. They were protected from physical abuse; however, fairness in business did not prevail.

Why there was a resurgence of anti-Jewish sentiment after 1390 remains unanswered—political uncertainties, fears related to the return of the plague, or other issues. The Jews in Basel decided to depart for areas under Austrian rule. The council's attempt to stop this exodus failed. The question of why the greater Basel authorities decided to banish Jews from Basel after 1397 is still unclear; no Jews lived in the city until the 1800s.

Single-domed synagogue consecrated in 1868

The Jews moved to the surrounding countryside and were subject to heavy traveling taxes and duties. An attempt by the city to have them banished from these areas was not successful. With the crowning of the antipope Felix V in 1440 during the Church Council, an appeal was issued to the population to desist in the molestation of the Jews.

During the 1500s Basel developed into a center of studies pertaining to Jewish research and culture. Censored publication of Jewish works in Hebrew was carried out by various printing houses, and the Hebrew language continued to be taught at the theological faculty of the university. Yet the Jewish population was required to remain outside the city walls.
With the introduction of the Helvetic Republic in 1798, they began to emigrate from Alsace into Basel. Religious services took place on a regular basis after 1805 at various locations. Residency permits were granted on a restricted basis—in numbers and duration, and with changing additional hindrances.

In 1849 a revision of the laws finally granted all sons born or raised in Basel the right of domicile. Slowly other rights were given, including the freedom of trade and religion, thus enabling growth of the community. The first synagogue was at Unterer Heuberg (1849/50). Full emancipation in Switzerland occurred relatively late, in 1866. This was realized due to pressure from England, France, Holland and the United States, which negotiated trade agreements and insisted on equal rights for all Jews living in the country. In 1874 the revised Federal Constitution finally granted them the same equal rights concerning freedom of conscience and religion as enjoyed by all Swiss citizens. A dramatic demographic change then took place, with Jews arriving from Alsace, France, the cantons of Aargau, Zurich and Basel-Landschaft; immigrants arrived later from Germany and Eastern Europe.

With this growth, the synagogue (with one dome) consecrated in 1868 on Eulerstrasse proved too small; an enlarged building (with two domes) was dedicated 25 years later. However, the right to bury their dead within the city was not granted until 1902. Previously the bodies were transported to Hegenheim in Alsace for burial. A second synagogue at Ahornstrasse was founded in 1927.

Around the turn of the century, textiles, including trade with products from the flourishing silk-ribbon industry, were the prevailing occupations of the community. Others were engaged in the food and wine business; Jewish banks were established—the Dreyfus Bank in 1813.

In 1897 Basel was host to the first World Zionist Congress, which created the original program of the Zionist movement. Its political aim was to establish a home for the Jewish people in Palestine, secure and under public law. The meeting took place in the Stadtcasino under the presidency of Theodor Herzl. A photograph of Herzl shows him leaning on the balcony of the Three Kings Hotel. Several subsequent Zionist Congresses took place in Basel as well, the last in 1946, a year and a half before the creation of the State of Israel.

The Jewish Museum of Switzerland on Kornhausgasse opened in 1966.

Konrad Witz's painting (part of *The Mirror of Salvation Altarpiece* purportedly intended for St. Leonard's Church) of the *Synagogue* is at the Kunstmuseum Basel.

In addition to the tombstones in the Jewish Museum's courtyard, the Historisches Museum Basel preserves examples from the 13th and 14th centuries, originally in the first Jewish cemetery on Swiss territory.

Tombstone from the Jewish Cemetery at Petersplatz, 1313

A complete inventory of the remaining 2850 tombstones in situ at the Hegenheim cemetery was published in 2004.

In celebration of the 200th anniversary of the third community (1805), a new publication on Jewish history in the area was published in 2005.

The Reformation and Iconoclasm

With a subject as complex and contentious as the Reformation, we can only aspire to present a brief synopsis.

During the 14th and 15th centuries, the power of the pope and his bishops began to decline both politically and spiritually. The Reformation ushered in an awakening in the population no longer willing to be subservient to the doctrines of Rome. Revolutionary changes took place in church politics, procedures and practices, and in the prevailing social structure and political power.

As a consequence of the Church Council (1431/48), Basel's excellent printing firms flourished and the university was founded. This offered freethinkers the opportunity to pursue their philosophical and religious beliefs and hypotheses, attracting many reform-minded individuals. It was a time of mobility and transition. Differing thoughts, at that time heretical ideas, were ignited by the availability of books and the need for change. Johann Amerbach's publication (1490/1506) of the extant writings of Augustine is said to have had a formidable impact upon the leaders of the reform movement. Martin Luther's teachings centered upon the concept of Augustine's doctrine of grace.

If a date could be attributed to the arrival of the Reformation one could cite 10 December 1520, the day when Luther burned the books of Canon Law outside the gates of Wittenberg—a bonfire which set Europe aflame.

In England, Henry VIII and Elizabeth I strongly led and supported religious reforms. In southern Germany and Switzerland, it was Luther, Zwingli and Calvin together with the middle and peasant classes who would fight and die for reforms. Strasbourg, an imperial free city, and surrounding regions were caught up in the movement. Zwingli and Calvin spent time in Basel before becoming reformers. Zwingli studied at the university (1502/06) and later became the leading reformer in Zurich. Calvin arrived in Basel at the end of 1533, having fled Paris. His 'Institutes of the Christian Religion' (1536) published in Basel, established him as the 'pope' of French Protestantism. Shortly after his move to Geneva, the city became home to the Swiss-French reformers. In Basel the leading reformer was Oekolampad. (Other proponents were Myconius, Oporinus, and Thomas Platter).

Shortly after noon on Tuesday 9 February 1529, over 200 protesters broke into the Cathedral, shattering the doors and chopping up the rood screen, altarpieces and panel paintings; statues, crucifixes and stained-glass windows were smashed. From the Cathedral the iconoclasts moved onto St. Martin's, St. Alban's, and St. Peter's churches continuing their havoc until four a.m.

With the iconoclastic destruction in the city 'complete', the masses were on the verge of crossing into Kleinbasel when the town council requested an hour to consider their demands. Within the hour they conceded and religious reforms were put into place. Three days later a blanket pardon was issued for all iconoclasts. This practical resolution ended the revolt; it is perhaps testimony to the seriousness of the underlying causes preceding these events.

Erasmus, a Catholic and humanist, supposedly witnessed these events and took refuge in Freiburg im Breisgau not returning until 1535, one year before his death.

The leaders of the Reformation in Basel did not sanction violence; they recognized the necessity of a transformation and separation between ecclesiastical and secular power.

What prompted this iconoclasm? For the perpetrators, the precious and sacred objects no longer held their original purpose as holy items to be shared with the public. They were now material property of the canons and clergy, devoid of their sacredness. The combination of an increasing accessibility to books and translations of the Bible, and an awakening among the populace that they no longer needed to rely on the Vatican to interpret the Scriptures, put an end to their dependency.

Johannes Oekolampad, Rittergasse

The university suffered from the confusion caused by this revolt. Normal academic activities slowly resumed in 1532 under professors expressing new philosophical and theological doctrines. The upheaval in the city was a two-edged sword. With the departure of Catholic professors 'in disgust at the triumph of heresy' and deaths from the various sweeps of the plague, openings were created for new teachers at the university.

Limits of power needed to be addressed by Protestants and Catholics alike; abuses existed on both sides. Zurich Protestants were defeated in 1531 during the Battle of Kappel where Zwingli died 'fighting like a wild man'. This and later battles briefly halted the spread of Protestantism in Switzerland and resulted in a shaky coexistence. The *Sonderbundskrieg* (the civil war in 1847) won by the Protestant troops of the Diet under the command of General Dufour (1787-1875), resulted in the Protestants gaining the balance of power, but not a political monopoly. This afforded the necessary equilibrium vital to the stability of the Swiss Confederation after 300 difficult years. The Reformation in Basel coupled with the iconoclastic consequences was milder than in other cities. The monasteries and convents closed down. In some cases, choice was given to the nuns and monks to remain on the premises. The destruction of religious objects, however, was catastrophic. As a bishopric, the number of precious ecclesiastical treasures was immense. The day following the destruction, fires burned outside the churches—12 burned at the Cathedral. Change had indeed come to Basel and it was to affect every segment of society. The word Protestant and its doctrine materialized, giving rise to a plethora of churches, followed by uncertainty.

After these reforms took hold, both Catholics and Protestants treated heretics harshly. Michael Servetus came into conflict with Calvin's beliefs; in 1553 he was burned at the stake in Geneva. The Anabaptists were also considered a threat to the stability of the social structure. After his death David Joris, who had a considerable following in Basel, was identified as leader of the Anabaptists. His body was exhumed and he was posthumously tried for his heretical past. Sebastian Castellio, an important precursor for the freedom of religious expression, was called before Basel's clergy and magistrates. He died of natural causes while a second legal process was being prepared.

From 1550 to the 17th century, French Protestants, the *Huguenots*, were increasingly under attack as heretics. Literally thousands fled to Switzerland and other countries seeking refuge from persecution. Basel was a haven. The city benefited from the work ethic, vision and active social conscience of these 'spiritual' pioneers. Banking, sundry businesses and industries profited from their presence. Before 1550 small numbers had immigrated to Basel. After the St. Bartholomew's Day Massacre in Paris on 24 August 1572, large numbers came seeking asylum. A second wave arrived after the revocation of the Edict of Nantes in 1685, when 200,000 Huguenots escaped France. Due to this influx, for the next 100 years the highly sought-after and prized Basel citizenship became difficult to obtain. The Huguenots played a prominent role in furthering Basel's silk-ribbon manufacturing and were instrumental in the development of the chemical and banking industries.

Thus, rising out of the ashes of the *Bildersturm* / iconoclasm and the turmoil of reform there was ubiquitous change in the political and social development of Basel, and indeed Switzerland. This achievement strengthened and shaped its citizens, its culture and its industries—and continues to influence and affect us after almost 500 years.

Oath pledging on the Rütli, 1291

A GLIMPSE AT SWISS HISTORY

Foundation of the Swiss Confederation

The formation of the Swiss Confederation began with *Rudolf I von Habsburg* (1218–1291). In 1273 while besieging Basel, news arrived that he was now German King of the Holy Roman Empire. Rudolf ruled over part of Switzerland, Alsace, Germany and later Austria, becoming the first Habsburg of European-wide importance. The ancestral seat, the castle of *Habsburg* / Hawk's Castle near Brugg, Aargau, gave its name to the dynasty; the family reputedly originated in Alsace.

The *Vierwaldstätte*, the four cantons of Uri, Schwyz, Unterwalden and Luzern, which include Nidwalden and Obwalden and border the *Vierwaldstättersee* / Lake of the Four Cantons, unhappy with their suppression by local Habsburg overlords, joined forces. This was the beginning of independence. At great personal sacrifice, the inhabitants of Uri purchased their valley back from the Hohenstaufen rulers and thus became keepers of the Gotthard Pass. Rudolf I had grant-

Rudolf I von Habsburg

ed Uri *Reichsfreiheit*, which meant that Uri answered only to the emperor and not to lesser bailiffs. Schwyz and Unterwalden also claimed *Reichsfreiheit*, but their charters were of questionable legality and Rudolf was not prepared to accept them. Uri, Schwyz and Unterwalden also questioned their owing loyalty to the ecclesiastical institutions of Einsiedeln, Engelberg and the Fraumünster in Zurich. Chaos reigned.

In August 1291, Uri, Schwyz and Unterwalden gradually began to form a league for mutual protection, later the *Confoederatio Helvetica* / Swiss Confederation. To make this pact, Walter Fürst of Uri, Werner Stauffacher of Schwyz and Arnold von Melchthal of Unterwalden, each accompanied by ten men, secretly met in the dark of night in the meadow at Rütli *(Rütliwiese)* near Seelisberg. They refused to accept judges not of their own choosing and laws not of their own making.

Editor's note: These were the First Swiss Men / FSM = Fürst, Stauffacher and Melchthal. This alliance gave birth to the legend of William Tell.

Battles Towards Independence

The Habsburgs refused to accept the Swiss claim for independence. In 1315 the *Eidgenossen* / Confederates won the Battle of Morgarten fought on the borders of Schwyz and Zug against the Habsburgs.

During the Battle of Sempach in 1386, the Habsburg Archduke Leopold III perished along with the legendary Confederate hero Arnold von Winkelried from Unterwalden, who had gathered to his body the pike points of the enemy, thereby opening a hole in the Austrian line.

Editor's note: A short quote from the poem by Sir Walter Scott (1771-1832) The Battle of Sempach: "I have a virtuous wife at home, A wife and infant son: I leave them to my country's care, The field shall yet be won! He rushed against the Austrian band, In desperate career, And with his body, breast and hand, Bore down each hostile spear; Four lances splintered on his crest, Six shivered in his side, Still on the serried files he pressed, He broke their ranks and died!"

For each Confederate who died, nine Austrians and most of Basel's noblemen fighting alongside the Austrian Habsburg forces succumbed. Basel was then allowed to buy back the lease of Kleinbasel, which had been mortgaged in 1375 by Bishop Jean de Vienne to Leopold III.

The battle of St. Jakob-on-the-Birs in 1444 fought just outside the city walls was against the Armagnacs, a powerful group of Frenchmen who were in opposition to the Burgundians. This battle, followed in 1499 by the Swabian War, would influence Basel's later decision to pledge allegiance to the Confederation in 1501.

The victorious battle against the Burgundians was at Murten / Morat. *Karl der Kühne* / Charles the Bold, alarmed by the determination and unity of the Confederates, took possession of Grandson for a short period, but was routed and lost his *Gut* / military equipment and possessions. He continued on to Murten; at the castle 2,000 Bernese blocked his passage. The threat of losing this strategic position was such that 20,000 Swiss came to its defense; on 22 June 1476, the Battle of Murten ended in a complete Swiss victory. It was here that Charles lost his *Mut* / courage. He then fled to Geneva and subsequently moved on to Nancy, where in 1477 he was defeated, died and lost his *Blut* / blood. Children in Switzerland learn: in Grandson Charles the Bold lost his *Gut,* in Murten his *Mut* and in Nancy his *Blut.*

Charles the Bold fleeing the Battle of Murten in 1476 by G. Anderegg

The aftermath of the Burgundian War caused social unrest between the poor mountain dwellers and the prospering cities. A civil war was prevented through the diplomacy of *Niklaus von Flüe* (1417–1487). Known as *Bruder Klaus,* he was a wise and pious hermit from Sachseln, so respected that he was able to influence the cantons into signing the *Stanser Verkommnis* / the Convention of Stans in 1481, which reunited the territories. Bruder Klaus was canonized in 1947.

The *Bruder Klaus Kirche* on the Bruderholz in Basel is dedicated to his memory.

Political conflicts between France and the Italian duchies intensified during the 15th and early 16th centuries. The area around present-day Ticino, dominated in the south by the Duke of Milan and in the north by an alliance of the three cantons, was drawn into battle. With help from the Confederates, the Milanese forces were defeated in 1478 at Giornico.

On the other hand, Swiss mercenaries led by Cardinal Schiner (c.1470-1522) fought for the Dukes of Milan. After a series of victories, defeat came in 1515 at Marignano under Francis I of France. Urs Graf, himself an avid mercenary, depicts scenes of the battle in a most dramatic way. A series of drawings are in the *Kupferstich-Kabinett* / Engraving Room at the Kunstmuseum Basel. The Swiss artist Ferdinand Hodler (1853–1918) produced heroic paintings showing the returning survivors. Most Swiss museums have representations of the Battle of Marignano in their collections.

Battlefield, 1521 by Urs Graf

The battle convinced the Confederates to resist foreign conflict; it was the beginning of a new policy of self-imposed neutrality. This neutrality, formally recognized in 1648 at the Treaty of Westphalia, followed the Thirty Years' War (1618/48), a long struggle involving all the powers in Europe. Johann Rudolph Wettstein, mayor of Basel, represented Switzerland during the negotiations and signing of the treaty. The Wettstein Bridge and Square, and the Wettstein March for fifes and drums, are in his memory.

The Swiss Mercenaries

The demand for Swiss mercenaries prospered in direct consequence of their reputation as spirited, courageous and reliable fighters, the precarious economic situation and the ongoing power struggle between the different warring factions. From the 15th until the 18th century, many were engaged in Germanic and Italian territories; the Bernese were in the service of the French kings until the Revolution. These mercenaries were not always volunteers. They became available through treaties (called capitulations) with the Swiss Diet, the cantons and foreign powers; reciprocation was through payment in money, corn, salt, or other commercial goods. The men regarded these periods favorably and returned home with their pay and booty.

Swiss men continued hiring themselves out as mercenaries, but under the jurisdiction of a Swiss regimental leader and swearing loyalty to a Swiss regimental flag. These contingents were in the service of European courts. Because of the traditional alliance between Switzerland and France—dating from the Everlasting Peace of 1516—the Swiss mercenaries played their most important role fighting for France. The men of the Swiss regiment, one of four in the service of the French, who fought and died in 1792 while defending the Tuileries of Louis XVI during the French Revolution, are a fine example of exceptional bravery. The *Lion Monument* in Lucerne commemorates their dedication. The inscription reads *"Helvetiorum Fidei Ac Virtuti"*—To the Loyalty and Courage of the Swiss.

In some cantons, the patrician classes evolved from the commanding officers returning with their booty and pensions.

The Swiss Guards

Pope Julius II (1503/13), the warrior-pope, formed the *Cohors Helvetica /* the Swiss Guards in 1506 using them as papal mercenaries against the French. In 1527 during the Sack of Rome, 147 of the 189 guards were slain while protecting Pope Clement VII. The corps prolonged the battle against the troops of Charles V, thus enabling the Pope to escape by a passageway leading from the Vatican to Castel Sant'Angelo.

Raphael's paintings, some of which masterfully portray the fashion of 16th-century Rome, likely inspired their Renaissance-style uniform of striped blue, red and yellow, the Medici colors. The contemporary uniform was designed and introduced in the early 1900s.

Nowadays the Swiss Guards number between 100 and 120 and continue the tradition of protecting the Pope. Investiture of new members is held each year on 6 May—the anniversary of the massacre in 1527.

The Late 16th and 17th Centuries

Switzerland was now composed of 13 autonomous cantons whose land mass corresponded to approximately one-half of the Swiss territory, the other territories being subordinate to them. These 13 cantons had one central institution, the *Tagsatzung* or Diet, an assembly of delegates from each canton with no inherent power to coerce its member states.

Much time and effort was devoted to forging a sense of unity among the various cantons. Conflicts arising from the Reformation hampered these efforts. Almost an equal number of cantons adopted the Protestant ethic and beliefs as those who held to the Catholic precepts and loyalty to the pope. A number of bloody skirmishes followed in various cantons. In 1579 Lucerne became the de-facto capital of Catholic Switzerland with the installation of the papal nuncio.

Cities developed along natural trade routes and gradually accumulated wealth and prominence, while the peasants in the countryside barely managed to feed themselves. Taxes were imposed. However, it was not always a losing proposition. During the Thirty Years' War, refugees streamed into Switzerland and the peasants profited by their presence. Produce prices and farmland increased in value. With the end of the war, refugees returned home; prices dropped and the peasants could no longer meet their obligations. Resentment increased, revolts intensified. However, against the troops called out by the Diet, the peasants had no hope of success.

In spite of the continuing religious and economic differences, the 13 cantons reached an agreement with the Defensionale of Wil in 1647, whereby the frontiers would be defended against any aggressor; a mixed council of war composed of Protestants and Catholics would direct a force recruited from all parts of the Confederation. The acceptance of the principle of defending neutrality was a significant step towards a national identity and sense of purpose.

The 18ᵗʰ Century

The cantons followed different political policies, with some ruled by a patrician aristocracy, and others by a people's assembly. This situation, coupled with religious disagreements, led inevitably to the Villmergen Wars, the second of which resulted in the Peace of Aarau on 11 August 1712. The establishment of true equality for both sides increased decisively the influence of Berne and Zurich in the Confederation.

During the 18ᵗʰ century, almost every form of government existed throughout the Confederation. Trade corporations and craft guilds ruled Basel, Zurich and Schaffhausen. Patrician families ruled Berne, Fribourg, Solothurn and Lucerne. The oldest cantons continued to observe their earlier forms of direct democracy.

Bishops and autocratic princes ruled St. Gallen and Neuchâtel. The search for a national identity assumed secondary importance, whereas the pursuit of economic gain was paramount—founded on a belief that contentment, prosperity and industry were indeed interrelated.

Yet all was not calm. In 1723 Citizen Jean Davel attempted to free Vaud from 'the yoke of Berne' for which he was duly executed. Uprisings in various territories and cantons, while posing problems for the new Confederation, were generally dealt with in a united and efficient manner.

The 19ᵗʰ Century

At the beginning of the 19ᵗʰ century, Napoleon Bonaparte was the dominant force in Europe. In 1798 his troops crossed into Switzerland and defeated the Bernese. At that time Berne was not the capital—this occurred in 1848—but a wealthy territory extending from the lower Reuss River (which later empties into the Rhine) to the Lake of Geneva. Napoleonic troops who plundered where they could to finance their military campaigns, stole Berne's gold. To this day restitution has not been made.

Switzerland had been a loose confederation of cantons, each with its own borders and laws. Napoleon established the Helvetic Republic (1798/1803) and installed a new government based on the Paris model. Personal equality was adopted, weights and measures standardized and the Napoleonic Code introduced; the Code is still the basis for judicial decisions. The Helvetic Senate was the parliament and convened in Aarau. All seats of independent authority and all former subordinate territories received the same equal rights as the 13 cantons. Free cities and valleys, prince-bishoprics, princely abbeys, sovereign convents, monasteries and city aristocracies were suppressed. A new constitution abolished borders between cantons. As the Swiss, especially those residing in the mountainous cantons, totally rejected the idea of a Helvetic Republic; it existed only on paper. Chaos reigned again.

Napoleon summoned the representatives of the cantons to Paris in 1802 to work on a new constitution. He referred to himself as a 'man born in a land of mountains to understand how mountain people think.' The Basel State Chancellor Peter Ochs, of brilliant gifts and equally conversant in French as well as German, was head of the Swiss delegation.

The Act of Mediation of 1803, an outcome of the Napoleonic negotiations, restored political sovereignty to the old cantons under a loose federal constitution. Louis d'Affry (1743-1810) of Fribourg, the first *Landammann* / President of the Helvetic Republic, negotiated and defended the country's neutrality against Napoleon. St. Gallen, Graubünden,

Basel soldier, Napoleonic era

Aargau, Thurgau, Ticino and Vaud took their places as full cantons bringing the membership in the Confederation to 19. Geneva, Valais and Neuchâtel joined in 1815. Following a referendum in 1978, part of the Jura separated from Berne; it legally became the canton of Jura on 1 January 1979.

After Napoleon's defeat at Waterloo, Swiss neutrality was recognized by the rulers of Austria, Prussia and Russia and reaffirmed in 1815 at the Congress of Vienna.

While Switzerland's external borders and its role as an independent state were being affirmed and accepted by the major European powers, conflicting forces within the country engaged in periodic armed conflict. Following the formation in 1803 of Canton Aargau, with a constitutional 50:50 representation of Catholics (for the most part conservatives) and Protestants (for the most part liberal), their counterparts throughout the country found themselves increasingly at odds over divisive issues, such as the role of the Jesuits within the Confederation. Particularly affected was Lucerne, where the parliament appointed the Order responsible for the education of priests. This resulted in liberal-led outbreaks in Vaud in February 1845; in the spring of the same year, *Freischaren* / armed insurgents marched on Lucerne. They were defeated in two pitched battles before the *Tagsatzung* prohibited any further armed marches. The policies of both conservative and liberal cantonal governments continued to diverge, culminating in the formation of a secret alliance of the Catholic cantons of Lucerne, Uri, Schwyz, Unterwalden, Zug, Fribourg and Valais—the *Sonderbund* /special alliance—patterned after the same coalition formed during the cantonal wars in the wake of the Reformation.

The pope, Prussia and Austria attempted to interfere on behalf of the Catholic alliance, but the liberal majority in the *Tagsatzung* held firm; in 1847 the Sonderbund was declared illegal. Both sides elected military commanders and the *Sonderbundskrieg* / civil war commenced on 3 November 1847 when the Sonderbund forces attacked Ticino and Aargau. The war won by the Protestants was over by the end of the month. Thanks to the strategy and great speed of the Diet forces led by General Dufour (1787-1875), a prolonged and bloody civil conflict was avoided. The Jesuits were banned from Switzerland; their residences and schools closed. It was not until a referendum held in 1977 that they were allowed to return.

In 1848 the Swiss wrote their constitution, using the American Constitution and the Declaration of Independence as models.

Origin of the Swiss Flag

The Swiss national flag evolved from war flags. During the Middle Ages, the cross was used on coins and seals and carried into battle on the banners of warring parties as a symbol of Christian faith. As the cantons went to war carrying regional banners, it soon became apparent that a commonly recognizable sign of unity would be helpful. As early as the Battle of Laupen in 1339, troops wore a long, narrow white linen cross on their clothing. After the defeat of Napoleon in 1814, returning mercenary troops were presented with an honorary flag bearing this same white cross on a red field. The cantons continued to use their own flags and  uniforms; at this time an armband with a white cross, which would eventually appear on the federal flag, was adopted by all troops.

General Dufour argued that cantons carrying the same flag were more likely to have a feeling of solidarity. In 1840 a rule went into effect that the new flag would replace all cantonal flags for the armed forces. The flag went into war once—with Dufour's Diet Army when it suppressed the Sonderbund forces in the short civil war of 1847. The white cross had five equal squares on a red field; it was officially adopted in the Constitution of 1848.

Attempts to refine the flag followed. In 1889 the Federal Assembly ruled that it was keeping the white cross, but that it would change from five equal squares to one in which the arms were one-sixth longer than they were wide, bringing it into conformity with the cross on the state seal of 1815.

Switzerland has no presidential or ceremonial flag. At times of national crises, the Federal Assembly appoints a commanding general who receives a special standard, an unadorned national flag with red and white fringe— identical to a cavalry guidon.
General Guisan (1874-1960) carried the last such flag during the mobilization of 1939/45.

New Directions

With the increasing interdependence of nations, a new chapter in Swiss history opened. Organizations such as the International Red Cross (1864), the International Labor Organization (1919) and the League of Nations (1919), which later became the European Office of the United Nations, established their headquarters in Geneva. Pro Helvetia, created in 1938, is an autonomous, permanent Swiss institution whose mission is to preserve and promote Swiss culture, both at home and abroad.

During the two world wars, Switzerland defended its frontiers and maintained its neutrality. The Red Cross acted as an intermediary for the countries at war. The mobilization during WW I was under the leadership of General Wille (1848-1925), in 1939 under General Guisan. In 1940 the general and his officers assembled on the Rütli meadow near Seelisberg and repeated the vow of the *First Swiss Men.* The general announced his new defense system—the so-called national redoubt, the objective being to fortify the Alps. To this end, the bulk of the Swiss military was stationed in the mountains. With the end of WW II in 1945 came the demobilization. Relief work was carried out for war victims; the Pestalozzi children's village, for the care and education of war orphans from all over the world, opened in Trogen, Appenzell.

Pestalozzi with the Orphans of Stans by Konrad Grob, 1879

Helvetia Taking in Refugees, postcard, 1915

The story of Switzerland is one of working together towards unity, as expressed in its motto—*One for All and All for One.* We should also like to quote Voltaire: "In history, Switzerland will have the last word." On that note, our abbreviated history lesson ends and we close with Helvetia and William Tell.

Helvetia is the Latin name for Switzerland, home of the Helvetians (Helvetii). The appellation is used to describe the allegorical female figure which personifies the Swiss State. Whereas William Tell was the main symbol during the Helvetic Republic period (1798/1803), this honor gradually was accorded to Helvetia. With the founding of the Federal State in 1848, she received her position as the uniting and protective Mother of the Nation and began appearing on stamps from 1854 to 1942, and on coins up to the present.

Helvetia by Albert Walch
(1874)

William Tell by Ferdinand Hodler
(1896/97)

The Legend of William Tell

William Tell, alleged son-in-law of Walter Fürst, was a brave huntsman. One day while visiting Altdorf, the capital of Uri, with his son Walter, he was arrested; he refused to honor the hat of the Habsburg bailiff Gessler, which was placed on a tall pole for all to pay due respect. Gessler then ordered Tell to take his crossbow and pierce an apple placed on his son's head. Tell hesitated; Gessler insisted. Tell's valiant son persuaded his father to go ahead. Tell succeeded; Gessler, however, discovered a second arrow inside Tell's shirt

William Tell open-air performance near Interlaken

and asked its purpose. Tell replied that had he killed his son, the second arrow would have been for Gessler. Immediately rearrested he was taken in Gessler's boat to Brunnen in Canton Schwyz. During a heavy storm, Tell was pressed into service to maneuver the boat and somehow managed to jump ashore at today's Tell Chapel. Later, he apparently ambushed and killed Gessler in the *Hohle Gasse* (a path through a hollow) at Küssnacht. The play *Wilhelm Tell* by Schiller (1804) is performed every summer at the open-air theater near Interlaken, with local residents playing the roles. The legend is commemorated with wall paintings by Ernst Stückelberg at the Tell Chapel on the Lake of Uri.

Editor's note: This legend is likely based on an 11th-century Norwegian fable. It first appeared in Switzerland in 1470 in the 'Weisse Buch von Sarnen'; plays were already enacted in the 16th century.

The Swiss National Museum, Museumstrasse 2, Zurich, is devoted to Swiss cultural history.

The Swiss National Museum, Château de Prangins, Vaud, depicts life as it was in Switzerland from 1700 to 1900. (Katherine McCormick, an American, owned the château; she later deeded it to the US government).

Johann Jacob Bachofen by Hieronymus Hess, 19th century

BIOGRAPHICAL SKETCHES

We present chronologically, as in the 1986 edition, the first six sketches (Erasmus, Amerbach, Wettstein, Euler, Burckhardt and Böcklin) by Dr. Hannah Katz.

Erasmus: 1469–1536

Had we met Erasmus in 1514 when he first came to Basel to visit his printer and publisher Froben, he might have disappointed us; he would not have met our expectations as one of the great men of history. He was a somewhat frail looking person, constantly worried about being in a draft, catching cold, contracting the plague, or having to live through any kind of upheaval, such as war or revolution, both of which were frequent in his time. He wanted peace, quiet and comfort in which to do his work, and, having that, worked incredibly hard and passionately.

Born in Rotterdam, by 1514 Erasmus was acclaimed and praised throughout the intellectual world of 16th-century Europe. He corresponded with the leading men of his time, among them popes, emperors and kings. His training was both philological and theological. One of his major accomplishments was translating, editing and annotating the New Testament in Greek and Latin.

Editor's note: The New Testament had already been translated from Greek by St. Jerome (c. 342-420), but Erasmus detected that the Greek had been corrupted. He differed with Jerome's Latin that was done at the bidding of the Roman hierarchy. Erasmus translated with the express purpose of putting it into the hands of the common people of his day.

He was the first writer and publicist to rely on the printing press for the widespread diffusion of his ideas; he wrote in a beautiful clear Latin, often witty or satirical—but always clever and skillful—about religious, political and social issues of his time. He was a foe of credulity and ignorance and wanted to see the good and the pure triumph in every sphere; he pleaded constantly for reform, and he meant reform, not revolution. This attitude placed him in opposition to Luther and other reformers, although all of them propagated some of Erasmus's ideas.

Albrecht Dürer's St. Jerome in his Study, Basel, 1492

His views on various subjects such as education or hygiene were strikingly modern. It took several centuries for them to be accepted and adopted. He advocated that children should be taught with love rather than severity and that they should learn through play. He condemned the lack of fresh air, as well as several people drinking from the same goblet, as conducive to sickness—surprising ideas for his contemporaries.

When Erasmus appeared at Froben's front door in 1514, he was evidently in high spirits. He told Froben, to whom he was a stranger, that Erasmus had sent him to look after his books. How long he continued this practical joke is not known.

Erasmus traveled for a great part of his life. He had invitations from all corners of Europe; it is remarkable that he spent almost eight consecutive years in Basel. Froben and others became his close friends; that was only one reason why the city was so attractive to him. Basel was also relatively peaceful, and Erasmus liked the climate!

He resided in Basel through most of the 1520s. His best-known work, 'In Praise of Folly', came into the hands of the 18-year-old Hans Holbein the Younger (1497-1543). Holbein illustrated the margins of the book for his pleasure and that of Erasmus. The book is still published with these drawings. Holbein painted Erasmus several times while both resided in Basel. When Holbein left for England, Erasmus gave him letters of introduction to Sir Thomas More, which helped Holbein establish good connections at the English court. He eventually became the court painter under Henry VIII.

When the Reformation movement reached Basel in 1529, the town was on the verge of revolution. Rioting mobs destroyed much beautiful church property. Erasmus immediately fled to Freiburg im Breisgau, despite the fact that his former student, Oekolampad, led the movement. When he returned in 1535, Basel had become a Protestant town. Once again, he resided with the Froben family who had moved to a newly built house at Bäumleingasse. Erasmus's apartment was spacious and comfortable; it is now open to the public. Over the ten-year-period before his death, Erasmus sold his library of 413 books to a Polish baron, one of his former students. The sales contract stipulated that Erasmus would retain the use of his library as long as he lived. The purchaser had to pay half the price at once, and the other half after Erasmus's death; the sales price was 600 gold guilders, representing three years' salary for a university professor. These books are now scattered around the world or lost.

Erasmus died at seventy, a year after returning to Basel. The town felt honored by his presence. Although a Catholic, he received an official funeral and was buried in a prominent position in the Cathedral. The epigraph on his gravestone states that a tribute to his memory is unnecessary, as he has rendered himself immortal.

Editor's note: The Erasmus Walk—the historical heart of the city—is signposted. Further information is available at the tourist office.

Bonifacius Amerbach: 1495–1562

Amerbach, who studied law, became professor at the University of Basel and consultant to the city government. The first to collect Hans Holbein's art, he and his son compiled a valuable collection—the *Amerbach Kabinett*. The most precious part of the collection, Holbein's paintings and drawings, are at the Kunstmuseum Basel. The few objects inherited by Amerbach from Erasmus, along with items collected by his son Basilius, are at the Historisches Museum Basel.

In 1535 he was rector of the university; aside from his personal relationship with Erasmus, he realized that Erasmus's return from Freiburg im Breisgau, where he had fled during the Reformation, would increase the attractiveness of the university. Erasmus died one year after his return. Amerbach was forty-years old.

In addition to his hobby of art collecting, his job and various other tasks, Amerbach had to fulfill the stipulations of Erasmus's testament: to manage and distribute the fortune left by Erasmus. He invested 5000 *Goldgulden* / guilders, the sum remaining after all obligations had been discharged. The income from this investment was used to establish a foundation that would distribute money for charitable purposes. He also shipped three barrels of Erasmus's books to Poland. His most challenging task was receiving needy people. For 25 years he listened to their pleas and decided who was worthy of a donation. Amerbach accomplished this tedious task with great patience and benevolence. He had to listen to untrue stories, deal with lazy students, or console those who had walked from Rotterdam to Basel because of a rumor that every

citizen of Rotterdam, Erasmus's birthplace, could spend a year in Basel on money received from the foundation. All of his decisions were recorded faithfully in a ledger. Although he kept a large leather purse with five divisions to facilitate the equal distribution of money to the poor people mentioned in the testament, (e.g., old people, needy students, poor maidens in need of a trousseau, etc.), he eventually fell to borrowing from one partition to fill another as it became empty. His desire to help was greater than his inclination to be systematic.

Amerbach helped innumerable people by paying their rent, medicine, furniture, food and clothing. Erasmus knew his friend well. All of his requests were honored with much devotion and no pay. The small sum left to Amerbach by Erasmus had no relationship to the labor and time involved in executing his will.

Bonifacius Amerbach should not only be remembered as a friend to Erasmus and Holbein, as a lawyer who amassed a remarkable art collection, but also as a shining example of a 16th-century social worker.

Johann Rudolf Wettstein: 1594–1666

Wettstein, in addition to being a noteworthy mayor of Basel, played a most important part in the history of Switzerland. His life and his career were as remarkable as the man himself. He was married at the age of 16 to a 22-year-old girl from a good family for purely practical reasons. Anna Maria, no longer considered young, needed a husband. The marriage provided Wettstein with a good financial start, but more importantly offered him the possibility of a political career in Basel. Wettstein's family was not wealthy, and, furthermore, had moved to Basel shortly before his birth, which meant they were not entirely accepted. Without the connection provided by the marriage, holding public office was out of the question.

The marriage, unfortunately, proved to be a mistake and cast a shadow over Wettstein's entire life. His wife was the nagging type, while he was both aggressive and easily hurt. He had a keen sense of humor, lacking in his wife; he was courageous and ready to master any situation except in his own home. During the first years of marriage, Wettstein was so unhappy that he finally fled to Venice. While there, he entered into military service and wrote home asking for a divorce. His mother opposed his request and asked him to return, which he did. Although still unhappy at home, he was useful and intelligent in public affairs. He was promoted within his guild and held a number of important positions in the government; in 1645 he became mayor. By then he and his wife had nine children.

In 1646 the European states engaged in The Thirty Years' War, assembled their statesmen and delegates at a peace congress in Westphalia. The Swiss cantons had not taken part in the war, and at first did not plan to attend the congress. Basel, however, was having difficulties with the German Imperial Court of Justice, which claimed the right to judge cases involving some of the city tradesmen. The court also ordered the city to pay taxes. Basel had claimed exemption from imperial jurisdiction as a right of long standing. In order to settle this matter, Basel, with the

reluctant backing of nine cantons, decided to send Wettstein to Westphalia.

The three cantons around the Lake of Lucerne refused to endorse this mission. They did not consider it worthwhile to spend money on something that did not in the least concern them. They had no common frontier with a foreign country and therefore did not feel exposed. For them the entire issue was purely theoretical. Wettstein remained in Westphalia for over a year. With French backing, his mission broadened from a simple confirmation of freedom from imperial jurisdiction to a demand for recognition of the Swiss cantons as a sovereign state. The Swiss Confederation had existed as such for many years, but was not officially recognized by law; hence the demands of the imperial court. The French, who were interested in any development that would contribute to a weakening of the German Empire, wholeheartedly backed Wettstein's diplomatic efforts. It took great perseverance and much hard work on Wettstein's part to conclude successfully his mission. Moreover, he suffered a major handicap—reluctant and lukewarm backing from home. The very people whose interests he represented were unwilling financially and morally to back him. Some citizens of Basel even believed the money wasted.

Other diplomats lived well, or even splendidly, while Wettstein had to live in small and shabby apartments, to rent worn carriages and to dress modestly. Success, however, crowned his efforts. The final document of the peace congress contained a formal recognition of the independence of the Swiss Confederation.

One additional accomplishment needs mention. In 1661 the library and art collection started by Bonifacius Amerbach and continued by his son Basilius, was on the verge of being sold to Amsterdam by Basilius's heirs. Wettstein persuaded the city government and the university to buy this unique collection for Basel.

Editor's note: Spielzeugmuseum in Riehen was his residence; the Wettstein Fountain and Wettstein Bridge are named in his honor.

Leonhard Euler: 1707–1783

Euler was born in 1707. His father, a clergyman, expected him to become a theologian and he did begin his studies in this field. Professor Johann Bernoulli, an eminent scholar and his science teacher, persuaded Leonhard and his father that he should study science. At the age of twenty, young Euler applied unsuccessfully for a teaching position at the University of Basel. At that time if there were no general agreements among the university authorities, the two or three candidates drew lots for the available teaching positions. Euler decided to try his luck at the newly established academy at St. Petersburg in Russia where Bernoulli's sons taught; after a while, he was appointed professor of physics and mathematics. He had the remarkable gift of being able to express himself clearly and simply about the most intricate scientific problems. In 1733 he married a Swiss girl in St. Petersburg.

Fascinated by his science, he ceaselessly worked out new combinations and formulae at an astonishing speed; he explained differential and integral calculus; he wrote textbooks understood by people without a special aptitude for mathematics. In the following years, he became well known and decided to move with his family to Berlin. Euler's motives for moving were mostly political, as conditions in Russia had become turbulent due to ineffective rulers. Frederick the Great was pleased to have him join the Prussian Academy of Sciences. His amazing productivity continued while in Berlin. He contributed his thoughts and ideas to fields as varied as astronomy, shipbuilding, navigation, turbine-drives, and studies of light, color and musical theory. The French Academy in Paris named him a nonresident member, a distinction of high honor when Paris was the recognized center of European culture.

In spite of his talents and honors, he remained modest and patient. After teaching for two decades in Prussia, he returned to St. Petersburg. Order had been restored under the reign of Catherine the Great. This time his reasons for returning were personal. Frederick II never showed gratitude for Euler's achievements. Although it was important to the king to have a brilliant academy of sciences, his chief interest belonged to the arts. Euler also lacked social graces and dexterity, serious disadvantages in Frederick's eyes. Catherine, on the other hand, liked Euler and was grateful to have him return; his presence increased the intellectual brilliance of her academy—she personally welcomed him back.

An operation in 1771 failed to help his deteriorating eyesight. Six years after his return, he was blind. With the aid of devoted students, he continued to teach and to produce exciting scholarly works. Translations of his works appeared in many languages, both during his lifetime and after his death in 1783. The university in Basel lost out on a great scholar.

Editor's note: Euler's portrait is in the Aula at the Naturhistorisches Museum and at the Kunstmuseum Basel. The Hotel Euler carries his name, as does Eulerstrasse.

Jacob Burckhardt: 1818–1897

Jacob Burckhardt's independent thinking and passion for history led him to new ways of looking at historical documents. Until then, historical research had been confined mainly to the political aspects of history. Jacob Burckhardt went further; he wanted to know and to show how people lived in former times, and what they thought. He was interested in their likes and dislikes, their joys and fears, their art and literature, and their cuisine. For example, he investigated the psychological atmosphere in Rome during its decline and fall. He fashioned a verbal-portrait of Napoleon; he researched the cooking habits of the ancient Greeks; he described the daily life of a Parisian lady frequenting the court of Louis XIV. He lectured on painting—its changes in style and subject matter as related to history; he spoke about poets and painters, about different religions and discussed the relationship between painting and the Bible. His interests were extensive.

Two of his most famous books: *'Die Kultur der Renaissance in Italien'* / The Civilization of the Renaissance in Italy (1860) and *'Weltgeschichtliche Betrach-*

tungen' / Reflections on History (1905) expound his views on the political future. He taught at the universities in Bonn, Berlin, Zurich, and for many years in Basel.

There was much more that made Jacob Burckhardt an outstanding individual in addition to his pioneering work in exploring the relationship between art history and cultural history. He was a fascinating lecturer; when he spoke, his audience was spellbound. Inspired by his material and by his travels, he talked as if he saw the subject—a visionary with hindsight, an artist painting the past, an actor making it come alive. His language was natural. The appropriate words seemed to flow. His voice was agreeably sonorous; he had a wonderful sense of humor. He transmitted his immense scholarly knowledge in an entertaining manner, a rare gift. There can be no doubt that his lectures were a great attraction and a delight.

His private life was austere. All of his concentration was devoted to his academic endeavors; he never married. A dark, deep staircase led to a few small, narrow and poorly furnished rooms in his quarters on St. Alban-Vorstadt. Evidently his work was not financially rewarded, but this did not seem to bother him. One of his students in describing Burckhardt's outward appearance as an elderly gentleman is remembered as saying: of medium height with very short-cropped hair, a mustache and baggy trousers. The head is wonderful—special and spirited.

He carried a blue briefcase every day as he walked past the Cathedral on the way to his classes. At seventy-five he stopped lecturing. He died four years later.

A former student who succeeded him at the university said in his inaugural address, that he did not dare praise Burckhardt: only gratefulness and veneration seemed appropriate. A number of inspired students continued his work, but the magic of his own presentations remains unique.

Editor's note: Other works by Burckhardt: 'Recollections of Rubens', 'The Age of Constantine the Great', 'The History of Greek Culture' and 'Cicerone'. A memorial tablet is at Burckhardt's lodgings, St. Alban-Vorstadt 64, Haus Zur Roten Tanne. Jacob Burckhardt-Strasse carries his name. A Jacob Burckhardt Walk—past and present in harmony—is signposted. Further information is available at the tourist office.

Arnold Böcklin: 1827–1901

Böcklin was born when Jacob Burckhardt was nine-years old. He received drawing lessons as a boy, and at the age of 18 went to Düsseldorf, Germany to attend art school. In 1848, after spending a few years at the school, he began to travel. His first stop was Paris where he was not only impressed with the city, but also surprised and frightened by the February Revolution with its bloody and brutal scenes. He soon found himself penniless and returned home. Unknown and without work, he became so depressed that he thought of dying. Instead, he fell in love with a neighbor's daughter.

At the time a stay in Rome was indispensable for an aspiring painter. Burckhardt, who recognized his young friend's extraordinary gift, encouraged him to go. In 1850 he left for Rome; two weeks after Böcklin's departure, his bride died of brain fever. Although this terrible misfortune affected him deeply, he decided to remain in Rome. He studied its art and architecture and familiarized himself with the surrounding landscape. Two years later, he interrupted his stay and hiked back to Switzerland over the Gotthard route. One can observe from his paintings how closely he studied the Alps, noting their wild formations and deep ravines.

In 1853 he returned to Rome where he married a pretty, well-educated Roman girl. Jacob Burckhardt was his witness at the wedding ceremony.

For years Böcklin's economic situation remained a crushing worry for him and his growing family. Added to this was the constant threat of illness and death; cholera epidemics being a constant threat, both in Rome and in Munich, where the family lived in 1873/74.

Böcklin and his wife had 13 children. Six died young. Böcklin himself fell seriously ill several times, normal dangers in the 19th century. Böcklin's reaction to these experiences was always deeply emotional. Just as he was easily touched by beauty and joy, he became easily depressed by fears and losses.

Some of his paintings inspired composers. The famous *Toteninsel* / Island of the Dead (1880) is a fine example. Sergei Rachmaninoff (1873-1943) created his symphonic poem *The Isle of the Dead* in 1908 after Böcklin's painting. This painting was so popular that up until the beginning of the 20th century, a reproduction of some type was in most middle-class homes in Germany and Switzerland.

Toteninsel, 1880

He gradually found friends and patrons who supported him. From 1860/62 he held a professorship at the painting academy in Weimar; nevertheless, he could not be persuaded to stay on any longer. Work was promised in Basel and he returned in 1865. He had obtained some private commissions and sold his first painting to the city.

The Basel Museum Committee asked him to paint three frescoes to decorate the walls going up the inside staircase in the museum at Augustinergasse, today two museums: Museum der Kulturen Basel and Naturhistorisches Museum Basel. The sketches submitted for the first two frescoes were accepted and Böcklin set to work. The third sketch created an uproar. It was a picture of the god Apollo riding one of several horses as they soared towards heaven. People climbing the stairs would have been able to admire the bodies of the horses from below; it would have been a most naturalistic sight. This was the crucial point. It clashed with the puritanical views and the aesthetic ideals of the time. There is little doubt that even the first fresco, which depicts two fat demigods (Tritons: half-man, half-fish) carrying a goddess through the water, also offended some sensibilities. The horses, however, were more than the committee could take. Since Jacob Burckhardt, as a member of the committee, had been partly responsible for naming Böcklin to paint the frescoes, it fell to him to tell his friend that he should veil the bodies of the horses with clouds. This criticism ended their friendship. Böcklin complied, but he was furious. Looking at this fresco today, one can sense his anger. The clouds are badly painted and the horses seem to drown in them. He finished his murals, but added three heads—Medusa with terribly glaring eyes, and two masks with grim and stupid countenances. He could not have been more explicit. The entire drama is played out on the stairway at Augustinergasse.

Despite these differences, Böcklin was asked to decorate a wall of the newly built Kunsthalle with sculpted stone masks, which turned out to be very witty.

In 1871 he left Basel for Munich; in the following years he became well known. His drawings and paintings, of which the Kunstmuseum Basel has acquired a goodly number, are executed with verve and animation. Classical sagas, allegories, striking landscapes, portraits and self-portraits bear his special imprint. His preoccupation with death is obvious. One of his self-portraits, in the *Nationalgalerie Berlin*, shows him with brush in hand concentrating on his canvas while Death, almost touching him with horrible, bony fingers, stands behind him playing the fiddle.

In 1887, the year Böcklin turned 70, Basel christened the Arnold Böcklin-Strasse and honored him with a large exhibition of his works. At the vernissage, Burckhardt's successor at the university, Heinrich Wölfflin, praised Böcklin's art, diplomatically including the frescoes. He also called attention to the brilliant colors of Böcklin's latest works. They seemed festive to him. "Many people," he said, "cannot conceive that Basel, where the joy of life has always been subdued and veiled, is his home town. But as long as Arnold Böcklin is honored in our town, the festive radiance we enjoy here today will never entirely disappear."

Böcklin died in 1901 near Florence. There can be no disagreement about the words carved on his gravestone: *"NON OMNIS MORIAS"* (I shall not wholly die).

Editor's note: A retrospective of Arnold Böcklin's paintings was held at the Kunstmuseum Basel in 2001.
A memorial tablet is at Gerbergasse 4.

Bachofen family coat of arms

Johann Jacob Bachofen: 1815–1887

Johann Jacob Bachofen, born into an important silk-ribbon manufacturing family, inherited one of Basel's greatest fortunes. Because of alliances established over generations through marriage—the Burckhardt, Merian and Hoffmann families—a sound financial and social standing was secured for him. His mother, Valerie, was of the distinguished Merian family.

Bachofen studied law, the humanities and philology at the universities of Basel, Berlin and Göttingen. In 1841 at the age of 26, he received his doctorate in jurisprudence and became a professor of law at the University of Basel. One year later he was named criminal court judge, and in 1844 was elected to the legislature. This provoked uproar in the liberal press, aimed more at the Basel establishment than at Bachofen. Shortly after he resigned from these positions, thereby ending his academic and political careers.

His intellectual energy was then directed to that of a private scholar. He detached himself from community life in Basel, entered into discussions with Nietzsche (who at that time was teaching philology at the university) and corresponded with others of similar interest outside his native city. His learning and insight made him one of the best interpreters of ancient myths and sagas and led him to explore the depths of the human soul. He devoted much of his time to the study of the symbols of death and resurrection; to Bachofen humanity consisted of the solidarity between the living and the deceased. The accidental death of his sister so affected him that mourning was a normal condition and a central theme of his writings. He searched for life in graves—antiquity, he stated, is at its greatest in its graves. With his sense of symbolism, he contributed to a better understanding of religion and modern psychology.

His most famous work *'Das Mutterrecht'* / Myth, Religion and Mother Right, published in 1861, is dedicated to his mother. It sets forth the precept that matriliny (descent through women) and matriarchy (rule by women) were two aspects of the same institution elevating women to the same status occupied by men in a patriarchy.

At various times the Bachofen family owned an impressive number of some of Basel's finest residential and commercial properties: a factory in the old *Friedhof* / cemetery in the Petersgasse, the *Rollerhof* in the Cathedral Square and several villas in the countryside, including the *Ebenrain* near Sissach. They escaped the summer heat in Basel by retreating to their residence on Klybeck strasse in Kleinbasel. The baroque *Weisses Haus* on Rheinsprung was purchased in 1811; it remained the headquarters of their company until its dissolution in the early 20th century. The Bachofen family coat of arms is over the entranceway and inside the building. A villa designed by Melchior Berri on St. Alban-Graben (the Antikenmuseum Basel und Sammlung Ludwig) is where Bachofen was born—precisely in the garden house, the *Ritterhof*—and lived for 50 years. In 1865 Bachofen married Louise Burckhardt; in 1870 they moved into their home at Münsterplatz 2, designed by Christoph Riggenbach. A son was born one year later. The house is on the site of a former medieval baptismal chapel (zur *Johanneskapelle*). During extensive renovations, remains of the chapel were rediscovered.

In 1921 the Bachofen house on the Münsterplatz, which had been acquired by the city from Louise Bachofen, served as a branch of the Kunstmuseum. 293 paintings from the Bachofen Collection, many purchased by Louise Bachofen, were bequeathed to the museum.

During his Italian journeys, Bachofen purchased funerary lamps and ancient objects, most of which had symbolic and religious meanings. These he willed to the city of Basel. Some are now on view at the Antikenmuseum Basel und Sammlung Ludwig as the Bachofen Collection.

Bachofen's epitaph could well be his own statement—that not to be crowned with success is not the same as failure. He is revered in Germanic language and anthropological studies— a prophet except in his native city.

Louise Burckhardt-Bachofen, 1865

Karl Barth: 1886–1968

Karl Barth is considered by some to be the greatest Protestant theologian of the 20th century and by others, the greatest since the Reformation. Barth inspired and led the renaissance of theology that took place from about 1920 to 1950. Born in Basel to Fritz Barth and Anna Sartorius, he grew up in Bern where his father was a professor of New Testament and early church history. Barth studied theology at the university in Bern and at several universities in Germany. In 1913 he married Nelly Hoffman, a talented violinist; they had five children.

Barth earned the reputation as a radical critic of the prevailing liberal theology and social order. In his commentary *'Epistle to the Romans'* published in 1919 (a second, thoroughly revised edition was published in 1922 and translated into English in 1933), Barth stressed the discontinuity between the Christian message and the world—not only the modern world, but also the world of any era.

He held several professorships in Germany: in 1930 in systematic theology at the University of Bonn. His opposition to Hitler's regime (along with his refusal to pledge allegiance to Hitler) and his articles in opposition to National Socialist ideologies (*'The Barmen Declaration'*) led to his suspension from his chair at the university in 1934, and his expulsion from Germany in 1935. That same year his native Basel offered him a chair in theology; from that position he continued to champion his causes until his retirement in 1962. Barth

made regular visits to the Basel prison. His sermons, *'Deliverance to the Captives'*, emphasized his passion for the word of God and his social concerns. In Barth's sentiment, there is a sharp difference between religion and 'faith', which relates to the word of God.

A multivolume work, *'The Church Dogmatics'*, first volume (CD I/1) published in 1932 and volume IV/4 published in 1967, remained unfinished upon his death in 1968. *'The Christian Life'* was published posthumously in 1976.

In 1971 the Karl Barth Foundation and Archives opened in Basel. The Foundation's main objective is to publish his collected works. The Archives are located at Barth's former residence, Bruderholzallee 26. His grave is at the Hörnli Cemetery.

The Center for Barth Studies established in 1997 is part of the Princeton Theological Seminary Libraries System. The Center is amassing a complete collection of writings by and about Karl Barth; it is a clearinghouse for Barth scholarship and activities.

"With an ear open to your musical dialectic, one can be young and become old, can work and rest, be content and sad: in short, one can live." Karl Barth: *'A Letter of Thanks to Mozart'*.

Sebastian Brant: Strasbourg 1458–1521

In 1474 Sebastian Brant, a German humanist and poet, arrived in Basel to attend the university. He began studying philosophy, changed to law and succeeded in lecturing and practicing in both professions.

His poems, written in Latin and German, professed his religious and political ideals, praising Christ, the saints, the Virgin and her Immaculate Conception. He decried the paintings adorning lawyers' offices in Basel and commented that the clocks of Basel were one hour ahead of those in the environs. This alludes to when Basel was surrounded by enemies, both inside and outside the city gates. The conspirators agreed to coordinate their efforts in order to seize the city. The city watchman, however, learned of the plan and advanced the

city clock by one hour. This confused all. After informing the magistrate of this treachery, forces were mounted; the enemy weary of the siege retreated. By order of the magistrate, and until 1798, the clocks remained one hour in advance, ringing one o'clock in the city and twelve in the environs.

For almost two decades, Brant worked as a corrector in the printing houses of Basel. During this time, he married and had seven children.

In 1494 his *'Narrenschiff'* / Ship of Fools poem, a bitter satire on the follies and vices of the time, which was to have an impact on the cultural climate in Europe, was published in Basel. It tells of how a ship loaded with fools sailed to fools' paradise, Narragonia. Translations into French and Latin followed in 1497 and English in 1570. Hieronymus Bosch (c.1450-1516) painted *The Ship of Fools* (at the Louvre) based on this poem.

After Basel separated from the Holy Roman Empire and subsequently joined the Confederation in 1501, his situation in the city became untenable. Returning to Strasbourg, he accepted a governmental position; over the years he served in various official capacities, the last as emissary to the newly elected Emperor Charles V.

Editor's note: Brant lived in the Haus zum Sunnenlufft (1494) at Augustinergasse 1.

Dispute over Basel's Time, 1778

Johannes Froben:
Hammelburg, Franconia c.1460 – Basel 1527

Johannes Froben arrived in Basel, studied at the university and in 1492 became a citizen. Printing was a thriving activity in the city; Berthold Ruppel had founded a printing press in 1468. A short time later there would be over 70 printing establishments in operation, about the same number as today.

Froben's first publication, a Latin Bible, appeared in 1492. In 1496 he entered into partnership with Johannes Petri and in 1500 with Johannes Amerbach and the bookseller Wolfgang Lachner, whose daughter Gertrud he would marry. Eventually Froben controlled seven presses. He revolutionized printing in Basel —popularizing the Roman font, introducing italic and Greek fonts, experimenting with smaller and cheaper books and employing artists, e.g., Hans Holbein the Younger, as illustrators. His printing establishment *zum Sessel* at Totengässlein 5 (the small lane of the dead), once the property of the Eberler family, was acquired by Froben shortly after his arrival in Basel.

Between 1515 and 1520, Froben was the most renowned printer in the German-speaking area: a brilliant and sensitive publisher, he championed Basel's position as the leading printing center for German, French, Flemish and Italian clients.

His proofreaders, perhaps the word correctors would be more appropriate, were famous scholars and included Nicolaus Episcopius and Oekolampad. The proximity to the previously seldom used manuscript collections of Alsace and the Palatinate aided the advancement of his enterprise.

About 250 of his publications have been catalogued. They include the first New Testament printed in Greek and Latin, edited and annotated by Erasmus (1516), who after 1514 entrusted all his works to Froben. Erasmus praised Froben's noble nature and his capacity for affectionate friendship.

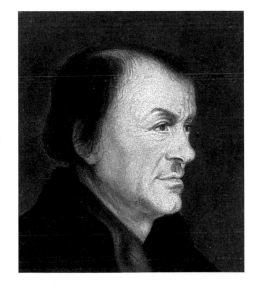

Froben printed the works of Velleius Paterculus (1520) and Tertullian (1521), both edited by the humanist Beatus Rhenanus (1485-1547).

The first child baptized in the Cathedral after Basel joined the Confederation in 1501 was Froben's son, Hieronymus.

The funerary memorial of the master of printers in the *Eberlerkapelle* at

St. Peter's Church bears a text in Hebrew, Greek and Latin, possibly by Erasmus. The sculpted decorations are believed to be from a design by Hans Holbein the Younger—tributes to the prince of his trade from two exceptional men.

Emperor Heinrich II: Bavaria 973 – Göttingen 1024
Empress Kunigunde: Luxembourg c.980 – Kassel 1033

Heinrich was one of the three patron saints (with Maria and Pantalus) of the Basel Cathedral from 1347 to the Reformation in 1529, and of the bishopric of Basel from 1347 until today. Heinrich and Kunigunde were still very important for Basel after the Reformation, rather like 'patrons' of the city.

The Hungarian invasion of Basel in 917 left the cathedral built by Bishop Haito (805/823) in ruins. In 1006, the childless King Rudolph III of Burgundy gave the western part of Switzerland (which included Basel) to his nephew, the King of Germany, Heinrich II. Basel thus became the doorway to Burgundy, France and Italy, thereby sparking economic and cultural growth for the city. The future German King and Holy Roman Emperor was born in 973, the last of the Saxon dynasty of emperors. Well-educated and destined for the priest-

On western facade of the Cathedral

hood, he was crowned king in 1002 and ruled the Empire until 1024. As a conscientious, pious and practical leader he worked for cooperation between church and state, which obliged him to travel throughout the Empire in order to quell opposition and bring about or maintain peace. Successful and admired as a soldier and ruler, Heinrich answered the plea of Pope Benedict VIII in 1013 to put down a rebellion in Rome. As a reward, the Pope crowned him Holy Roman Emperor in 1014. During his reign Heinrich made three visits to Rome.

When Heinrich married Kunigunde of Luxembourg, daughter of the Duke of Luxembourg sometime before 995, he was already Duke of Bavaria. She became queen upon the crowning of Heinrich as king, and empress upon his

Empress Kunigunde Walking on Red-hot Plowshares by W. Katzheimer

crowning as emperor. They had no children and were devoted totally to each other. Heinrich valued Kunigunde's intelligence and companionship as consort, advisor, aide and representative, both at home and during their travels.

In addition to bestowing upon Basel the golden altar frontal (1015/19) probably from Bamberg, Germany, now at the Musée de Cluny in Paris, the Heinrich Cross (1000/50), now in Berlin, and other church treasures, he contributed to the rebuilding of the Basel Cathedral. He was present at its consecration in 1019.

Golden altar frontal (antependium), 1015/19

Together they established and endowed the religious community in Bamberg: building a magnificent cathedral, creating a bishopric and supporting pious and religious foundations.

Upon Heinrich's death in 1024, Kunigunde, together with her brothers, ruled the Empire for a short period until King Konrad II assumed power. On the first anniversary of her husband's demise, she retired to a convent founded by the couple where she remained the rest of her life.

In 1146 Heinrich was canonized, the only Holy Roman Emperor to receive such honor. Kunigunde was canonized in 1200.

In 1347 relics of the imperial pair arrived in Basel from Bamberg. Shortly thereafter, Heinrich was designated patron saint of the Cathedral, together with the Virgin Mary and St. Pantalus. *See Basel history.*

The Cathedral of Bamberg houses an impressive marble cenotaph by Tilman Riemenschneider (1513) with bas-relief scenes from the lives of the imperial couple. Their skulls are housed in a crystal case in a chapel in the crypt. The separation, distribution and sale of saints' bodily parts for religious, political and economic reasons were common practices in the Middle Ages.

Over the centuries, legends developed pertaining to the couple and in particular to Kunigunde. One such tale is illustrated by showing her walking barefoot over red-hot plowshares and surviving unscathed, a trial proving her saintly purity.

Basel elected to join the Swiss Confederation on 13 July (1501), the anniversary of Heinrich's death.

Representations of the holy pair can be found in various locations in Basel: among the sculpted figures above the clock on the city hall; on the western facade of the Cathedral; kneeling in adoration at the feet of Christ on the copy of the golden altar frontal in the Historisches Museum Basel, and more.

Hans Holbein the Younger: Augsburg 1497 – London 1543

Hans Holbein the Younger received his first lessons in art from his father, a respected master. After leaving Augsburg with his brother Ambrosius—during their travels they worked as journeymen—they arrived in Basel in 1515 hoping to find work as book illustrators.

It was with the publisher Froben that Hans Holbein immediately found employment. His first works to come down to us intact are the illustrations on the margins of Erasmus's satire, *'Encomium Moriae'* / In Praise of Folly (1515), an auspicious beginning. Erasmus, who had arrived in Basel in 1514, befriended the young Holbein.

An early work by the brothers was a sign for the schoolmaster Oswald Myconius. In 1516 Holbein received a commission for the double portrait of *Bürgermeister* / Mayor Jacob Meyer zum Hasen (1482-1531) and his wife Dorothea Kannengiesser.

Meyer was the first mayor of Basel elected from the merchant class, not from the nobility.

Self-portrait (1542/43)

There is evidence that in 1517/18 Hans Holbein left Basel for Lucerne where he worked alongside his father decorating the house of Mayor Jakob von Hertenstein.

Soon after his return to Basel in 1519, Holbein painted the portrait of Bonifacius Amerbach, a simple and striking masterpiece in portraiture. Ambrosius disappeared at this time; perhaps he left the city, or he succumbed to the plague.

When Hans the Younger married the widow of a tanner, he obtained the status of burgher. In 1519 he joined the guild *zum Himmel* and became a master of his trade; his brother had previously joined the guild. Both his citizenship and his marriage would keep Holbein returning to Basel for the rest of his life.

Wall paintings, designs for glass, drawings for engravers and for book illustrations bear witness to his talents. It is difficult to conjure up an image of how Basel must have looked at that time with his genius evident in so many public buildings. Only a few fragments of Holbein's wall paintings have survived; fortunately his designs are preserved and many are at the Kunstmuseum Basel. In 1521 he received the commission to decorate two walls in the new *Grossratssaal* / cantonal parliament chamber of the city hall. Drawings have survived, giving us a satisfactory idea of the quality and scope of his œuvre. In 1523 a portrait of Froben was executed—and his first portrait of Erasmus. This painting bestowed upon Erasmus such marvelous dignity that it led to a great demand for Erasmus portraiture (these circulated much as our photos and images do today).

Due to the religious agitation and social unrest in 1524—a precursor to the Reformation—Holbein left Basel for France. In all probability, he encountered Leonardo da Vinci's work, as well as that of other contemporary Italian artists. (Leonardo died in 1519 in the Loire Valley and is buried at Amboise).

Holbein received the commission for the folding wings of the swallow's nest organ in the cathedral. (The organ no longer exists; the painted wings are in the Kunstmuseum Basel). Emperor Heinrich II and Empress Kunigunde are on the left-side panel with a view of the cathedral between them; the Virgin and St. Pantalus are on the right-side panel with a group of angels playing trumpets.

Holbein's drawings for the *Dance of Death (Pictures of Death)* woodcuts were done in Basel between the years 1523/26. Hans Lützelburger, an accomplished collaborator, interpreted the designs. A masterpiece emerged with Holbein's ability to communicate a sense of fatality in an era of plagues, wars and famines, and Lützelburger's talent in conveying these emotions via the woodcuts.

With permission granted by the city fathers, Holbein left Basel in 1526 for a two-year leave in England. He carried letters of introduction from Erasmus to Sir Thomas More, Henry VIII's chancellor. To paraphrase Erasmus—the arts in Basel had frozen. Upon his return in 1528, he purchased a house at St. Johanns-Vorstadt 22. Despite finding Basel in the throes of an upheaval with reformers about to do away with the old regime, he continued to paint. The portrait of his wife and two children executed at this time is a powerful yet tender work. Holbein's œuvre did not escape the iconoclastic frenzy and rampages of 1529. His painting of *The Last Supper*, influenced by Leonardo's painting (a copy of which he likely saw during his trip to France), was damaged; a fragment escaped destruction.

With the loss of his predominantly wealthy Catholic clientele, Holbein's prospects in Basel dramatically declined. Nevertheless, in 1530 he finished the third wall in the great council chamber at city hall. With this commission the city councilors hoped to persuade him to remain in Basel (a few fragments survived later renovations). The same year he was called before a citizens' committee of inquiry questioning his religious beliefs; the following year he was working in Freiburg im Breisgau, where Erasmus had fled.

A year later Holbein left Basel for England; his previous contacts ensured him royal commissions. A short return visit was necessary in 1538 to negotiate a pension and a two-year leave of absence in order to maintain his citizenship rights. His wife and two children remained in Basel on St. Johanns-Vorstadt and his wife drew on his pension.

Holbein returned to England as a royal painter and into the tumult of Henry VIII's court and marriages. He died there in 1543 from the plague and is buried in St. Andrew's Cemetery.

The contents of his last studio in Basel entered the Basilius Amerbach Collection; the latter would provide the foundation for the public art collection opened in 1662, today the Kunstmuseum Basel.

The works cited—and more—are at the Kunstmuseum Basel, either on exhibit or in the *Kupferstichkabinett* / Engraving Room.

The wings of the *Oberried Altar* (1520s) commissioned by Hans Oberried, a Basel council member, are in the University Chapel at the Cathedral of Freiburg im Breisgau; the central panel was lost during the iconoclastic turbulence.

Editor's note: There is a memorial plaque at St. Johanns-Vorstadt 22, the home of Holbein and his family.
A Holbein Walk—encompassing both sides of the Rhine—explores Basel from part of the old town and continues over into Kleinbasel. Information in English is available at the tourist office.

David Joris (Johann von Bruck): Bruges? c.1501 – Basel 1556

One day in early April 1544, three elegant Flemings requested and received residence rights in Basel. Asked if they were noble Netherlanders, Johann von Bruck (von Brügge) replied that the other two men were noble, but that he was not. A multilingual servant in their entourage named Heinrich Van Schor most likely assisted them. Von Bruck left almost immediately to assist in bringing his large family to Basel; we now know that he and the glass painter David Joris, who then applied for citizenship *in absentia,* were one and the same. Johann von Bruck was known in the Netherlands to be in charismatic opposition to the Catholic Church, and at the head of a major Anabaptist sect. Politico-religious chaos reigned at this time and executions of Protestants were commonplace and brutal.

Joris was born to a Dutch-Flemish family, many of whom died of the plague during his childhood. His chosen profession was that of glass painter. He married and had 11 children.

Joris was first impressed with Martin Luther's principally pacifist evangelism. Luther had opened a can of worms due to the myriad frustrations and disillusionment with the Catholic Church. Because of Joris's radical anti-Catholic activity, in 1528 he was imprisoned in Delft, put in the pillory and had his tongue bored. To avoid further conflict he spent much time hiding from and avoiding the authorities. Consequently, his glass-painting business collapsed. At this point he turned his substantial talents to politics, charismatic writing and preaching. His hymns and sermons were particularly powerful. Self-educated, his chief spiritual inspirations came from his visions and from the teachings of fellow reformers.

Having become an extreme pacifist Anabaptist with a growing family and increasing financial difficulties, Joris espoused contradicting philosophies, presumably to obtain supporters. In 1535 the conflicts of the militant Anabaptists in Munster, Germany were in full swing. They had seized the city, resisted a long siege and tried to remodel society along biblical and prophetic lines. The Catholic bishop, however, reinforced his depleted troops, surrounded the city and trapped 7000 women and 2000 men inside. A wartime mentality prevailed. Anabaptist priests became bigamous as well as brutal in order to survive, hoping at least to enjoy their last days. It seems that Joris avoided the militant portion of this Anabaptist congress due to family responsibilities, coupled with his pacifist nature. After their ultimate defeat, the Anabaptists were regarded as terrorists. The horror was still fresh in the minds of Baslers when Joris arrived in the city.

David Joris by Dutch Master of the 16th century

After the execution of his mother in 1538, Joris and his family were offered support and a place to live near Antwerp.

Supported by various Flemish followers, in 1540 he published a most successful *'Wonderbook'* notable for its illustration of the New Man, in which God the Father is in the head, Christ in the heart and the Soul in the genitalia. His sermons advocated sexual freedom within a marriage; but, he warned of the dangers of breaking marital vows. It did not matter how many wives one had as long as all followed the teachings of God.

Joris, his family and supporters acquired substantial real estate, including the *Spiesshof* on Nadelberg, a house opposite for storage, the *Schloss Binningen* and properties near St. Margaret's Church in Binningen. He enjoyed a peaceful and wealthy life in humanistic Basel until his death in 1556, shortly after that of his wife.

In 1559 Nikolaus Meynertsz van Blesdijk, a son-in-law, who had earlier followed Joris but now practiced a different type of reformed theology, revealed and condemned Joris as an Anabaptist and a heretic. Heinrich Van Schor, who entered Basel with Joris, assisted in the denouncement. Horrified, pious Baslers exhumed his body, held a trial, convicted him of heresy and burned his remains along with some of his books and portraits. They ostracized his children, demanded repentance and fined them. The fines went uncollected; enough of Joris's personal material survived to fill 15 volumes in the Basel University Library, and his portrait hangs in the Kunstmuseum Basel.

Joris was a pacifist Anabaptist. He was misunderstood—considered a militant, a bigamist and a philanderer. With the revival of interest in his writings by theologians, some who consider him a genius, this nomenclature is apt to change.

It is rumored that the ghost of David Joris still wanders around the Spiesshof (now an office of the *SBB* / Swiss Railway System). An employee in the office was on a group tour of the Kunstmuseum where a portrait of Joris hangs. Upon seeing it he exclaimed, "I just saw that man yesterday in the Spiesshof!"

Christoph Merian: 1808–1858

Christoph Merian was born into a wealthy and well-established family. His father, Christian Merian-Hoffmann (1769-1849), was a successful merchant and wished that his son would enter into the family business, Frères Merian. Instead, the younger Merian dedicated himself to agriculture, which he studied in Switzerland and Stuttgart, Germany.

At the age of 24 he married Margaretha Burckhardt (1806-1886). As a wedding present he received his first farm, *Brüglingen*, now the Botanical Garden; it became one of the most productive farms in the region. Merian significantly increased the amount of arable land when he straightened the course of the Birs River, which meandered through the farm. In 1836 after receiving an inheritance upon the death of his mother, he bought the St. Jakob estate adjacent to Brüglingen. Thereafter, he continued to purchase land and eventually expanded his total land holdings to 311 hectares, stretching from the Gellert quarter to the Bruderholz.

Merian was the sole heir to his parents' vast fortune. He inherited 2.5 million francs from his mother's estate and a further 9.5 million francs upon the death of his father, making him the wealthiest man in Switzerland.

The couple remained childless; Basel and its people became their adopted children. The first public act of charity was a donation of 10,000 francs in 1836 towards the building of a new hospital. In 1854, 100,000 francs were offered to help reduce the price of bread. This was followed by a 200,000 francs donation in 1856 for the Basel Mission (the mission founded in 1815 was

near the Music Academy; new headquarters later built at Missionsstrasse); that same year they decided to construct *Elisabethenkirche*. A further 300,000 francs were given in 1857 for a new wing of the *Bürgerspital*. Christoph Merian finalized his will in 1857, leaving his vast fortune of 11 million francs plus his land holdings as a foundation to the city. The foundation went into effect in 1886 upon the death of Margaretha.

The *Christoph Merian Stiftung* / Foundation (CMS) is the largest philanthropic organization in Switzerland. Its purpose is to help the needy and to promote the well-being of the people through various channels. It supports numerous charitable causes, sponsors cultural events in Basel and has its own publishing house. The foundation is administered by a special commission and supervised by the Citizens' Council. With 900 hectares of land, the foundation is one of the largest landowners in Switzerland. The main source of income comes from agriculture and rental properties. Since its inception, it has been active in building hospitals, nursing homes, museums, e.g., the Water Mill Museum in the Merian Park at Brüglingen, restoring buildings, refurbishing entire sections of the city, and actively supporting nature, the environment and the arts in Basel.

Paracelsus: Einsiedeln 1493 – Salzburg 1541

Philippus Aureolus Theophrastus Bombast von Hohenheim, better known as Paracelsus, was a key figure in the birth of modern medicine, chemistry, pharmacy and homeopathy. A colorful and dramatic character, he was a voluminous writer and an alchemist with amazing intellectual accomplishments. He was equally irreverent, boastful and arrogant.

After studying in Switzerland and Italy, Paracelsus settled in Strasbourg in 1526 where he practiced medicine. In 1527 he was called to Basel to treat the leg of the publisher Johannes Froben who suffered from a serious and perplexing illness. Once cured, Froben was able to ride his horse to the book fair in Frankfurt. Paracelsus also gave medical advice to Erasmus, met the Amerbach family and mingled with some of the more prominent scholars of the Basel Reformation. Oekolampad was his patron. Paracelsus lectured at the university and became city physician and professor of medicine.

On St. John's Day in 1527, he challenged the revered conventional medical wisdom of the day (based on writers from antiquity) by throwing the classic medical texts of Galen and Avicenna into a bonfire in a dramatic show of scorn. His verbal abuse accompanied his physical actions; he called physicians "sausage-stuffers", "impostors", and "ignorant sprouts". These and other incidents forced Paracelsus to flee Basel.

PHIL.^{Pe} THEOPHRASTE BOMBAST
dit Paracelse
Né à Einstdeln près Zurich en 1493. Mort à
Salzbourg en 1541.

Years were spent moving from town to town, leaving behind manuscripts as he continued working on his medical philosophy. His legacy far outshines the volatility of his personality. The significance of his contribution to science and modern medicine is favorably compared to that of his contemporary Nicholas Copernicus to astronomy and physics. The effect of Paracelsus on medicine was enormous. In the end, many of his medical views prevailed.

During a time when people spoke of white or black magic, Paracelsus roared "No! There is only one magic. Good or evil dwells in the practitioner, not the art." He chose the epithet Paracelsus as a means of proving his superiority to Celsus—an eclectic Platonist who lived in either Alexandria or Rome in the second century—one of the first iconoclasts representing the most powerful pagan reaction against Christianity.

Editor's note: There is a Paracelsus Walk—narrow lanes and many steps—encompassing both sides of the Birsig River Valley. Information in English is available at the tourist office. Paracelsus lived and worked at zum Sessel, Totengässlein 5, the location of the Pharmazie-Historisches Museum der Universität Basel.

Thomas Platter: Grächen 1499 – Basel 1582

Thomas Platter's memoirs, written in 1572 at the request of his son Felix, are an important source of information on peasant and family life in 16th-century Europe. It is a remarkable story of the transformation of a child born into a poor peasant family, to that of a prosperous member of Basel's humanistic and intellectual elite. His story illustrates the effects on one individual of the societal and ideological changes brought about by the Reformation and the Renaissance.

Thomas Platter was born in the Upper Valais; as a child he worked as a goatherd; as a youth he and a cousin set off for Germany in search of schooling. They traveled with a group of boys supporting themselves by begging and singing, common practices of students at the time.

By his mid-twenties he had learned to read and write Latin. In Zurich he studied with Myconius, a friend of the reformer Zwingli. In 1522 after hearing one of Zwingli's sermons, he became a staunch advocate of the doctrine put forth by the Protestant reformers; he carried letters for the Zurich Protestant leaders to other Swiss cantons. By 1526 he had also mastered Greek and Hebrew. Myconius was one of his pupils.

He became an apprentice ropemaker, a skill he would practice later in Basel. He taught Hebrew at St. Leonard's School, where he met Oporinus who, along with Myconius, played a key role in his life.

Platter traveled between Basel, Zurich and the Valais until 1531 when he settled permanently in Basel. He attended classes at the university and in 1534 accepted a position teaching Greek. In 1536, along with Oporinus and two others, he became a partner in a print shop; in 1538 he established his own printing business. A salient work published by his firm was the first edition of Calvin's '*Christianae religionis Institutio*' / Institutes of the Christian Religion (March 1536).

From 1544 until his retirement in 1578, he taught full time and became rector at the *Schule auf Burg*, now the *Gymnasium am Münsterplatz*; the founding of the school is to his credit. Thomas Platter was an influential figure in the development of secondary education in Basel.

Married twice, the second time in his seventies, he had 10 children. Only three, Felix, Thomas Jr. and Magdalena, survived to adulthood; the others succumbed to the plague.

Editor's note: The Thomas Platter House at Gundeldingerstrasse 280 escaped destruction and was restored in 1974. It now houses city offices.
A Thomas Platter Walk—craftsmen and academics—meanders through the former craftsmen's district. Further information in English is available from the tourist office.

Konrad Witz:
Germany c.1405 – Basel, probably of the plague, c.1446

Konrad Witz arrived in Basel c.1431. Whether he came to Basel upon the invitation of dignitaries attending the Church Council (1431/48) or arrived hoping to secure commissions is not known.

In 1434 he was admitted to the *zum Himmel* guild, the same guild Ambrosius and Hans Holbein the Younger would later join. Shortly thereafter he painted the *Heilspiegelaltar* / Mirror of Salvation Altar, most likely for St. Leonard's Church. Of the thirteen original wing-panels, nine are in the Kunstmuseum Basel, two in the municipal museum in Dijon and one in the *Gemäldegalerie Berlin*. The central shrine has not survived. The altarpiece is based on a 14th-century Dominican devotional book. One year later Witz was a citizen of Basel.

The Basel *Totentanz* / Dance of Death (c.1440), formerly on the cemetery wall at the *Predigerkirche* / Preachers' Church, is attributed to Witz and his apprentices (although this is disputed) and was likely commissioned by some of the Church Council participants. During the 14th and 15th centuries,

Europe was tormented by plague epidemics and the Dance of Death became a popular artistic theme, a *memento mori*. The Basel Dance of Death does not exclude anyone from the clutches of Death; all join him in his macabre dance. Twenty-three fragments of the 60-meter-long painting were retrieved when the wall was demolished in 1805; nineteen are preserved in the Historisches Museum Basel (the other four are lost).

Destruction of the Totentanz wall at Predigerkirche, 1805

His perspective, his bulky figures, his expressive manner and his iconography must have impressed the bishop of Geneva who commissioned him to do an altar of St. Peter for the Geneva Cathedral (c.1444). Four of the panels are in the Museum of Art and History in Geneva. In *The Miraculous Draught of Fishes*, his only known signed work, Witz painted a precise and poetic landscape of the banks of Lake Geneva with Mont Blanc and the countryside in the background.

In 1443 Witz purchased the house *zum Pflug* on Freie Strasse. As early as 1447 the painter's father was mentioned as guardian of his widow Urselin von Wangen and the couple's five children. Eventually the house was sold for the benefit of the children. One daughter entered a convent where she remained until her death in 1471.

It was in the years 1896/1901 when Daniel Burckhardt, then curator of the Kunstmuseum Basel, identified Witz's paintings. During the restoration of the Geneva altarpiece, the following inscription was noticed *"hoc opus pinxit magister conradus sapientis de basilea MCCCCXLIIII."* Loosely translated— this work painted by master conradus sapientis of Basel, 1444.

All known paintings by Witz were done in the period 1434/44. The Kunst-museum Basel has 11 of the 20 recognized works.

Esther before Ahasver, c.1435

Bettina Eichin

122

PANOPLY
OF BASEL PERSONAE

Abt, Otto: 1903-1982 Basel; artist, member of the Group 33—a group of Swiss artists who in 1933 split from the existing society of artists, sculptors and architects in opposition to its policy concerning the arts.

Amerbach, Johannes: c.1440-1513, settled in Basel in 1475; printer and forerunner of the renowned Johannes Froben; father of Bonifacius Amerbach (1495-1562) and grandfather of Basilius Amerbach (1533-1591).

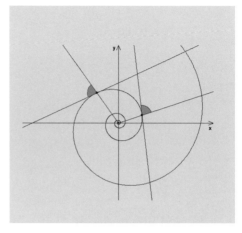

The 'real' Bernoulli spiral

Bernoulli family of eight mathematicians (from 1654 to 1807); the Bernoullianum at the university carries their name. Jacob (1654-1705) formulated the mathematical principle of the logarithmic spiral; his tombstone with a spiral (not the Bernoulli spiral) can be found in the cloisters of the Cathedral; it is engraved with the saying *'eadem mutata resurgo'*, freely translated—though changed, I rise again the same.

Bernoulli, Hans (1876-1959) and **Wilhelm** (1869-1909), Basel; architects.

Berri, Melchior: 1801-1854 Basel; architect. *See Architecture.*

Beyeler, Ernst: b.1921 Basel; gallery owner, distinguished collector of 20th-century art and friend to numerous artists. Co-founder in 1971 of the International Basel Art Fair, today Art Basel; together with his wife Hildy, created a foundation for their private collection in 1982. The Fondation Beyeler in Riehen / Basel, designed by the architect Renzo Piano, opened in 1997. In 2001 established The Art for Tropical Forests Foundation whose goal is to instill in artists, museums, collectors, the young, etc., an awareness of the fragility of the environment and to support these endeavors through the sale of art, museum tickets and the like.

Bock, Hans the Elder: c.1550-1624 Germany; mannerist artist who became a citizen of Basel in 1572. Painted murals at *Rathaus* / City Hall and on house on Nadelberg once belonging to Theodor Zwinger (1533-1588), Basel humanist, physician and university professor.

Bruckner, Trudl: b.1916 Basel; in 1956 founded Riehentor Gallery which specialized in contemporary Swiss art; co-founder in 1971 of the International Basel Art Fair, today Art Basel.

Burckhardt, Carl: 1878 Lindau – 1923 Ligornetto. Grew up and studied in Basel; artist, sculptor and innovator of freestanding sculpture in Switzerland. In 1904 received the commission to execute the bas-reliefs for the door of St. Paul's Church, Basel. Between 1905 and 1910 produced the polychrome marble *Venus* at the Kunsthaus, Zurich, and the metopes on its facade. Between 1914 and 1921 executed the allegories of the Rhine and the Wiese for the fountain at the *Badischer Bahnhof* / German train station; in 1923 executed *Sankt George* at the top of the stairs on the Kohlenberg. The bronze sculpture of the *Amazone* / Girl Leading Horse, corner of the Middle Bridge, was cast posthumously.

Burckhardt, Carl Jacob: 1891 Basel – 1974 Vinzel, VD; diplomat and historian; ambassador to League of Nations in Danzig, 1936/39.

Burckhardt, Johann Ludwig (Sheikh Ibrahim): 1784 Lausanne – 1817 Cairo; son of the Basel silk-ribbon manufacturer Johann Rudolf Burckhardt. Engaged by the African Association (originally the British Association for Promoting the Interior Parts of Africa) to discover the source of the Nile. Two important discoveries were the temple of Ramses II at Abu Simbel, Egypt buried under the desert sand, and Petra in Jordan, once the capital of the Nabataeans. His diaries, along with his maps, are preserved in the British Museum, London. He was so captivated with life in that part of the world he assumed the name *Sheikh Ibrahim* and adopted the Islamic faith. His boyhood home is now the stately Kirschgarten Museum.

Castellio, Sebastian: 1515 France – 1563 Basel; religious refugee from France in 1545, he arrived in Basel from Geneva after serious disagreements with Calvin. In 1553 became professor of Greek at the university. A pioneer of the idea of principled religious freedom; his pleas for tolerance with interpretations of the Bible were not accepted by leading Protestant reformers. He argued that persecution of heretics was anti-Christian. Joined with Joris in denouncing execution of Servetus. Because of these views a legal process opened; before the trial got underway, he died of natural causes.

Cohn, Arthur: b.1928 Basel; film producer and multiple-Oscar winner. Before turning to film production, he was a journalist, author and student of international law. Cohn has a reputation for producing films of uncompromising vision and artistry. Awards include an Honorary Doctorate of Fine Arts from Boston University and title Commander of the Order of Arts and Letters by the French Government; a commemorative plaque is set in the pavement at Spalenberg near the Hotel Basel.

Cratander, Andreas: c.1490 as Andreas Hartmann, Strasbourg – 1540 Basel; worked as printer and corrector for the printing firm Adam Petri. Established his printing company, which printed the works of Oekolampad. Became a Basel citizen in 1519 and a member of the guild zu Safran in 1530.

Cuse, Nicolas de: 1401 Germany – 1464 Italy; philosopher, theologian and astronomer. He arrived in Basel in 1432 during the Church Council (1431/48).

Dienast, Johann Conrad: 1741-1824 Basel; art collector whose collection was given to Kunstmuseum Basel. From 1780 to 1813 held the post of *Stiftschaffner* / administrator of estate of former St. Peter's Monastery; since 1463 its revenues have been assigned to the university. To prevent his collection from being broken up, in 1797 he gave it to his daughter and upon her death to his granddaughter Emilie Linder.

Dürer, Albrecht: 1471-1528 Nuremberg, Germany; important artist and draftsman of German Renaissance art. Visited and worked in Basel (1490/94).

Eichin, Bettina: b.1942 Bern; lives and works in Basel, sculptor. Works represented in public and private collections in Germany, Switzerland and beyond. In 2005 honored for her work to bring equal opportunities to women. Her *Helvetia auf der Reise* is on the cover. *See Outdoor Art.*

Faesch, Remigius: 1595-1667 Basel; lawyer, born into an accomplished family of goldsmiths and stonemasons. Descendant of Jakob Meyer zum Hasen, the Basel mayor who supported Hans Holbein the Younger. Contents of the Faesch Museum once at Petersplatz were given to the university. In accordance with his will, it was united with the Amerbach cabinet in 1828; both are now part of the Kunstmuseum Basel.

Federer, Roger: b.1981 Basel; ranks number 1 in World Tennis; winner of numerous championships—Australian Open, US Open, Wimbledon, and many more. In 2004 founded Roger Federer Foundation, which supports young people in South Africa. In 2005 named World Sportsman of the Year.

Fehlbaum, Rolf: b.1941 Basel; director of Vitra AG, Birsfelden founded by his father in 1934. The firm has furnished headquarters of major companies—Coca Cola and Daimler Benz—the offices at the EU Commission in Brussels and the Bundestag in Berlin. Founder of the Vitra Design Museum in Weil am Rhein, Germany. *See museums.*

Fuchs, Leonhard: 1501-1566 Bavaria; German physician and botanist. His most important publication, the *'De Historia Stirpium commentarii insignes'* / Notable Commentaries on the History of Plants, a work with more than 500 meticulous drawings and precise plant descriptions, was printed in Basel in 1549. Fuchs was interested in the medicinal properties of plants and their reputed powers. In 1753 Carolus Linnaeus (1707-1778), a Swedish botanist, scientifically defined the labeling of plants and named the plant fuchsia in his honor. In the summer, the *Fuchsientreppen* / fuchsia stairs at the Merian Park Botanical Garden, Brüglingen are a special attraction.

Gelpke, Rudolf: 1873 Basel – 1940 Waldenburg; engineer and pioneer in Rhine navigation and shipping; responsible for proving the Upper Rhine was navigable to Basel, thereby allowing large vessels to pass through the city and beyond. Founder of the *Basler Personenschiffahrts-Gesellschaft* and the *Schweizerische Schiffahrtsvereinigung* / societies for passenger traffic and shipping on the Upper Rhine; also founded the journal of shipping, *'Die Rheinquelle'*. He was engineer for the Zurich street-car system and a tunnel in the Ticino. An important personality, he contributed greatly to furthering the shipping potential of Basel, thereby improving its economy. The Kleinhüningen port itself is his memorial. *See Basel and Its Waters.*

Graf, Urs: 1485-1527 Solothurn; draftsman, designer, goldsmith, painter, printmaker and mercenary—a wild sort of character. Graf raised the status of drawing to an independent art by signing and dating his works. In 1512 he purchased citizenship in Basel and entered the *Hausgenossen* / goldsmiths' guild. He fled Basel in 1519 but was invited back to be the die-cutter at the city mint; disappeared from Basel shortly before his death. The Kunstmuseum Basel has a fine collection of his drawings.

Hebel, Johann Peter: 1760 Basel – 1826 near Heidelberg; popular poet, theologian and professor. His works have a distinct flavor of fidelity, naiveté and humor, married with a certain freshness and vigor. He wrote in Basel dialect. Author of the song, *'z Basel am mim Rhy'*.

Heintz, Daniel: c.1530 Italy –1596 Bern; Renaissance architect and stonemason who worked inter alia, in Bern and Basel; in 1559 he became a Basel citizen. *See Architecture.*

Herzl, Theodor: 1860 Budapest – 1904 Vienna (in 1949 his remains were reinterred on Mount Herzl in Jerusalem). A journalist and leader of the quest for a Jewish state; in 1897 convened the First Zionist Congress in Basel during which time he stayed at the Three Kings Hotel. "In Basel I founded the Jewish state. Maybe in five years, certainly in fifty, everyone will realize it." Commemorative plaque inscribed in Hebrew and German is in the music hall of the Stadtcasino.

Heusler, Andreas: 1834-1921 Basel; university professor who published books on the history of Basel.

Heusler-Ryhiner, Andreas: 1802-1868 Basel; *Ratsherr* / senator and founder of the precursor of today's *Basler Zeitung*; a contemporary of Bachofen and Burckhardt.

Heynlin, Johannes: 1430 Germany – 1496 Basel; humanist who studied in Erfurt, Leipzig, Paris and Basel. In 1474 he was preacher at St. Leonard's parish; c.1487, preacher at Cathedral and later that year entered the Carthusian monastery.

Iselin, Isaak: 1728-1782 Basel; Basel's state chancellor. A friend of Pestalozzi, both of whom believed in the importance of elementary education. In 1777 he founded the *Gesellschaft zur Förderung des Guten und Gemeinnützigen (GGG)*. This society for social welfare is still active today; it was the first philanthropic institution in Europe founded by a layperson. *See Outdoor Art.*

Jaspers, Karl: 1883 Germany – 1969 Basel; philosopher. In 1932 published his work *'Philosophy'*; from 1948 was professor of philosophy at university in Basel; also wrote on history, theology and politics. In 1967 became a Basel citizen.

Kämpf, Max: 1912-1982 Basel; artist and draftsman. In 1948 he founded the *Kreis 48* / Circle 48 whose members painted principally in gray and blue tones. A wall painting (*Meer*) is at the *Wirtschaftsgymnasium und Wirtschafts-mittelschule* / High School of Business and Economics at Andreas Heusler-Strasse.

Koch, Joseph Anton: 1768 Tyrol – 1839 Rome; painter of landscapes, historical, religious and mythological scenes; a member of the Nazarene art group. Some of his works are at the Kunstmuseum Basel in the Dienast Collection.

Linder, Emilie: 1797-1867 Basel; artist, collector, supporter and benefactress of the arts. Granddaughter of Dienast and friend of the Nazarene artists (Overbeck and Koch). The Kunstmuseum Basel received her collection and that of her grandfather. Perhaps the most valuable paintings are the two panels from Konrad Witz's *Mirror of Salvation altarpiece* (c.1435) likely painted for St. Leonard's Church. She donated a vast collection of Nazarene art, which includes, inter alia, *Macbeth and the Witches* by Joseph Anton Koch.

Littmann, Klaus: b.1951 Basel; owner of Littmann *Kulturprojekte* which organizes cultural events/happenings, e.g., Sculpture 2000, Frontside 2001, the angel's room on the Cathedral spire 2002, Sidewalk paintings 2003, Punkt-leuchten 2004 (project at the former tourist office, now part of the Three Kings Hotel renovation), the *Spiegel* Cover Illustrations exhibition, 2005.

Loos, Cécile Ines: 1883-1959 Basel; poet. '*Der Tod und das Püppchen*' / Death and the Doll (1939) is a recollection of her traumatic childhood. The Cécile Ines Loos Anlage is located at the end of St. Alban-Rheinweg in the area known as the *Breite*.

Luginbühl, Bernhard: b.1929 Bern; sculptor, draftsman, filmmaker and friend of Tinguely. The Museum of Fine Arts Bern and the Jean Tinguely Museum Basel held a jointly organized retrospective of his works in 2003. *See Outdoor Art.*

Mangold, Burkhard: 1873-1950 Basel; artist and draftsman, a pioneer in Swiss graphic and poster lithography. A multidisciplinarian, he painted numerous city- and seascapes. Wall painting of the Rhine port in the *Bahnhofbuffet* Restaurant at the *SBB* / main railway station; in the main post office building, scenes of the Rhine port in 1910 and of the former *Kaufhaus* / customs and warehouse on Freie Strasse as it was in 1853; the *s'graffiti* building / scratched facade painting at Spalenberg 22, the first grocery store in Basel. The Kleines Klingental Museum mounted a retrospective of his works in 2004.

Merian, Amadeus: 1808-1889 Basel; architect.
See Churches and Architecture.

Moser, Karl: 1860 Baden – 1936 Zurich; one of the most significant Swiss architects of his generation: *Pauluskirche* / St. Paul's Church, Basel, 1898; *Kunsthaus*, Zurich, 1910; *Badischer Bahnhof* / German train station, Basel, 1912/13; *Antoniuskirche* / St. Anthony's Church, Basel, 1925/27; plus other works throughout Switzerland and Germany. *See Churches and Architecture.*

Münster, Sebastian: 1488-1552 Germany; a humanist summoned to Basel by Oekolampad; taught Hebrew studies at the university. The Petri printing firm published '*Cosmographia*', his celebrated book on geography. In 1535 he became a citizen of the city.

Myconius, Oswald: 1488-1552 Germany; schoolmaster and theologian who arrived in Basel in 1510; served as schoolmaster at St. Theodore's Church, St. Peter's Church and preacher at St. Alban's; appointed professor at the university; a friend to Thomas Platter. In 1516 he commissioned a schoolmaster's sign from Ambrosius and Hans Holbein the Younger as an aid in promoting learning, now in the Kunstmuseum Basel.

Nietzsche, Friedrich: 1844-1900 Germany; philosopher and author who at 24 years of age was offered the position of professor of classical philology at the university in Basel. Friend to Jacob Burckhardt, Johann Jakob Bachofen and Franz Overbeck. Memorial plaque is at Schützengraben 47.

Nobel Prize winners: In addition to Carl Spitteler mentioned later, Basel has produced the following Nobel Prize winners
1948 Paul Hermann Müller in medicine
1950 Tadeus Reichstein in medicine
1978 Werner Arber in medicine
1984 Niels K. Jerne, jointly with Georges J. F. Köhler, in medicine
1987 K. Alexander Müller in physics
1987 S. Tonegawa in medicine
1996 Rolf M. Zinkernagel in medicine
2002 Kurt Wüthrich in chemistry

Ernst Beyeler

J. L. Burckhardt
(Sheikh Ibrahim)

Arthur Cohn

Cécile Ines Loos

Burkhard Mangold

Peter Ochs

Wibrandis Rosenblatt

Andreas Ryff

Maja Sacher-Stehlin

Rudolf Gelpke   *Johann Peter Hebel*   *Theodor Herzl*

Mathilde Paravicini

Aeneas Silvius Piccolomini
Pope Pius II

Rudolf Riggenbach

Carl Spitteler   *Jean Tinguely*   *Alexander Zschokke*

Ochs, Peter: 1752 Nantes, France – 1821 Basel; politician, jurist and historian. He arrived in Basel in 1756 and later studied at the university. The signing of the Peace Treaty between France, Spain and Russia in 1795 took place at his residence, the *Holsteinerhof* on Hebelstrasse. As city chancellor, he headed the delegation to Paris during the negotiations with Napoleon for the Act of Mediation of 1803.

Oekolampad (Oecolampadius), Johannes: 1482 near Heilbronn, Germany – 1531 Basel; humanist and reformer, he arrived in Basel in 1515 to work as corrector (critic and proofreader) for the printer Froben. In 1522 he lodged with the printer Cratander on Petersgasse. He was appointed professor of theology after receiving his doctorate from the university in 1523. In 1525 became preacher of St. Martin's Church. Leader of the Reformation in Basel. *See Outdoor Art.*

Oeri-Hoffmann families: Patrons of Basel's cultural life—founders of the Emanuel Hoffmann Foundation, the Maja Sacher Foundation, the Contemporary Art Museum / *Museum für Gegenwartskunst* and through the Sacher / Hoffmann families, the Museum Jean Tinguely. Founders of the *Puppenhaus* / Doll House Museum, the *Schaulager* / Depository of the Hoffmann Foundation's art collection and research center; financial supporters of the *FCB* (Football Club of Basel). Purchased and donated to the city the *Laurenz Bau* (former Basel branch of the Swiss National Bank), which adjoins the Kunstmuseum Basel and now houses its library.

Oporinus, Johannes (Herbster): 1507-1568 Basel; printer, secretary to Paracelsus and professor at the university. In 1542 printed a Latin version of the Koran; in 1543 printed the seven-volume treatise on anatomy by Vesalius. Owned one of the finest Renaissance libraries, which after his death was regrettably scattered around the world. The University Library possesses some of these books along with assorted letters and memorabilia.

Overbeck, Franz: 1837 St. Petersburg, Russia – 1905 Basel; scholar and professor of New Testament theology and church history, devoted friend of Nietzsche.

Overbeck, Friedrich: 1789 Lübeck, Germany – 1869 Rome; artist and cofounder of the artistic movements the *Lukas Bund* / Brotherhood of St. Luke and the Nazarenes; his works are represented at the Kunstmuseum Basel as part of the Dienast Collection.

Paravicini, Mathilde: 1875-1954 Basel; humanitarian who during WW I helped evacuate the endangered and wounded from occupied France; she later brought war-traumatized children to Switzerland for a three-month respite. In 1942 received an honorary doctorate from the university for her endeavors; in 1947 received title of officer in the French Legion of Honor. For 40 years she directed a school for sewing and tailoring. The Mathilde Paravicini-Strasse is in the Gellert neighborhood.

Pellegrini, Alfred Heinrich: 1881-1958 Basel; an important 20th-century artist who worked in various media and styles. He produced many wall paintings in Basel and Germany. *See wall paintings / Outdoor Art.*

Petri: a family of printers active in Basel: Johannes (1441-1511), Adam (1454-1525) and Heinrich (1508-1579).

Piccolomini, Aeneas Silvius, / Pope Pius II: 1405-1464 Italy. The 27-year-old Piccolomini arrived in Basel during the Church Council (1431/48) as secretary to Domenico Capranica, bishop of Fermo. Later sent by the Council to arrange an alliance with the king of Scotland; antipope Felix V sent him to pay homage to the newly installed Emperor Frederick III. He gained the Emperor's favor, becoming his secretary. As his representative he pledged allegiance to the legitimate pope, Eugene IV. Later bishop of Siena; in 1456 received cardinal's hat and was crowned Pontiff in 1458. As Pope, granted permission in 1459 for founding of Basel's university. Rebuilt Corsignano, his town of birth, today's Pienza, according to his vision of the ideal Renaissance city. The wall paintings of the Piccolomini Library in the Siena Cathedral, painted by Pintoricchio (c.1452-1513), narrate the story of Piccolomini's life.

Platter, Felix: 1536-1614 Basel; son of Thomas Platter, he was a physician and art collector. In 1562 appointed Dean of the Faculty of Medicine at the university; in 1571 named City Physician and Professor of Practical Medicine. Physician to the courts of German princes; as a skilled anatomist he contributed to the fields of epidemiology and pathology. Felix Platter Hospital carries his name. Portrait by Hans Bock the Elder (1584) is in the Kunstmuseum Basel.

Portmann, Adolf: 1897 Basel – 1982 Binningen; a zoologist who in 1931 began his professorship at the university. His research focused on the early development of animals and humans.

Reuchlin, Johannes: 1455-1522 Germany; humanist and student of Hebrew and Cabbala. He studied in Freiburg im Breisgau, Paris and Basel; in 1474 came to Basel with Johannes Heynlin. He was instrumental in rescinding an imperial edict to destroy the *Talmud* and other Hebrew writings. His was the first Hebrew grammar and dictionary written by a Christian.

Riggenbach, Christoph: 1810-1863 Basel; architect.
See Churches and Architecture.

Riggenbach, Rudolf: 1882-1961 Basel. *'Dingedinge'* (a fond nickname); when he could not think of the name of something, he asked, "what is / or pass me that *'dinge-dinge'.*" A bon vivant, art historian, curator of historical monuments and the first director (1939/54) of Klingental Museum, which he saved from being converted into a school. *See Outdoor Art.*

Rosenblatt, Wibrandis: 1504-1564 Basel; *Four times widow.* The destiny of this woman illustrates the tragic game of life and death in the turbulent 16th century. Married at 20 to Ludwig Keller; widowed three years later; married three reformers—Oekolampad, Capiton and Bucer—all who succumbed to the plague. She gave birth to 11 children; went into exile in England with last husband, Bucer, returning to Basel after his death. The Black Death took her also. Wibrandishaus (a home for senior citizens) is opposite the Oekolampad-kirche at Allschwilerplatz. Commemorative signs are at Martinskirchplatz 2 and on Rheinsprung.

Ryff, Andreas: 1550-1603 Basel; politician, chronicler and silk merchant. In 1582, along with Basilius Amerbach, he carried out the first excavations at the Roman settlement of *Augusta Raurica* / Augst. Negotiated the settlement of the 1591/94 *Rappenkrieg* / the 'penny' war.

Sacher, Paul: 1906-1999 Basel; married to Maja Stehlin-Hoffmann; long-time director of the Musik-Akademie Basel; musician and benefactor who promoted and conducted early music, and supported contemporary music. Founded the *Kammerorchester Basel* / Basel Chamber Orchestra (also that of Zurich), the *Schola Cantorum Basiliensis, Freunde alter Musik Basel* / The Friends of Early Music and the *Paul Sacher Stiftung* / Foundation.

Sacher-Stehlin, Maja: 1896-1989 Basel; promoter and supporter of the arts; daughter of Basel architect Fritz Stehlin. Maja founded the Emanuel Hoffmann Foundation in memory of her first husband and financed the construction of the *Museum für Gegenwartskunst* / Contemporary Art Museum. Maja-Sacher Platz is near the Museum.

Sarasin, Jacob and Lucas: Silk-ribbon manufacturers during 18th century whose homes, the Blue House and the White House (built between 1762 and 1771), are on Rheinsprung. *See Architecture.*

Servetus, Michael: 1511 Spain – 1533 Geneva; a polymath—student of law, theology, mathematics and medicine—he arrived in Basel (1530/31) just after Reformation with the aspiration of discussing his conclusions concerning the Trinity and infant baptism with Erasmus. Erasmus had already departed for Germany; he lodged with Oekolampad, but wore out his welcome. Left for France where he resided some 20 years under the pseudonym *Villeneuve*; met Calvin in Paris. After acquittal by the Inquisition for mixing astrology and medicine, he settled in Lyon. Resumed contact with Calvin, at which time his identity was revealed to the Inquisition in Vienne—he was arrested, escaped and rearrested. Calvin asked that he be beheaded; the council insisted that he be burned at the stake. It is alleged that, "before his ashes were cold, cries for religious tolerance were heard". Servetus's beliefs are the founding doctrine of the Unitarian Church. Memorials honoring him are in France, Spain, Geneva, the United States and the United Kingdom.

Spillmann, Fred: 1910-1986 Basel; internationally renowned couturier. First fashion show presented in Paris in 1937. The Historisches Museum Basel presented a retrospective of his life and creations in 2003.

Spitteler, Carl: 1845-1924 Liestal; Nobel Prize winner (1919) in literature for his epic *'Olympian Spring'*. Studied at the *Pädagogium* / Cathedral School under Wilhelm Wackernagel and Jacob Burckhardt.

Stehlin, Fritz: 1861-1923 Basel; member of family of architects—Johann Jakob the Elder (1803-1879) and Johann Jakob the Younger (1826-1894).
See Churches and Architecture.

Steiner, Rudolph: 1861 Kraljevec, Croatia – 1925 Dornach. Austrian philosopher, scientist and artist who formulated the philosophic theory known as anthroposophy—"knowledge produced by the higher self in man". In 1913 built the first *Goetheanum* at Dornach as a school of spiritual science. After it was set aflame and burned down in 1922, he redesigned a new building in molded concrete that became the center of the Anthroposophic Society. It is possible to visit the center; performances in eurhythmic movement take place throughout the year. Known worldwide for its presentations of the complete *Faust* by Goethe.

Stoecklin, Niklaus: 1896 Basel – 1982 Riehen; artist and illustrator. A leading pioneer in *Neue Sachlichkeit* / neo-realism art in Switzerland. His output includes posters (for which he won the 1941 Swiss poster of the year award), portraits, botanical drawings and scenes of many of the streets and events beloved by Baslers. *See wall paintings / Outdoor Art.*

Studer, Hanns: b.1920 Basel; wood-block engraver, illustrator and stained-glass painter. Works are in various churches, hospitals and other locations throughout the city, and beyond, e.g., Zwinglihaus, University Hospital, City Hall and St. Theresa Church in Allschwil.

Stückelberg, Ernst: 1831-1903 Basel; portrait, historical and genre artist. In 1878/82 decorated the William Tell Chapel on the Lake of Uri. The Kunstmuseum Basel mounted an exhibition of his works in 2003; *The Earthquake of Basel* painting is in the museum collection. Nephew of architect Melchior Berri.

Tinguely, Jean: 1925 Fribourg – 1991 Bern; artist and sculptor. Tinguely adopted Basel and Fasnacht. Museums dedicated to his works are in Fribourg and Basel. Created kinetic art; public pieces in Basel are the *Fasnachtsbrunnen* / Fasnacht Fountain at the Theater Square and pieces outside the eponymous museum. He was married to the artist Niki de St. Phalle (1930 -2002).

Vesalius, Andreas: 1514-1564, in present-day Belgium; humanist, physician and father of modern anatomy. In 1543 Oporinus published his opus—the first complete textbook on anatomy with illustrations by a student of Titian. Vesalius attended and lectured at the university. He was court physician to Charles V of Spain and his son Philip II. The Anatomisches Museum Basel preserves the skeleton used during his lectures.

Wackernagel, Rudolf: 1855-1926 Basel; historian, city archivist and author of the four-volume *'Geschichte der Stadt Basel'* / History of Basel. For some years the Wenkenhof in Riehen was his home.

Zschokke, Alexander: 1894-1981 Basel; sculptor and artist who studied in Germany; a professor at the Academy in Düsseldorf, he returned to Basel in

1937. From 1953/64 he was a member of the Commission of the Kunstmuseum Basel. His numerous fountains and public sculptures are located throughout the city. *See Outdoor Art and Fountains.*

Zurkinden, Irène: 1909-1987 Basel; artist and a member of the Group 33. Recipient of various art citations and prizes.

Zwinger, Theodor: three men of the same family with the same name: (1533-1588), (1597-1654), (1658-1724). All served as rector / headmaster of the university in Basel. Bock painted the facade of the first Zwinger's house at Nadelberg; the designs have survived.

Zwingli, Ulrich (Huldrych): 1484 at Wildhaus, St. Gallen - 1531 in the battle at Kappel during the Reformation. Theologian, humanist and reformer. Graduated University of Basel in 1504; he valued his correspondence with Erasmus. During his service as chaplain with the Swiss forces, he developed his opposition to the mercenary system; later appointed priest at the *Grossmünster* / Cathedral in Zurich.

Andreas Vesalius

TRADITIONS

Fasnacht

Fasnacht is Basel's carnival. It is a three-day action-packed event different from most carnivals. The Basel event does not take place before Lent, but during the first three days of the week after Ash Wednesday. This underscores the break with the Catholic church after the Reformation of 1529.

The roots of carnival celebrations are a reflection of pagan rites, jousting tournaments and military inspections. In 1376 an argument broke out between Basel's citizens and the knights during a tournament arranged by the Duke of Austria. The ensuing confrontation led to the city being fined and the duke escaping to Kleinbasel. This event is known as the *Böse Fasnacht* / the Bad Fasnacht and is Basel's first such recorded event.

In the Middle Ages all armed men were under the strict control of the guilds; once a year they were called up for inspection. After this inspection they paraded through the streets, ending up in a *Trinkstube* / drinking hall to solidify their camaraderie.

Some celebrations once promoted by the Catholic church were curtailed after the Reformation, and no celebrations were held during wartime. The Fasnacht we now celebrate bears witness to continual refinements.

Since 1834 the official start of Fasnacht is at the stroke of four on the Monday morning after Ash Wednesday. When the clock at St. Martin's Church rings four bells, all the city lights go off, a hush quickly falls over the city and suddenly the slow piccolo playing and drumming starts. With the glow from the various-sized lanterns carried by the marchers, a magic spell envelops the city. *Morgestraich* (early-morning stroke) has begun. *Die drey scheenschte Dääg* / the three most wonderful days, for which many have been preparing since the close of the previous Fasnacht, are underway. Spectators are waiting to see and hear the processions playing their piccolos and drumming their way through the city streets.

The *Cliquen* / marching societies, which originated in the mid-19th century as cultural, sporting and social associations meet year round; music is rehearsed. Until two months before carnival, drumming is practiced on rubber pads mounted on wooden blocks, after which time actual drums are used. Themes, usually based on some political or social blunder of the past year, are chosen and carried out in all aspects of the cliques' presentations, from costumes to floats. The more one knows of the local and federal scandals or happenings of the past year, the more one can enjoy the abundant satire and humor. Designs for their colorful and elaborately executed lanterns illustrate the chosen theme in a direct and often whimsical fashion.

The larger, transparent lanterns are carried on the shoulders of strong men (some of whom are hired by the larger cliques as carriers). Those not involved in piccolo playing or drumming carry smaller lanterns. To add a further touch of mystery, every marcher wears a different costume topped with a light perched on his or her head. The processions follow no planned route, often criss-crossing each other's paths as they wind their way through the narrow medieval cobble-stoned streets.

Before dawn, spectators and musicians leave the streets in search of a restaurant or café for the traditional Fasnacht breakfast. *Mählsuppe* / roasted flour soup with grated cheese, *Ziibelewaaie* / onion tart and *Kääswaaie* / cheese tart, are washed down with beer or white wine, or for the less adventuresome, tea, coffee or hot chocolate. First mention of this breakfast, with hot chocolate as the beverage, was in 1861. Once fortified, it is time to re-enter the almost surrealistic outdoor Fasnacht feeling before going home to rest up for the eclectic afternoon and evening activities.

The cliques return in the afternoon for the cortège, which follows a pre-determined route. Members of the group are dressed alike wearing fanciful costumes and masks. The piccolo playing and drumming continues, lanterns are carried but not illuminated, and other cliques—generally not the marching groups—parade marvelously executed and imaginative floats. Leading each group is a drum major, sporting a remarkably tall mask. Oranges, flowers and *Räppli* / confetti are handed out or launched from the floats to and at the spectators. A word of caution: do not be enticed to get up close to the revelers as you might be grabbed and carried along, ending up with an entire bag of confetti poured down your back.

Along with the traditional Fasnacht tunes, the almost revered *Guggemuusig* is in evidence. Guggemuusig groups consist of brass bands playing renditions of popular tunes, all slightly off-key and definitely out-of-tune. Many of the instruments are homemade. Stove-pipes, faucets, horns and all types of gadgets and bric à brac are put to use in their fabrication; they must be seen and heard to be believed.

In the evening the groups parade at random through the streets and squares. The *Schnitzelbänggler* / mummers go from restaurant to restaurant and table to table, singing in falsetto voices their *Schnitzelbängg* / satirical rhymes derived from local events, to the consternation and delight of the audience. *Zeedel* / handbills, which provide insight into the subject matter, are distributed.

All day Tuesday the lanterns are on display at the *Münsterplatz* / Cathedral Square, an incomparable location and opportunity to appreciate at close range the artistic talents employed in their creation, while basking in the glow of these illuminated works of art.

Tuesday afternoon is Children's Fasnacht. The city comes alive when young children, accompanied by their proud parents, parade through the streets dressed in their innovative and enchanting costumes. Many find this the most peaceful and reassuring part of Fasnacht, demonstrating that the tradition of Fasnacht will never die out.

In the evening, *Guggemuusig* groups amuse all with their concerts. After their 'gigs' at Barfüsserplatz, Marktplatz and Claraplatz, they roam the streets playing their original musical renditions, gathering dedicated followers as they move along.

Wednesday afternoon the indefatigable cliques go out for a final 'letting go,' continuing their piccolo playing, drumming, parading and celebrating. The haunting tunes continue to drift over the medieval rooftops into the early hours of Thursday, when Fasnacht officially ends—exactly 72 hours after *Morgestraich* rang out. With the *Ändstraich* comes the closure to three unforgettable and colorful days of contagious enthusiasm, intensity, laughter, ridicule, gaiety, sadness, music and parading, all mingled with a general feeling of goodness and well-being.

Traditional Fasnacht Figures

The *Waggis* is a parody of an Alsatian peasant with an oversized head, enormous eyes, bulbous nose, buckteeth and a dust-mop wig. His wild hair can be in flaming orange, yellow, red, pink, or chartreuse. His costume of peasant shirt, neckerchief and wooden shoes is identical to that once worn when he came to town to sell his produce at the market. He may drag a bone on a leash, carry a club, or a string bag filled with onions and carrots; he is the epitome of the impish Fasnacht spirit with his mastery of the put-down. By disguising his voice with his mask, he cuts down friend and foe with great relish; he is a loud and playful character.

The *Alti Dante* / the old aunt, a popular figure dressed in Biedermeier-period clothing, is the essence of politeness and prudishness. She wears a wig under her elegantly designed hat, a long dress, carries a net bag and usually a parasol. Who is hiding behind the costume can be yet another surprise of Fasnacht. (Originally, the old aunt was a take-off on a market vendor from the Markgräflerland dressed up for a day in the city).

Other major characters are *Ueli*, the grinning court jester who wears a costume dotted with bells; the *Harlekin*, a harlequin figure; *Dummpeeter*, a trumpeter in Rococo-period dress; *Pierrot*, the traditional clown and the *Blätzlibajass* who sports a costume made of several hundred pieces of colorful material. What a sumptuous array of costumes there must be hanging in many a Basel wardrobe!

Fasnacht Hints:

Purchase the *Blaggede* / Fasnacht badge, the sale of which helps defray some of the costs for the participating groups. Do not impede the festivities in any way. Never throw anything back at the revelers, or pick up the confetti from the street! During *Morgestraich* do not use the camera flash.

In general, join in the celebration in a considerate and unobtrusive manner.

144

Vogel Gryff

A fascinating festivity of Kleinbasel is the *Vogel Gryff*. The yearly gathering and celebration of the three Honorable Societies of Kleinbasel takes place on the 13, 20 or 27 January. The *Wild Maa* / wild man rides down the Rhine on a platform supported by two boats. He begins his wild dance to the accompaniment of drums and many cannon shots. The boats must never cross the middle of the Rhine, which would bring him onto the main Basel side and allow the spectators the opportunity to jeer him; he must always keep his back turned towards Grossbasel. Ivy leaves and a garland of apples are part of his adornments; he carries a large sapling fir in his hands. This follows an ancient custom symbolizing the abundance of spring. Upon arrival at the Kleines Klingental Museum around 11 a.m., the time-honored figures of the *Vogel Gryff* / griffin and the *Leu* / lion, representing the other two honorable societies, greet him.

According to strict rules, certain dances are performed at various locations throughout Kleinbasel and on the Middle Bridge, but only up to the middle of the bridge. The fabulous figures neither tread on nor look to the left bank of the Rhine (the city side), nor does the Wild Maa, who wears a frightful and heavy copper mask, turn his head in that direction.

The trio makes its rounds throughout Kleinbasel, all the while paying honor to the guild masters. Upon arrival at the *Waisenhaus* / orphanage, they carry on with their vigorous dancing. At a scheduled time the three take a break for a well-deserved meal, after which dancing resumes and the festive atmosphere continues until around 10 p.m.

Chienbäse

A yearly event held at the Rathausgasse in Liestal, the Sunday after Ash Wednesday, and the night before *Morgestraich*. The street is transformed into one enormous fire with *Holzbesen* / burning wooden brooms and fire carts throwing light, heat and ashes everywhere. These 'brooms' weigh up to 30 kilos. The tradition most likely originated before the Reformation. Several bans have been imposed, but the burning still goes on. A procession of cliques, playing their tunes and displaying their lanterns, is now part of this unique revelry.

Legends: The Basilisk

Basilisk stems from the Greek word *basilikos* meaning 'little king,' and the beast itself may herald back to the cobra of ancient Egypt, the king of all serpents. The legend of the Basilisk, embellished over time, stems from the Middle Ages, the last time a 'sighting' was reported.

It is an evil, mythological beast hatched from a slimy egg laid by a cock. A serpent or toad must have sat on the egg for nine years. With the wings of a bird, the tail of a dragon and the head of a cock, it is among the deadliest of beasts: its breath scorches; its skin, covered with poison, kills upon contact; its eyes are so powerful they kill with a single glance. In fact, the only way to kill a Basilisk is to have it look at itself in a mirror, thus killing itself with its own deadly stare.

In the 15th century, a nine-year-old cock was tried in Basel's public court on the charge that it had laid an egg. It was declared guilty and executed by the official hangman.

A Traditional Basilisk Legend

Early one morning, while the city of Basel was still fast asleep, Leni, a baker's daughter, began her morning chores. She went to the well, as she did every morning, for a bucket of water, but the thick, putrid steam that was pouring out of it that morning frightened her. She called to her father who came running out of the bakery. He leaned into the well to have a look at what was therein, and fainted from the venomous strength of the fumes.

Leni, even more frightened than before, called for help and slowly doors and windows began to open. The neighbors came out of their homes, carried the baker into his shop and called for the city guards. When the guards arrived, the master guard tied a rope around his waist and had his men lower him into the well; he was quickly overcome by the fumes and pleaded to be pulled back up.

As the guards and the townspeople who had collected around the well were deciding what to do next, Peter, the youngest of the baker's apprentices, volunteered to go into the well for a look. Leni begged him not go, but he gently stroked her cheek and had the guards lower him. Peter withstood the fumes for a long time. When they finally pulled him back up, he told everyone he had seen a most horrific creature at the bottom of the well. It looked like a rooster with the legs of a toad, the tail of a dragon and foul-smelling steam pouring out of its beak. Its eyes were liquid fire.

A man in the crowd announced that Peter had seen a Basilisk, a monstrous creature born from an egg laid by a rooster and hatched by a toad. Its eyes were so deadly it could kill with a single glance. Everyone was terrified!

Peter could not sleep that night. Finally, he took the mirror off his wall, tied it to a long stick and ran to the door in the basement of the bakery that led to the well shaft. He opened the door and held the mirror towards the beast. The Basilisk looked at itself in the mirror and exploded into a million pieces. Peter was proclaimed a hero and shortly afterwards married Leni. They lived happily ever after.

Wilhelm Bubeck won a competition in 1884 for the design of a sidewalk fountain and the first appeared shortly thereafter. Of these original fountains, 28 remain. In 2002 the commune of Anwil, Basel-Landschaft commissioned a Basilisk fountain. There are over 1000 representations of the Basilisk throughout the city and with a renewed interest in the creature, the number is apt to increase. The home of the Basilisk is allegedly beneath the dark bottom of the fountain at Gerbergasse 48.

The Basilisk of Basel
Inscription on the well on Tanner's Hill
Gerbergasse 48

Within the Darkness of this Well,
As Legend tells us, used to Dwell
A Basilisk of Aspect wild
(To hold our Shield he's now Beguil'd)
In later Years a Judgement Seat,
And Place where Rev'llers used to Meet,
This Spot was named, from Guildhall nigh
The Tanners' Well, as none Deny.
For many Years the Spring was still
Today, Behold, and drink your Fill.
The murd'rous Dragon long has fled,
Yet Basel, a different Dragon dread!
Discord, that sunders Kin from Kin,
Will rend you if you let him in!

Translation Anton R. Obrist

The Legend of St. Ursula

A legend dear to Basel is that of St. Ursula (c.380) and her 11,000 virgins. Ursula, the daughter of a minor king in England was a Christian. Betrothed to the son of the major king, she refused to marry, as he was a heathen. While waiting for his conversion, she decided to make a pilgrimage to Rome. Part of the journey took her up the Rhine to Basel. Supposedly she was accompanied by eleven virgins (or according to another source, 11 decent young women), which over time and an incorrect translation has been magnified to the awesome number of 11,000. While in Basel she met Bishop St. Pantalus, the legendary first bishop of the city, who accompanied her to meet Pope Cyriacus. During their pilgrimage by foot from Basel to Rome, they gathered countless ardent followers; this ended up with the emperor perceiving them as a personal threat. Their return journey once again brought them to Basel. Upon arrival in Cologne they were attacked and killed by the Huns (perhaps the emperor had something to do with this action). The Guebwiler Chapel in the Cathedral and a steep passageway leading from Rheinsprung up to St. Martin's Church, commemorate the 11,000 virgins and the unlucky Ursula. *(Elftausendjungfrauen Kapelle and the Elftausendjungferngässlein).*

The Ghost of Spalen

Every stormy night the Spalen ghost rushes about between the Spalentor and Spalenberg. No one can exactly describe it, although its passing is frequently heard and felt. Only fleeting glimpses have been caught with varying descriptions of a seahorse, a pig, a dragon or a griffin. Should anyone attempt to catch a glance when the sounds of its flying footsteps are heard, they are duly punished by waking up on the morrow with a very swollen face. A bold soul who recklessly poked his head far out the window to satisfy his curiosity, was struck with such a sudden and exaggerated inflammation that the window frame had to be removed before his head could be drawn in.

Holidays and Commemorative Days
Religious Holidays and 'very local' events are not mentioned

National Day
1 August celebrated in Basel and throughout the county as the National Holiday. It commemorates the founding of the Confederation in 1291 by the three original cantons —Uri, Schwyz and Unterwalden. Festivities include fireworks, on the Rhine 31 July and on the Bruderholz 1 August, speeches, folklore events and family gatherings.

Banntag
Ascension Day celebration in Basel-Landschaft. A holiday-tradition which originated as a Catholic event and later became political. It has evolved into a walking and folk festival during which the residents 'control' the *Bann-steine* / boundary stones marking one village from the next. Older boundary stones are in the inner churchyard at St. Argobast in Muttenz. Some regions offer open-air church services.

1 May
A cantonal holiday honoring workers much like Labor Day in the United States.

Battle of St. Jakob-on-the-Birs
26 August recalls the battle in 1444 when a contingent of Swiss confederates fought to their death against the armies of the Dauphin of France, the Armagnacs. Even though the Swiss lost the battle, the prince, who later became Louis XI, was so impressed with their courage that he spared the city. In 2004 the holiday was suppressed.

Dies Academicus
The yearly celebration of the University of Basel, founded in 1460, takes place in November. On this day professors walk in procession to St. Martin's Church dressed in the robes of their various disciplines. The rector addresses the audience of academics, politicians, economists and other learned people. Honorary degrees and prizes are bestowed upon individuals who have contributed to the cultural, medical, legal, social or academic environments.

St. Nikolas / *Santiglaustag*
6 December rings *Santiglaus*, the embodiment of goodness, into homes; from his book, he cites the good and bad deeds of children and adults during the

past year and encourages improvement. Questions are asked before a poem is recited, or a song is sung. Traditionally, nuts, chocolate, apples, pears (now tangerines) and presents are distributed. *Schmutzli*, his assistant and the dark side of *Santiglaustag*, originated in the *Schwarzwald* / Black Forest.

Dressed in black and his face blackened with soot, he carries a switch made of birch twigs. His former frightening and dreaded image is now tempered—nowadays he also carries Santiglaus's bag of goodies. The traditional *Grättimaa*, a sweet yeast bread in the shape of a little man, is a definite must for supper!

Fairs

In 1471 Emperor Frederick III granted Basel permission to hold two fairs in perpetuity, one in spring and one in fall. The majority of the fairs takes place at the *Messeplatz* / Exhibition Square unless otherwise indicated. Up-to-date information is available from the tourist office.

Muba / Swiss Trade Fair

First fair was held in 1917 at the Stadtcasino, Barfüsserplatz. This is now the largest spring fair in Switzerland, exhibiting items ranging from home furnishings to sports equipment to health and fashion—all on display and available at discount prices. Special events are organized and guest countries featured.

BASELWORLD

The world's largest watch and jewelry industry fair occurs in April. Thousands of national and international exhibitors present their creations to the trade audience, from watches, jewelry, precious stones to allied sectors. Many manufacturers use BASELWORLD as their exclusive exhibition venue. Newly discovered trends give the show a tremendous impact on the industry. It attracts over 85,000 visitors yearly, covers 150,000 m² of floorspace and has an enormous turnover; it was originally part of Muba.

Art Basel

The prestigious modern and contemporary art fair has been held every June since 1970. It enjoys a worldwide reputation for the quality and variety of art represented by 270 international art dealers who yearly vie for exhibition space. Attendance varies from between 50 and 60,000 art-hungry aficionados. A daughter branch of Art Basel opened 2002 in Miami, Florida—Art Basel Miami Beach (ABMB)—a contrasting venue, but one generating equal success.

Herbstmesse / Autumn Fair

This lively event takes place at Petersplatz, Barfüsserplatz, Münsterplatz, the Kaserne, the Messeplatz (a wine and household fair) and lately overflows into other areas of the city. It includes amusement rides and a vast variety of stands selling everything imaginable—the *Hääfelimäärt* / ceramic market at Petersplatz, used books, crafts, clothing, pots and pans and all the goodies necessary to stave off hunger and thirst.

The traditional opening of the *Herbstmesse* takes place at St. Martin's Church, the oldest parish church in the city, 14 days before St. Martin's Day, when at 11:30 a.m. the doors of the church open. Approximately 40 people climb into the church tower. At 11:55 the *Messeglöckner* (fair's

bell-ringer) holds a left-hand glove out the tower's window, while blowing a signal on a Polish war horn. One minute before noon silence is requested. Precisely at noon the bells ring out, heralding the opening of the fair; with the last stroke, children bolt to the rides, as the first three trips are free.

Weihnachtsmarkt / Christmas Market

A Christmassy feeling radiates from mid-November to just before Christmas in front of and around the Historisches Museum Basel, Barfüsserplatz. Other locations vary; the main train station is the latest venue.

Christmas market at Barfüsserplatz

Music in Basel

An appreciation and love of music develops at an early age, as documented in the 16th-century *Basler Liederhandschriften* / hand-written songbooks of the Amerbach family. Basel city and Basel country offer well-organized music education programs taught at local music schools. Music education culminates at the *Musikwissenschaftliches Institut der Universität Basel* / The Institute of Musicology at the University of Basel, one of the most renowned such institutes with a well-founded reputation in research and teaching. The city has two additional research and education institutes of world acclaim: the *Paul Sacher-Stiftung* / Paul Sacher Foundation and the *Schola Cantorum Basiliensis.*

The Schola Cantorum Basiliensis was founded in 1933 by Paul Sacher and specializes in the study of early music—medieval, renaissance, baroque and classical. It is an integral part of the *Musik-Akademie Basel* / Music Academy of Basel. The original purpose of the Paul Sacher Foundation was to preserve his vast music library and collection. It is now an international research center for music of the 20th and 21st centuries. These teaching and research institutes attract talented musicians and musicologists to the city.

Numerous local orchestras and choirs perform regularly in Basel. The most familiar are the *Kammerorchester Basel* / Basel Chamber Orchestra, the *Neues Orchester Basel* / New Basel Orchestra, Basel Sinfonietta, the *Basler Gesangverein* / Basel Choir and the *Sinfonieorchester Basel* / the Basel Symphony Orchestra. The symphony orchestra came about in 1997 from the merger of two existing orchestras, the Radio Basel Orchestra and the Basel Symphony Orchestra. Performances are held on a regular basis in Basel and worldwide. A leading baroque orchestra, *La Cetra,* based in Basel enhances its manifold music programs.

The main concert subscription series with performances in the Stadtcasino— the concert hall built in 1876—are primarily under the aegis of the *Allgemeine Musik Gesellschaft (AMG).*

Basel is host to esteemed soloists, choirs and orchestras. In addition to the venues mentioned, other productions take place in many churches and music halls.

Basel is also a destination for enthusiasts and students of organ music. The numerous churches in the city house an enviable array of historical organs

Painting of swallow's nest organ in cathedral at Sion, VS by Cynthia Large

and reproductions from all epochs of history beginning with the *Schwalbennestorgel* / swallow's nest organ from the late Middle Ages to the great organs of the 18th century—several by the famous Silbermann family—continuing into the 21st century. Swallow's nest organ is a term used to signify the shape, location and housing, i.e., in the form of a swallow's nest. The Cathedral, Predigerkirche and St. Peter's Church each had such an organ. In 1528 Hans Holbein the Younger painted the wings of the second organ (1474) for the Cathedral. The two painted-panels are in the Kunstmuseum Basel. A reconstruction of the Predigerkirche swallow's nest organ is in situ.

Any discussion of musical tradition in Basel must include Fasnacht. Drummers and *piccolo* (a small flute) players practice all year in preparation for the event. An astonishing number of people are adept at playing both instruments with great skill and enthusiasm. The saying that Baslers are born with a drumstick or piccolo in hand could well be true.

Fasnacht cliques actively promote music education for children. Teaching of the drum and the piccolo starts at an early age. To quote Peter Habicht, author of '*Lifting the Mask—your guide to Basel Fasnacht*' – "learning how to play the piccolo is not terribly difficult but, the drum that is where Baslers excel". Drumming is not easy.

It requires at least three to five years of study before reaching a level of proficiency, and life-long practice thereafter. Drummers worldwide recognize the traditional Basel drum.

(Another Basel tradition equally as well recognized, which often travels in a miniature Basel drum, is *Läggerli*, the world-famous gingerbread biscuit).

On a different note, Basel also caters to those who enjoy musicals, jazz, rock, pop techno and hip-hop. Specialized clubs are scattered throughout the city and a string of yearly musical festivals satisfy all tastes. Major events drawing up to 50,000 spectators are staged at *St. Jakob-Park* / the football stadium. Other large-scale presentations are performed at the Musical Theater in Kleinbasel.

During the traditional Bebbi-Jazz festival in August, the entire innercity is transformed into a mesmerizing jazz scene. Over 50 groups play—free—to thousands of enchanted spectators.

To complement Basel's strong musical tradition, the *Musikmuseum* (one of the four museums of the Historisches Museum Basel) displays 650 instruments from an inventory of 2500—the largest collection in Switzerland—and features more than 200 interactive musical examples.

The variety of musical opportunities offer yet another means of sampling—a cultural experience.

Stained Glass

Stained-glass design and production has a long and noble history in Basel and throughout Switzerland. From early religious works, to later armorial panels, to present-day contemporary designs, Basel continues to be an important center in this art field. No historical study of stained glass would be complete without references to the city's centuries-old tradition.

Early works were mostly religious in nature and provided a steady source of income to both designers and artisans. It evolved into an even more flourishing art after the Reformation with the change in direction of design to that of commemorative windows and panels.

Hans Stocker, Antoniuskirche

Between 1550 and 1650 over 50 glaziers and glass painters worked in Basel. A renaissance occurred in the early 19th century (Hieronymus Hess, 1799-1850).

In addition to the collection at the Historisches Museum Basel (some roundels are ascribed to David Joris), and designs by artists such as Hans Holbein the Younger and Urs Graf at the Kunstmuseum Basel, one can appreciate stained-glass windows in numerous locations in the city. For example: at *Antoniuskirche,* (Otto Staiger, 1894-1967 and Hans Stocker, 1896-1983); panels in the *Rathaus /* city hall, guild houses, the main post office (Burkhard Mangold, 1875-1950); over the entrance to the *Kunstmuseum Basel;* in the entrance hall of the *Spiegelhof* (Charles Hindenlang,

1894-1950), at the *Zwinglihaus* and the *Fischerstube* (Hanns Studer, b.1920). The *Schützenhaus*, a public restaurant and the meeting place for the *Feuer-schützen* / the Society of Riflemen—the building dates from 1561/64—has an impressive collection of historical, biblical, mythological and classical-inspired panels.

Hanns Studer, Zwinglihaus

MARGARETHA
MERIAN-BURCKHARDT
FRAMED BY...

THE FIRST BOOK ILLUSTRATION BY
MATTHAEUS MERIAN · BASEL · 1610
SHOWING MUNATIUS PLANCUS AS
CITYGUARD (L.) AND A MESSENGER (R.)

ABSTRACT OF SOME BASEL INDUSTRIES

A Brief History of the Development of Banking

First mention of moneylenders and bankers in Basel was in the 13th century. At that time they formed a closed union, and business was carried out in an exchange arcade. All members enjoyed the privilege of judicial immunity and, with the exception of goldsmiths, had the exclusive right to deal in silver. The profession of moneylender was hereditary; new applicants were only accepted if all members agreed—the privilege could not be sold or transferred.

With the arrival of the Lombards from Italy in the middle of the 13th century, additional competition was added to that already present between the unions (guilds) and the Jewish moneylenders. In the 14th and 15th centuries, Basel was the economic and banking center for the Austrian-controlled regions and present-day German-speaking Switzerland. With the influx of church dignitaries and foreign participants attending the Church Council of Basel (1431/48), a more complex and riskier market evolved.

Around 1470 the question of setting up a municipal exchange bank was considered; in 1503 the first public bank opened. Unsuccessful credit operations led to its liquidation in 1744, and finally to its dissolution in 1746.
Despite the nationalization of money exchange, private moneylenders persevered and entered into other financial and commercial ventures.

A total transformation of the economic orientation of Europe took place following the discovery of America. Overland trade routes succumbed to the maritime trade centers in Antwerp, Amsterdam and London.

The expansion of this overseas trade resulted in new forms of businesses, which generated an increase in credit transactions, along with a commensurate increase in fraud and bankruptcy. The moneylenders maintained their activities in commerce and transportation, eventually becoming bankers. This growth, as well as an increase in the population, necessitated a corresponding increase in the number of banks and exchange offices.

A transfer and discount bank founded in 1843 soon failed. A positive result of this default was the establishment of the Bank of Basel that until 1907 issued bank notes. Thereafter, the Swiss National Bank became the sole note-issuing entity.

The Commercial Bank of Basel, the city's first large bank, was established in 1862. The Basel Bank Corporation opened in 1872; through mergers it evolved into Swiss Bank Corporation, today UBS AG—a fusion of Union Bank of Switzerland and Swiss Bank Corporation.

The Stock Exchange opened in 1876 and remained under the supervision of the chamber of commerce until the end of the century, when the government took control. All transactions are now processed electronically in Zurich.

The Swiss Bankers Association, the umbrella organization for the Swiss financial industry, was established at Basel in 1912. Virtually all the country's banks, auditors and securities dealers are members. The SBA's main purpose is to represent its members' interests in dealing with authorities both at home and abroad.

The second location of the Stock Exchange at Fischmarkt / Marktgasse

The BIS Botta and Villa building at Aeschenplatz 1

The *Bank für Internationalen Zahlungsausgleich* / Bank for International Settlements chose Basel for its headquarters in 1930, a decisive factor being the city's location at the railhead of three international railways. From its inception, the Bank was responsible for the receipt, administration and distribution of the annuities payable as WW I reparations, and for the service of the external loans earlier contracted to finance them. The duties of the Bank are to promote cooperation between central banks, and to provide additional facilities for international financial operations. The *BIZ* / BIS has branch offices in Mexico City and Hong Kong.

The BIS Tower at Centralbahnplatz 2

Today there are 35 banks represented in the city. They include 13 private, two major Swiss banks, the two cantonal, regional and major foreign banks—a clear indication of the on-going availability of domestic and international financial expertise in the city.

The Chemical and Pharmaceutical Industries

The chemical and pharmaceutical industries evolved out of the early print-ing, dye and silk-ribbon industries. Johann Rudolf Geigy-Gemuseus founded Geigy in 1758, trading in chemicals, dyes and drugs. Ciba *(Chemische Industrie Basel)* and Sandoz started up in the mid-to-late 19th century.

In the early years, the heart of these businesses was primarily supplying textile and silk dyes. Pharmaceuticals, herbicides and pesticides followed.

Fritz Hoffmann-La Roche was a pioneering entrepreneur convinced that the future belonged to branded pharmaceutical products. He was among the first to recognize that the industrial manufacture of standardized medicines would be a major advance in the fight against disease. In 1896 he founded F. Hoffmann-La Roche & Co. He attached great importance to product infor-mation as the link between the pharmaceutical manufacturer and doctors, pharmacists and patients.

Shortly after the foundation of the company, affiliates opened in Germany, Italy, France, the United States, the United Kindom and Russia. Roche has grown into one of the world's leading healthcare companies. The firm car-ries out its daily plant operations and research, while simultaneously intro-ducing advanced production facilities in its 1935/40 historical buildings designed by Otto Rudolf Salvisberg (1882-1940). Further expansions and renovations followed, 1960/71 by Roland Rohn (1905-71) and in 2000 by Herzog & de Meuron.

La Roche, Solitude Promenade

Lonza Ltd. was founded in 1897 as an energy company. Alusuisse acquired it in the 1960s; in 1999 there was a demerger and the Lonza Group Ltd. became an independent entity. Today it is a life-sciences driven company.

Clariant grew as a spin-off of Sandoz in 1995, and expanded through the integration of Hoechst specialty chemicals business in 1997. It became a manufacturer of intermediates and active ingredients for the pharmaceutical and agrochemical industry with the acquisition of a fine chemicals producer in early 2000.

Novartis ensued in 1996 from the merger of Ciba-Geigy and Sandoz. The name derives from the Latin *novae artes,* meaning 'new skills'. The Group focuses on carrying out the necessary research in order to develop and manufacture products designed to protect and improve health and well-being.

Syngenta evolved in 2000 from the merger of Zeneca (agrochemicals) and the agribusiness department of Novartis. With the knowledge acquired from its 'parents', Syngenta is now a global leader in providing innovative solutions and products for the enhancement of the food chain.

Biological, medical, scientific, chemical and pharmaceutical research undertaken in Basel is recognized and respected worldwide. The Noble Prize winners from the city reflect the breakthrough discoveries in these fields. A contributing factor to this success is the ongoing cooperation between the university and the private sector in pursuing research; the *Tropeninstitut* / Swiss Tropical Institute, the Biozentrum and the Friedrich-Miescher Institute are examples of this partnership

In 1996 more than 300 companies and research institutes located in the Upper Rhine formed the trinational BioValley Network, a sort of biotech Silicon Valley, whose purpose is to establish a biotechnology glomeration. As the economic activities in the biotech field are mainly carried out in Switzerland, a national BioValley Basel was launched in 2002 with the goal of making Basel even more attractive as a center for this technology.
Additionally, numerous public and private research institutions are active in the fields of basic and applied research and play an important role in future developments in the life-sciences industry—all of which contribute to the leading-edge medicine at the University Hospital.
Basel remains in the forefront of medical and scientific advancements with its on-going research and development in the expanding information and communication technology, nanotechnology, alternative and renewable energy fields, and in the field of agriculture, i.e., seed research.

1963

Major corporations in the pharmaceutical and chemical industries form the backbone of Basel's economy. Due to their adaptability and innovative strength, they continue to be highly successful and profitable. From a city of chemicals, Basel has rapidly become a city of research with an international and farsighted flavor.

A long-term project of Novartis is the Novartis Campus Park, which will transform its headquarters in the St. Johann area into a 'city within a city', incorporating the former factory complex and the Celtic settlement of some 2100 years ago into a 'campus of knowledge, innovation and encounter'. A project anticipated to last several decades.

Overview

History:
Geigy (1758)
Ciba and Sandoz (mid-late 19th century)
Roche (founded in 1896 as F. Hoffmann-LaRoche & Co)
Lonza Ltd. (1897)

Today:
Merger (1970) of Ciba and Geigy (Ciba-Geigy), renamed in 1992 as Ciba
Merger (1996) of Ciba and Sandoz, forming Novartis
Ciba Specialty Chemicals (Ciba SC) offshoot of merger
Clariant (1995) spin-off of Sandoz
Merger (2000) of agrocompany Zeneca, and agribusiness department of Novartis, forming Syngenta

Novartis and Roche (pharmaceuticals)
Syngenta (agroproducts)
Clariant and Ciba SC (specialty chemicals)
Lonza (custom manufacturer of, inter alia, chemical intermediates, biopharmaceuticals for the pharmaceutical and agrochemical industries and polymer intermediates).

The Salt (White Gold) Industry

Upon the advice of the professor and geologist Peter Merian, in 1834 Carl C.F. Glenck (1779-1845), a German entrepreneur and mining specialist, began systematically to explore for salt in the region. Saline deposits, traces of the ocean that covered central Europe 200 million years ago, were discovered in 1836 at the Red House in Muttenz. With this find, Switzerland's dependency on outside sources for salt ended. The newly established canton of Basel-Landschaft (1833) and later the canton of Aargau, were provided with a financial base, in the form of a salt tax, with which to develop their economy.

The discovery of salt in the Basel area attracted the chemical and bathing industries. In 1843 the Kaiseraugst saltworks were created as the first of three in the canton of Aargau. Rheinfelden followed in 1844 and Riburg in 1848. A concession was granted in 1846 to operate a brine-bath at Rheinfelden, today the spa and bath center. A natural outcome of the salt production was that the chemical industry, which needs salt for some of its products, located their factories at Schweizerhalle. The word *halle* has its roots in the late Roman *halla* as well as in the Greek *hals,* e.g., Reichenhall, Halle, Hallstatt; the latter gave its name to the early Iron Age because of the nearby salt mines.

The saltworks at Kaiseraugst ceased operations in 1847; in 1848 the salt-boiling pans from this former site were used to set up the Saline Riburg. In 1865, however, the Kaiseraugst saltworks reopened; in 1874 the three saltworks, all located in Aargau, united to form the *Schweizerische Rheinsalinen AG / Swiss Rhine Saltworks.* In 1909 the Schweizerhalle, Rheinfelden and Riburg saltworks merged, creating the *Vereinigte Schweizerische Rheinsalinen / United Swiss Saltworks on the Rhine.* The Kaiseraugst works closed, the buildings were torn down and the area flooded by the reservoir for the new power plant at Augst-Wyhlen. A 1973 agreement between the Swiss cantons regulates the sale of salt and guarantees the supply to all regions at fair and uniform prices.

Today the two facilities at Schweizerhalle and Riburg produce more than 400,000 tons of salt a year, with a turnover of roughly 70 million Swiss francs. About 40% of the production is designated for industrial use, 30% for de-icing roads, 15% for table salt, 7% for use in water-softening products, 5% for agricultural purposes and 3% for bath salts and medicinal purposes. All cantons, as well as the Principality of Liechtenstein, own the saltworks—with the exception of the canton of Vaud, which controls its own supply and cantonal monopoly at the saltworks in Bex.

In 1996, the one-kilo *JURA-SEL* package was used for an advertising campaign. Its motto: "Genuine for over 200 million years." In 1997 the *Salzkammer/* Salt Museum opened in the renovated Glenck villa in Pratteln.

The wooden salt drilling and pump houses are visible near Schweizerhalle, as well as at Riburg, a historical reminder of the origins of this industry.

In 2005 a new salt warehouse, capped by a 31-meter-high and 93-meter-wide cupola, making it the largest such construction in Switzerland, opened in Rheinfelden / Riburg.

The Silk-Ribbon Industry

Silk-ribbon weaving was once an important source of income to many people in the Basel area. It was the dominant industry from the late 1500s to the 1800s and built upon the silk trade established since the 1400s. Who first brought the craft of weaving ribbon to the area is difficult to pinpoint. Some say the French Huguenots fleeing religious persecution; others say the Italians, still others the Dutch or the Flemish. It is clear, however, that numerous waves of refugees from centers with international reputations for fine-quality textile production settled in Basel and developed the craft. Their influence on the economic life of the region, supported by farsighted decisions made by the Basel city council, would prove beneficial for centuries to come. Though the industry itself is no longer important to the region—the last factory closed its doors in 2001—ribbon weaving was key to the industrialization of the area, it gave birth to Basel's world-renowned pharmaceutical and chemical industry by creating the need for sophisticated silk-yarn dyes.

In the late 1500s when refugees first arrived, silk ribbon was crafted individually on single-ribbon looms. As more sophisticated looms were developed, a struggle ensued between artisans who wished to preserve ribbon weaving as a handicraft, and those who wanted to turn it into a large-scale industry. Basel's city council facilitated its development by allowing ribbon to be manufactured outside the city walls and away from the influence of the artisans' guilds, which represented local ribbon weavers. Then, in the second half of the 1600s, the council approved the introduction of manually operated and later water-powered ribbon looms that could produce up to 16 ribbons at a time. This was carried out in the face of massive opposition from the guilds and was the greatest change to take place in the ribbon-weaving industry.

The first manually operated ribbon loom on which multiple ribbons could be woven was reputedly smuggled into Basel from Holland by Emanuel Hoffmann-Müller, a wool weaver. In 1669 he established the city's first ribbon mill, which led to his reputation as a respected and successful businessman. He is the ancestor of all the Basel Hoffmanns, including Fritz Hoffmann, the founder of the pharmaceutical company, F. Hoffmann-La Roche & Co.

Silk ribbon also adorned French fashions, epoche Louis XVI, 18ᵗʰ century

First steps were taken towards the mechanization and industrialization of the process. By the 1720s, use of the new loom was commonplace; its operating principles remained practically unchanged until the 1900s. The ribbons produced on these looms were of high quality, luxurious, sophisticated and sought-after worldwide. They established Basel's position as the center for quality workmanship. It also gave the city a near monopoly in silk-ribbon sales.

The ribbons were used for garments, expensive fabrics, on precious objects and as fastenings. The industry continued to flourish during the 1700s with over 60 silk-ribbon weaving companies operating in the area. Basel ribbon producers went over to a cottage system of production, contracting work out to farmers in the surrounding countryside. A financial partnership of sorts developed between the city and the countryside. The farmers were able to maintain their subsistence-level income and get by in times of crisis, and the owners of ribbon mills continued to make profits. The home weavers took pride in their work and their indispensable contribution to the Basel silk-ribbon trade. France, England and the United States were large importers of ribbon from Basel.

The first large-scale, silk-ribbon factory opened in 1846. The industry reached its peak in the 1860s; by the 1870s business began to stagnate. The US market deteriorated as American entrepreneurs, who had purchased Swiss looms

and hired Swiss technicians and operators, began producing their own high-quality ribbon. Furthermore, the industry suffered from the European economic crisis that began in 1874 and by the ever-increasing levying of customs duties on imports. The industry went into decline near the turn of the century, as silk ribbon fell out of fashion.

Editor's note: Schappe needs mentioning. Raw silk thread is obtained by reeling off the cocoons of the silkworm, in theory producing endless fibers. Schappe, on the other hand, is spun into short fibers from silk waste which can include cocoons unsuitable for manufacturing the long, raw silk fibers. With this by-product, more people could dress in 'schappe silk' as it was cheaper, but still silk.

J. Sigmund Alioth founded the first mechanically driven schappe-spinning mill on the continent in 1824. More mills developed up to the boom years of 1865 to 1872. A decline in the number of operational mills began shortly thereafter, but production continued. In the 1920s, due to the constant improvement of artificial silk, the price of raw silk dropped dramatically, and it was even cheaper than schappe.

With change in fashion and increase in cheaper and new materials, the schappe industry, and textile production in general, slowly ceased operation.

A random selection of families connected with silk-ribbon manufacturing: Bachofen-Heitz, Burckhardt, Christ, de Bary, Dienast, Faesch, Iselin, Sarasin, Senn and Vischer.

A Summary of Basel's Industries

The Rhine attracted the original settlers: their fishing and farming along the banks and tributaries of the river were Basel's first industries. The draining of the wetlands, the canalization and damming of the tributaries were further attempts to use the waters to promote its fledgling economy. The major breakthrough occurred with the harnessing of the canals to turn the first mills for grain, which eventually were used to produce paper and drive printing presses and spinning mills. The remarkable growth of the printing industry in the days of Erasmus is a result of the number of paper mills in operation along the various streams and canals. From this there is a direct line to the introduction of dyes for the silk-ribbon output to today's chemical and pharmaceutical industries.

With its unique location straddling three countries, Basel functions as a traditional and important European transportation hub. The Rhine afforded a convenient means of south-north transit. Served by the three national railway lines as well as the tripartite EuroAirport, the city also lies on the north-south, east-west motorway system. Four thousand people are employed in the forwarding industry in the area, with additional employees abroad who have connections with forwarding activities in Basel.

Two of the largest worldwide concerns have their origins and headquarters here: Panalpina, with 18,000 employees, and Danzas-Air-Ocean, (owned by the German Post), with 40,000 employees.

The guaranteed source of water and excellent transportation facilities have allowed Basel's industries to grow and expand far beyond its confines. One could say that all the industries have their origins in its waters.

Pauluskirche

CHURCHES
AND MONASTERIES

Basel's churches and monasteries were built from the early Christian era to the present. Until the Reformation in 1529, they reflected the wealth of the city and its flourishing artisanal industries. Prior to that date one-tenth of the population was involved with the religious life of the city. Churches and religious buildings comprised one-quarter of Basel's buildings. After the Reformation no new churches were constructed until the mid-19th century when rich artistry and symbolism once again took form.

Many churches were associated with monasteries and convents. At one time there were ten monasteries in the area—within or outside the city walls; the epithet 'The Holy City' described Basel. As hotels did not exist, the convents and monasteries provided necessary accommodations. The best example of monastic life can be seen at Kleines Klingental Museum, the former Klingental Convent. The following is but a selection of some architectural, historical and artistic highlights of the existing buildings.

As with all older buildings, renovations are periodically necessary; therefore, dates of restoration work may not be current.

Albankirche / **St. Alban's Church**
Mühlenberg 5
Late 11th-century Romanesque origin; reconstruction occurred from 1270 onwards. After the Reformation the buildings were neglected; renovated and reduced in size in 1845, based on plans by Johann Jakob Stehlin the Younger (1826-1894).

Bishop Burkhard von Fenis / von Hasenburg founded the monastery outside the town walls in 1083. It housed the Cluniac monks.

To note: the singular row of columns once part of the Romanesque cloister.

St. Alban's Church (rear view) 1871

Allerheiligen /All Saints

Neubadstrasse and Laupenring
Building started 1950
Architect: Hermann Baur (1894-1980)
Bell tower and parvis lead to the single-nave hall church; an elegant concrete structure suffused with daylight.
Interior: baptismal marble font with metal cover by Hans Arp (1887-1966); stained-glass window and stone mosaic by Alfred Manessier (1911-1994); stone altar by Albert Schilling (1904-1987) and much more.

Antoniuskirche / St. Anthony's Church

Kannenfeldstrasse 35
Begun 1927 and consecrated in 1931; first church in Switzerland constructed in raw (exposed) reinforced concrete.
Architects: Karl Moser (1860-1936) and Gustav Doppler (1869-1944)
A transverse rectangular bell tower (fondly known as the souls' silo / *Seelensilo*) dominates the skyline, contrasting with the subordinate appearance of the elongated church which melds with the residential area. A harmonious blending of concrete, glass and steel.

Altar and pulpit by Moser; mosaics in choir by Hans Stocker (1896-1983); stained-glass windows by Stocker and Otto Staiger (1894-1967), each almost 5 meters wide and 14 meters high. Over the main entrance, the relief of the Angel of Judgment is by Max Varin (1898-1931).

Arbogastkirche /
St. Arbogast's Church
Kirchplatz, Muttenz
Built c.1359 and 1420; Romanesque and late Gothic.

The only remaining fortified church in Switzerland. In times of war people and cattle gathered inside for safety. Previous churches on the site date from 8th to 12th century, the latter partially destroyed in the earthquake of 1356. Rebuilt 1359, followed by several renovations from 1420 to late 20th century.

Exterior: *Bannsteine* / old border stones and gravestones in inner courtyard; charnel house with wooden overhang and exterior wall paintings. Interior: well-preserved late Gothic frescoes (school of Martin Schongauer, dated 1507) and memorial plaques. Well worth a trip outside Basel. Tram No. 14 will get you there.

Barfüsserkirche /
Barfüsser Church
Barfüsserplatz

The brothers of the Franciscan order (barefoot monks, i.e., *Barfüsser*) arrived in 1231; first church built 1253/56; rebuilt in 14th century after a fire in 1298; closed after the Reformation when it became property of the city. Reformed services held until 1794. In the mid-1800s the church served as a salt warehouse which accelerated the decay of the red sandstone. The monastery was demolished in 1843; a *Kaufhaus* / customs and

warehouse was built on the site. A close vote in 1882 saved the church from demolition. Since 1894 it has been the Historisches Museum Basel. Renovated to halt further decay in 1974/80 and 2003; returned to the late Gothic structure.

Interior: treasury of the Basel Cathedral; treasury of the guilds; noteworthy, late medieval tapestries from Basel and region; fragments of the Totentanz / Dance of Death frescoes; historical rooms; remarkable space. *See Museums.*

Clarakirche / St. Clara's Church

Claraplatz, Kleinbasel

Built c.1268; Gothic: used as a monastery by the Sack Brethren (an order of 13th-century hermits; the name derives from their rough garments). After the suspension of the Order it was given to the Franciscan nuns (the Poor Clares, c.1277). Dramatically altered over the centuries; in 1857/59 Amadeus Merian designed an extension doubling its size. Renovated in 1973/74.

Interior: to the right of the altar, a mid-15th-century Neapolitan sculpture of the Virgin Mary. Over the right-side door, figures of St. John, the Virgin with the Christ Child and a Crucifix by Albert Schilling (1939); over the left-side door, figures of St. Clara and Emperor Heinrich II. Mosaic by Hans Stocker (1931); painted glass designed by Giuseppe Scartezzini (1934/35). A stone block on left side of the nave is engraved with dates of the Church Councils held from 325 to 1962. The polygonal choir houses the Sunday Cross with base / *Sonntags Kreuz* (1450/75, Basel).

Editor's note: The Sunday Cross was allotted to Basel-Stadt in 1834 after the division of Basel into two half cantons; it was then given by the city to the Catholic community and deposited in St. Clara's Church.

Dom Arlesheim / Cathedral of Arlesheim

Built in two phases: from 1679/81, baroque, combining Italian and south German influence after design by Jakob Engel (1632-1714); significant Rococo renovation 1759/61 from plans drawn up by Franz Anton Bagnato (d.1757) and carried out by his son. Renovation in 1978/81.

When the city joined the Reformation in 1529, the Cathedral Chapter of Basel departed and remained outside the city for 150 years. In 1679 the chapter returned from exile in Freiburg im Breisgau and settled in Arlesheim; construction of the cathedral began.

The two-towered cathedral sets the backdrop for the impressive square, lined on both sides with period buildings—a setting which faithfully portrays the baroque epoch in the area and presents a picture of architectural harmony.

Interior: extraordinary wall paintings and side altarpieces by Giuseppe Appiani (1712-1742); stucco decoration and marble high altar by Francesco Pozzi (c.1779-1844), the main figures in the altarpiece by Appiani are that of Heinrich II and Kunigunde. First chapel on the north side, a 15th-century wooden figure of St. Odile (c.660-720), who according to legend founded the convent in Alsace at Mount St. Odile/ *Hohenberg*; choir stalls, sacristy and woodwork (1760/61). Organ built 1761 by Johann Silbermann (1727-1799) of Strasbourg. The crypt contains a modern altar and baptismal font by Albert Schilling (1904-1987). Suggestion: stroll through the nearby *Eremitage*, a romantic garden with ponds, grottoes and a hermit's chapel.

Elisabethenkirche /
St. Elizabeth's Church

Elisabethenstrasse 10

Built 1857/65, neo-Gothic; an important representation of this style in Switzerland.

Architects: Christoph Riggenbach (1810-1863) and Karl Wartner after design by Ferdinand Stadler (1813-1870).

Built over the site of a 13th-century hospital chapel dedicated to St. Elizabeth of Thüringen. First Protestant church built after the Reformation; endowed by Christoph and Margaretha Merian, it became their 'mausoleum'. It escaped demolition in 1968. The church was renovated in the early 1990s to create a multifunctional space. Now operates as one of the most open ecumenical 'city' churches in Europe.

Interior: a vaulted hall construction with two aisles, gallery / *emporium* and polygonal choir with painted glass windows by Christian and Heinrich Burkard of Munich (1865); inscription to the donors is at the base of central window. The crypt contains the sarcophagi of Christoph and Margaretha Merian. The pulpit, gargoyles and tympanum relief over the main portal of Christ and the Samaritan Woman at the Well are by Jacques-Ange Corbel of Paris. Tower is accessed by 228 stairs.

Heiliggeistkirche /
Holy Ghost Church

Thiersteinerallee 51 in the Gundeldingen quarter

Built 1910/12 as neo-Gothic basilica; partially renovated in 1975

Architect: Gustav Doppler (1869-1944)

Design: Max Meckel (1847-1910)

Interior: three-aisled nave; altars from the workshop of Joseph Dettlinger (1865–1937). The main altar is dedicated to the Holy Ghost; the altar on the left to the Virgin Mary—to her

right is the figure of Heinrich II and to her left that of St. Pantalus (two of the patron saints of Basel); the altar on the right is dedicated to St. Joseph. Wall paintings by Franz Schilling (1920/25); the altar table and ambo are by René Küng (b.1934), as is a clover-shaped fountain in the side courtyard and garden.

Josephskirche / St. Joseph's Church
Amerbachstrasse 9, Kleinbasel
Built 1901 in neo-baroque style; the Catholic church for lower Kleinbasel
Architect: August Hardegger (1858-1927)
Interior: stained-glass windows of the apostles; organ inaugurated in 1904 was renovated in 1992.

Kartäuserkloster, Margarethenkapelle, Waisenhaus.
Former Carthusian monastery, existing church, cloister and orphanage
Near Theodorskirche and Wettstein Bridge, Kleinbasel
Established in 1401 by Mayor Jakob Zibol, master of Basel's guilds, as a Carthusian monastery. The last monastery founded in Basel was given to the city in 1669; subsequently converted to the *Bürgerliches Waisenhaus Basel* / city orphanage and home for juveniles, and location for various teaching organizations. Many wealthy benefactors supported the monastery, which was a favored retreat during the Church Council of Basel (1431/48). Buildings planned by Brother John of Hungary. Hieronymus Zscheckenbürlin joined the order in 1487; as its last prior (1501/1536), he extended the buildings and commissioned masterful furnishings.

Editor's note: To visit the church, request key at office located inside archway entrance.

Church interior: entrance hall with tombstone slabs; choir stalls (c.1420s), two of the end panels represent the Annunciation, the other two SS. Peter and Paul; various heraldic shields, a few with intricate details. Stained-glass windows (some originals are at the Historisches Museum Basel); decorated bosses and keystone. Behind the wrought-iron gate are faded frescoes of the Crucifixion scene and a stained-glass panel with figures as represented by the three Honorable Societies of Kleinbasel. Also houses a small organ.
In the adjoining cloister: the Amerbach family funerary slabs and ten fresco panels depicting the works of St. Bruno of Cologne, founder of the Carthusian

Zscheckenbürlin's portrait by Master from Basel, 1487

order in the valley of the Chartreuse / Alps of Dauphine near Grenoble in 1084, painted (c.1440) during the Church Council. Wall tomb slabs in sacristy, lower choir and cloister of benefactors and several attendees of the Church Council, including a cardinal and a bishop.

In main building: stained-glass panels (1402-1577); the *Zscheckenbürlin Raum* / room (1509), a most remarkable Gothic space. The Zscheckenbürlin bed (1510/12) is in the Historisches Museum Basel; portraits of him are in both the Historisches Museum Basel and the Kunstmuseum Basel.

Kloster Klingental; Museum Kleines Klingental / Klingental Convent and Museum

Unterer Rheinweg 26, Kleinbasel

Gothic-period convent built in 1274; numerous alterations over the centuries. The former convent is considered the most illustrious and richest of the ten which existed in Basel during the late Middle Ages. Founded in 1274 by the Dominican nuns, who several decades previously established a religious community in Alsace. From Alsace they moved to the Black Forest, eventually settling in Basel. The name Klingental originates with its patron, the knight and minnesinger (*Minne* / love) Walter von Klingen, a friend of King Rudolph von Habsburg, who offered the nuns land in the Black Forest. His family remained closely attached to this religious community even in death, as members of the Klingen family are buried in the convent's cemetery.

The original building of the convent was laid out along the existing city wall in Kleinbasel and parallel to the Rhine. All rooms necessary for community life: chapels, chapter rooms, dormitory, dining rooms and kitchen were built. This representation of a medieval convent is today largely intact, albeit with later structural modifications. On the ground floor, a dining room with late-Gothic ceiling leads to the convent's kitchen with its vast chimney flue; on the upper floor, a small wooden-paneled dining room, two nuns' cells and an anteroom with wall paintings are all accessible to the public. The dining halls are available for rent.

Kaserne courtyard, 1860/63

Shortly after the original building was completed, construction of a cloister church began next to the city wall. For centuries the roof with its colored and glazed tiles and 28-meter high bell tower gave a lasting and impressive image to Kleinbasel. The church still stands. Since the 17th century its interior has been completely altered (stories added for military dormitories) and its use multifarious. Today it houses artists' ateliers.

The completion of the church did not stop future building projects for the convent. Next to the church, where the Kaserne now stands, the nuns built

Hans von Nussdorf,
master builder of the Cathedral

A misericord from a choir stall
at the Cathedral

a cloister, with frescoes of the Dance of Death, and other stately buildings. These buildings around the cloister, the Grosses Klingental, differentiate them from the original building, the Kleines Klingental. Following the completion of this construction phase, the nuns offered the original building for use by members of the convent's laity. The Kaserne was built in 1860 for military purposes (a garrison) by the architect Jakob Stehlin the Younger (1826-1894). It now serves as a school and a venue for leisure activities.

The Klingental convent (as were all the monasteries and convents in Basel) was closed following the Reformation of 1529. The Basel authorities advised all religious orders to leave their monasteries. A large number of the nuns and monks did so and married, while some ignored the council and moved into still standing monasteries. Some nuns at the Klingental Convent did not wish to depart. The last abbess, Walpurga von Runs, held on inside the convent until her death in 1557.

Since 1939 the original building—the so-called Kleines Klingental—has been a museum. *See Museums.*

Editor's note: The building itself, carved-wooden elements and original Romanesque and Gothic sculptures from the Cathedral; scale-model of 17th-century Basel based on the 1615 map by Matthäus Merian the Elder; a new model, 1:100, of the convent in 1510; medieval herb garden, are some of its attractions.

Leonhardskirche / St. Leonard's Church
Above Barfüsserplatz and near the Music Academy
Of Romanesque origin, 11th and 12th centuries; new church built after earthquake of 1356; 'people's church' built in late 15th century (late-Gothic period) by the cathedral master, Hans von Nussdorf; alterations at beginning of 18th century, and thereafter. The crypt is Romanesque. It is a fine example of a late-Gothic hall church (with three equally high naves).

Located in a dominant position overlooking the valley of the once open Birsig River. The monastery was founded in 1133/35 to house the Augustinian canons. Well-preserved crypt, supposedly dedicated to St. Maurice, survived the 1356 earthquake. In 1525 the last prior turned the monastery over to the city council. Church expanded in 1528, site of some of the first Protestant services in Basel. Monastery buildings became known as the *Lohnhof* when it came under the *Lohnherren* / the city building authority. Later served as the city's prison; remnants of the monastery were incorporated into the prison buildings. Now houses the *Musikmuseum*, apartments, clubrooms for the English-speaking community, the *Au Violon* Restaurant and the *Lohnhof Hotel*.

Entrance to the square affords a feeling of seclusion with the long cemetery hall punctuated by tracery windows, the porch of the main entrance to the church, the Lohnhof archway and the wall going down to the level of Barfüsserplatz. The statue of Rudolf Riggenbach adds joviality to the scene.

Interior: left of the entrance door is a fresco of St. James, Christ and Mary Magdalene. Further on between the ribs of the vault are the four symbols of the evangelists; after the stairs, the St. Theobald's Chapel with tombstone and kneeling statue of *Hüglin von Schönegg* (1386), Marshall of the Duchy of Spoleto, donor and bene-factor of the building. Further still is a 1480s stained-glass panel depicting St. Leonard (patron saint of prisoners) with chain and abbot's staff; numer-ous decorative bosses throughout the edifice. A magnificently carved oak pulpit (1720); numerous memorial plaques; bouquet decorations between the arches of the chancel screen cle-verly integrate the bishop's crosier, the emblem of Basel (1530).

Organ: Silbermann (1718/1771); re-constructed and enlarged in 1969. Chancel: high and narrow space with generous natural light. A carving of St. George slaying the dragon on 14th-century oak choir stalls. Stained-glass window of the Annunciation by

Antoni Glaser (1519); numerous memorial plaques; mural (1435) on the left side is attributed to the workshop of Konrad Witz. It was perhaps for St. Leonard's Church that the Mirror of Salvation Altarpiece / *Heilspiegelaltar* was commissioned; nine panels are in the Kunstmuseum Basel.

Editor's note: See biographical sketch on Konrad Witz.

Crypt: Romanesque; served as a wine cellar until the late 1800s.

Marienkirche / St. Mary's Church
Holbeinstrasse 28/32
Built 1884/86 in neo-Romanesque design; dramatically renovated 1958 and 1984/88. Architect: Paul Reber (1835-1908)
First Catholic church constructed in Basel after the Reformation.
Interior: stained-glass windows by Ernst Stocker (1906-1976); Stations of the Cross reminiscent of icon painting; Gothic-style sculpture of Madonna and Child perched atop the organ; a modern statue of Madonna and Child; tabernacle by Albert Schilling (1904-1987).

Martinskirche / St. Martin's Church
Martinskirchplatz, behind Globus Department Store and City Hall / *Rathaus*
Believed to be Basel's oldest parish church (the peoples' church); first mentioned around 1100. Oldest parts are in the tower; 13th-century Gothic building dedicated to St. Martin of Tours. Reconstructed after the 1356 earthquake; significant renovations in 1851. Both Zwingli and Oekolampad preached here. One of the earliest churches to effect reforms (1526).
Interior: fresco above funerary slab (c.1370); numerous memorial plaques; polygonal choir (c.1398); frescoes above entrance to choir depict Death, the Grim Reaper and SS. Martin and Lawrence (c.1440); pulpit (1495).
Exterior: over south portal, wall painting of St. Martin by Hans Rohner (1920).

Matthäuskirche / **St. Mathew's Church**
Matthäuskirchplatz / Feldbergstrasse 81, Kleinbasel
Built 1893/95 in neo-Gothic style; the Protestant church for lower Kleinbasel.

Münster / **Basel Cathedral and Cloister**
Münsterplatz
Romanesque and Gothic
First church on site was a 9th-century Carolingian edifice. Present Cathedral erected by Bishop Adalbero II was consecrated in 1019 in the presence of King Heinrich II, who together with his queen consort, Kunigunde, financed the building and donated valuable furnishings, e.g., the golden altar frontal now in Paris and the Heinrich Cross now in Berlin. Several representations of Heinrich and Kunigunde are both inside and outside the Cathedral.
Together with the cathedrals in Freiburg im Breisgau and Strasbourg, the Basel Cathedral is a noteworthy and influential sacred building of the Upper Rhine; it contains the foremost late-Romanesque building elements in Switzerland.

Several fires over the centuries and the devastating earthquake of 1356 destroyed parts of the building. Some of the master builders who helped rebuild the Cathedral: Johann Parler of Gmünd, architect and master stonemason (the fountain at the *Fischmarkt* in Basel, the Cathedral of Prague and churches in southern Germany), Ulrich of Ensingen (Cathedral of Strasbourg), Johannes Kun (Cathedral of Ulm) and Vincenz Ensinger (Cathedral of Constance). With the completion of the St. Martin Tower in 1500 by Hans von Nussdorf (d.1502), the rebuilding of the Cathedral was concluded; shortly thereafter, the terrace-bastion / *Pfalz* was renewed.
Extensive reconstruction of the Cathedral took place in the mid-19th century under Amadeus Merian (1808-1889) and Christoph Riggenbach (1810-1863), with further restoration in the late-20th century.

An organ housed in a 'swallow's nest structure' with wing panels painted by Hans Holbein the Younger was installed in 1519. The panels are now in the Kunstmuseum Basel. The present organ was installed in 2003; it weighs 27 tons, has 5,301 metal and 400 wooden pipes, as well as 23 window shutters. The 1460/70 Gothic cloisters (with traces of original Romanesque features near the entrance to the choir) were used for clerical processions during the Middle Ages; until 1861 they served as graveyards. It is home to over 100 memorial plaques and chapels.

The *Gallus Pforte* / The St. Gall Portal: to the left of the Cathedral entrance, named after St. Gall, a 7th-century Irish monk, who was instrumental in introducing Christianity to Switzerland. A perplexing, fascinating and outstanding late 12th-century Romanesque carved portal. Subjects: (tympanum) Christ at the Last Judgment with SS. Peter and Paul, the donors, and below them the wise and foolish virgins; (sides) niches formed by small pillars, the six acts of mercy, the figures and symbols of the four evangelists.

Above the St. Gall Portal is the *Glücksrad* / Wheel of Fortune. Fragments of the original wooden Wheel of Fortune Window (c.1230) are in the Kleines Klingental Museum.

On the Pfalz: beneath the Romanesque choir with the carved figures of elephants and lions decorating the facade, contrasting grey bricks outline the original 10th-century outer crypt.

The cloisters: the 1501 Utenheim memorial (a tribute to Wolfgang Utenheim by his uncle Christophorus, bishop of Basel (1503/1527) during the Reformation) with a crucifixion scene, severely damaged at that time; a plaque commemorating champions of the Basel Reformation; Hieronymus Froben, Felix Platter, Andreas Ryff and Isaak Iselin are buried here; memorial plaques for Johann Rudolf Wettstein and Jacob Bernoulli. Bernoulli's memorial is engraved with *eadem mutata resurgo* / though changed, I rise again the same, which refers to his logarithmic spiral. The bronze table sculptures (1990) at the Rhine end of the cloister are by Bettina Eichin. Oekolampad's statue (1862) stands outside the entrance to the cloisters.

Interior: in the northern aisle a stone bas-relief panel of the legend of St. Vincent (c.1100); in the southern aisle a stone bas-relief panel of six of the apostles of same date.

Choir stalls and misericords (c.1375), masterpieces of Gothic woodcarving and medieval iconography; (the choir stalls originally provided over 90 seats for the canons of the Cathedral).

Erasmus's memorial (1538) is in the northern aisle.

Sarcophagus (1281) of Queen Anna von Hohenberg, wife of King Rudolf von Habsburg, and their son Charles (a significant reason for pilgrimages to the city until the Reformation), is at the back of the choir.

Fascinating late-Romanesque capitals (c.1180) are in the choir.

Late-Gothic pulpit (c.1486) by Hans von Nussdorf; nearby on the floor is a drawing of a dragon (c.1170), symbol of evil cast to the ground.

Stained-glass windows in the choir: neo-Gothic windows in the upper gallery and neo-Romanesque windows in the ambulatory of the choir (mid 1800s); the Star of David window with Christ the King in brilliant red is by Melchior Paul Deschwanden (1857). Fragments of earlier stained glass are in the Kleines Klingental Museum.

Crypt: late-Romanesque frescoes (1019-1400); ceiling paintings devoted to the Virgin; Cathedral's oldest sarcophagus, that of Bishop Rudolph II who was slain defending the town against the invading Huns (917).

Exterior: richly decorated archivolt over main entrance; figures of Heinrich II holding a model of the Cathedral and Kunigunde a Greek cross (1420). The Seducer and the Foolish Virgin (c.1290) are from a former cycle of the Wise and Foolish Virgins (before the earthquake in 1356, they were part of the figures surrounding the entrance portal, as can be seen today on the cathedral at Strasbourg).

The St. George Tower with the figure of St. George and the dragon (which crashed to the ground in 1372 and was replaced soon thereafter) shows traces of white stone outlining part of Heinrich's Romanesque cathedral.

On the St. Martin Tower (1488/1500), the figure of the saint on horseback should be cutting his cape to share with a beggar; in the 1600s the beggar was removed and replaced with a tree trunk, perhaps alluding to a knight and not the saint. On the upper part of the tower is a portrait in stone of the master mason Hans von Nussdorf.

Original stonework and sundry wooden elements are in the Kleines Klingental Museum.

Pauluskirche / St. Paul's Church
Steinenring 20
Built 1898/1901 in Art Nouveau / neo-
Romanesque style
Architect: Karl Moser (1860-1936)
A visual marvel; located in a park-like
setting with changing seasonal plant-
ings; it is Basel's most popular church
for weddings.
Interior and exterior: painted glass
windows by Max Läuger (1864-1952);
organ housing by Karl Moser, organ
built by Zimmermann of Basel. Mosaic
frieze on both sides of the pulpit by
Heinrich Altherr (1878-1947); behind
the pulpit, the carved stone screen
with two angels and sculpted reliefs
are by Otto Kiefer (1874-1938), as is

the bronze statue of Michael the Archangel crowning the entrance gable.
Over the main portal, a carved stone relief of Christ helping a sinner rise is
by Carl Burckhardt; an elegant and highly decorated bas-relief four-pillared
tower; the five-bells housed in the tower were forged in 1901, they weigh
eight and a half tons; Moser's signature is on one of the pillars of the bell
tower.

Peterskirche / St. Peter's Church
Peterskirchplatz 7, in the university district
9th-century Carolingian burial church; later a Gothic seminary (collegiate)
church; rebuilt after massive damage during 1356 earthquake; tower completed
(c.1430). Several renovations followed.
Interior: in the choir: the bosses on the network of vaults represent the 12
apostles and their symbols; carved stalls (1494) by Ulrich Bruder of Constance with religious and humorous figures; founders' coats of arms on pillars;
epitaphs of Johann, Niklaus and Daniel Bernoulli, mid-to-late 18th century.
Stained-glass window (1901) of the Crucifixion.
Organ: Johann Andreas Silbermann (c.1770).

Editor's note: The organ originally was built for Theodorskirche; it was disassembled in
1916 and sold. The Historisches Museum Basel purchased the housing and pipes in 1951;
they were re-assembled and placed in Peterskirche in 1968.

Precious frescoes in various chapels: in the Martins (or Keppenbach) Chapel to the right of the choir, one fresco represents the Trinity with a three-headed God (c.1400); to the right and before the chapel, St. Dorothy (c.1510); on the Efringer Chapel wall, the south aisle, The Torments of Christ and His Burial (c.1350/60).

In the Maria or Eberler Chapel, to the left of the choir, frescoes commissioned by the country squire Eberler include the Deposition of Christ, the Death of the Virgin, St. Bernard of Siena, and more.

Also in the chapel is the funerary monument to the printer Johannes Froben, the epitaph written in Greek, Latin and Hebrew is reportedly by Erasmus; the decorations of the slab possibly executed after designs by Hans Holbein the Younger.

Predigerkirche /
Preachers' Church

Totentanz 19, near the University Hospital

Gothic structure built c.1233 as home church of the Dominican brothers invited to Basel by Bishop Heinrich von Thun. Church's basilica plan dates from reconstruction in 1269; rebuilt after 1356 earthquake; in the 1680s used as a warehouse; restoration 1976/78, and thereafter. The frescoes of the *Totentanz* / Dance of Death cycle from the former cemetery wall, often attributed to Konrad Witz or his circle (c.1435/40), were

demolished in 1805. Nineteen of the rescued fragments are in the Historisches Museum Basel.

Today it is the parish for the Old Catholic Church, i.e., independent of Rome.

Interior: Equally proportioned nave and choir are separated by rood screen (1269), reconstructed in 1978; on the left aisle of the nave, lancet windows with tracery of joined trefoils, some with 14th-century frescoes (John the Baptist and the Virgin), and more. 14th-century wall painting on one side of

the swallow's nest organ; a 'new' organ by Johann Andreas Silbermann and son Daniel (c.1767) with some features from the elder Silbermann (1718). The St. Mary's altar (c.1300) is now at the Historisches Museum Basel.

Exterior: a 15th-century small bell tower by Johannes Kun who assisted in the rebuilding of the Cathedral; a memorial plaque dedicated to Peter Ochs by Bettina Eichin is on the Totentanz street-side of the church.

Theodorskirche / St. Theodore's Church
Theodorskirchplatz 5, Kleinbasel near Wettsteinplatz
Built in late-13th century
Already the parish church of the village *Niederbasel* before the founding of Kleinbasel. Consecrated in 1277; St. Theodore's relics installed (1319); rebuilt following earthquake. After the Reformation, celebration of high mass continued until 19th century. Church was restored in 1836 after design by Amadeus Merian; restoration in 1942/48, and thereafter.
Interior: large fresco (late 1300s) of St. Christopher carrying the Christ Child presented in a unique frontal position; stone pulpit with the symbols of the four evangelists, the stone baptismal font (both c.1490/97) and more.

The Nuns of Klingental - well-born and self-assured
After the community of Klingental nuns settled in Kleinbasel, the convent became rich and successful. The nuns were mostly women from the local nobility who often brought substantial dowries, possessions and inheritances from their families.
In the Middle Ages most women were legally dependent on their fathers or husbands, but women who entered a religious community were bound to obey their mother superior rather than a male figure of authority; they enjoyed a certain degree of autonomy and scope for self-development.

In the prosperous convent of Klingental, the novices and nuns benefited greatly from this situation. They received a good education, mostly in reading and singing, but also in writing, painting, weaving or embroidery. Their most important tasks were to praise God and pray for the salvation of humankind, and to hold memorial services for the repose of the deceased. This activity was highly regarded by society and the sisters were handsomely rewarded with gifts as well as stipends from grateful families. The wealth of the convent grew accordingly. To assure the financial security of the convent, the nuns were allowed to keep their possessions and to oversee the management of their fortunes. They could, for example, sell houses and land, lend money, or collect revenue and payments in kind.

Since the convent was so successful and wealthy, it attracted disapproval and envy. First came the Dominican monks from the monastery, who would have liked to regain their tutelage over the rich convent—a tutelage which the nuns had rejected earlier by putting themselves under the protection of the Bishop of Constance.

Over time, the convent had turned from a pious community into a religious institution for ladies of rank. Besides owning property, sometimes a whole suite of comfortably furnished cells, the nuns enjoyed freedom of movement outside the enclosure for visits in town, could hold private receptions for relatives and friends, and even were rumored to go bathing in the Rhine. The convent became a target of frequent verbal attacks.

By the mid-15th century there was a general demand for monastic reforms. The criticism was directed at wealth and poor discipline, with appeals for a return to a modest and pious life in seclusion.
Klingental's wealthy and self-assured sisters did not correspond to this ideal. When the criticism became more insistent (one accusation was chattiness during choir services)—*"es ist ein Gemach uff dem dormenter, das ist ein recht swetzhuss"/* in the dormitory it's a real chat-house—the nuns tenaciously defended their freedom and opposed any attempt at reform.
The situation escalated in January 1480. The zealous new Provincial of the Dominicans had obtained a Papal Bull from Pope Sixtus IV authorizing him to initiate reforms at the convent. Along with ecclesiastical and political officials from Basel, he entered the enclosure of the convent by force, violating the nuns' rights, and started reading the papal order aloud. But the assembled nuns drowned out his voice by clapping their hands, singing and shouting, while laysisters banged lids and pans. Later they could claim that they did not hear anything and were therefore not obliged to obey.

Furious about these 'incorrigible and shameless women', the Provincial had them shut in their cells and ordered thirteen reformed nuns from Alsace to move into the convent and carry out the reforms. The Klingental nuns were eventually given a choice between leaving the convent or accepting reform. All but one departed to other convents or to the homes of their families. Once outside the Klingental, they launched a successful campaign for their cause, enlisting influential relatives and political figures. In the meantime, the convent had substantial economic losses since the inexperienced young nuns from Alsace did not know much about asset management.

Within three years the situation had changed dramatically. The Roman Curia and the Council of Basel, the two powers upon which the Klingental reform ultimately depended, decided to drop the matter, and in May 1482 the

attempt to reform the convent was abandoned—the Pope revoked his Bull. The 'old' Klingental sisters allowed back into the convent, recovered all their possessions and rights, while the reformed nuns had to leave. Furthermore, a huge fine was levied against the Basel Dominicans to make up for the convent's financial losses.

The nuns had successfully fought for their Klingental and their relative freedoms. The convent flourished again, and ideas of reform were not carried out seriously. Fifty years later a more powerful and more radical movement, the Reformation, would put an end to monasteries and convents in Basel. It was the end of an era. For many women it was also the end of an experiment to ensure the possibility of creating an individual and independent way of life and self-determination.

St. Johannstor

ARCHITECTURE

Basel has a wealth of architectural treasures waiting to be seen and heard. They will tell their stories if we look and listen.

Editor's note: "There was an old owl who lived in an oak, the more he saw, the less he spoke. The less he spoke, the more he heard, why can't we be like that wise old bird?"

Highlights of some private and public buildings will only serve to whet one's appetite for the broad palette of architectural periods evident in the city—representative of its vast cultural experience—which will please both the novice and the expert. We start with the Celts—builders of the first city walls—and finish with the Elsässertor, a multipurpose complex, hoping to pique your curiosity. *See Churches and Monasteries for ecclesiastical architecture and Museums for details on the museums mentioned.*

Murus Gallicus / Gallic wall, vestiges in the Archaeology Park, Rittergasse 4, is part of the earliest city wall in Basel; a Bronze Age fortification and settlement, however, did exist. The Murus Gallicus was composed of timbers providing resilience (even against a battering ram); it was faced with stone providing protection from fire and was embedded in the earth.

Over the centuries, Basel built three more city walls. From the 11th to the 19th century it was a fortified city. The first or inner wall (1080/1100) known as the *Burkhard'sche* began a short distance from the Cathedral Hill. The second or middle wall (1200/50) followed the Burkhard'sche but was higher, stronger and had deeper *Graben* / moats; it was severely damaged by the 1356 earthquake. It was extended from St. Alban-Graben to Steinenberg and then ran parallel to the first wall down to the Rhine. A third or outer wall (1361/98) incorporated the *Vorstädte* / the suburbs of the expanding city. Of the five gates built, three still stand: St. Albantor, St. Johannstor and Spalentor; Aeschentor and Steinentor were demolished in the late 1860s. Spalentor was

Detail of Matthäus Merian's 'bird's eye' view map, 1617

the main city gate towards France, hence more elaborate. Near St.Albantor a walkway and battlements are visible.

Kleinbasel's fortifications began in 1255/70 with a moat and subsequently two gates: the Riehentor and Bläsitor. The walls were reinforced and lengthened during the 1300s. Paintings at the Kunstmuseum Basel and the scale model of the city at the Kleines Klingental Museum show the Middle Age fortifications with the numerous turrets, towers and battlements.

Editor's note: Remnants of the earlier city walls are in the Archaeology Department's Exhibition in the basement of the Hotel / Restaurant Teufelhof on Leonhardsgraben; a tower (Lohnhof-Eckturm) from the first wall on Kohlenberg can be visited (key is at the Musikmuseum); further information on other vestiges of old Basel is available from the Archaeology Department and the tourist office.

In the 16th and 17th centuries, a series of stone-gunners' and artillery positions were built along the wall providing additional defense. Examples of 17th-century posts are at Elisabethenschanze, Steinenschanze and St. Johannsschanze. These areas became parks with the razing of the walls in the late 1860s.

Romanesque buildings: best represented by elements of the Cathedral, the remaining columns at the former St. Alban Cloister, and certain features in the churches of St. Martin, St. Peter and St. Leonard.
See Churches and Monasteries.

Several buildings on ***Rittergasse*** / the Knights Street give evidence of early land ownership by the German Knights of Ramstein. Walk the street: look and listen.

* *Ramsteinerhof* 17: first mentioned in 1327. Residence of the antipope Felix V (elected in 1440 during the Church Council); reconstructed in 1727/32. The building now has five numbers: 7, 9, 13, 15 and 17. The complex is best viewed from the Rhine side.
* *Hohenfirstenhof* 19: came into the possession of the city in 1523. Completely reconstructed in 1583; later changes, notably in 1830. It is also best viewed from the Rhine side.
* *Deutschritterkapelle* 29 / Former Chapel of the Teutonic Knights: built 1268/87; renewed after 1417; secularized in the 16th century and completely renovated in 1844 after Melchior Berri's plans. Now an architect's office.

Ramsteinerhof, Rittergasse 17

The earthquake of 1356 with its aftermath of fires destroyed most of the city's densely packed wooden houses, as well as many stone structures. With the aid of dendrochronology, surviving elements of several pre-earthquake buildings have been verified. Parts of solidly built churches, patrician and public houses survived; extensive rebuilding in the late 16th century was carried out in a relatively short period with the assistance of master craftsmen from outside the city: e.g., the Parler family of Gmünd, Ulrich von Ensingen of Strasbourg, Johannes Kun of Ulm and Vincenz Ensinger of Constance.

Editor's note: Houses often have an early date on the facade; this refers to the first recording of the house and not necessarily to the present structure.

Gothic buildings date from 1356 to the early 1500s; either intact buildings or surviving elements are throughout the old part of the city: on Gemsberg, Heuberg, Leonhardsberg, Schlüsselberg, Martinsgasse, Rheinsprung, Rittergasse, and beyond.

- *Bischofshof*, Rittergasse 1: rebuilt 1451/58. Spacious meeting room decorated with frescoes; it served as library for the university and assembly room during the Church Council (1431/48).

- *Rheinsprung*: two adorable houses below St. Martin's Church built in the 15th century retain the form of craftsmen's cottages of the era, combining atelier, shop and living quarters.

Up the Rheinsprung   ***...and down***

- *Haus zum Luft*, Bäumleingasse 18: built in 1479 for the printer Michael Winzler; in 1531 became the property of printer Johannes Froben. Erasmus lived his last year here; the upstairs room is open for visits. Gothic inner-door frames. It now houses the Erasmushaus bookshop.
- *Löwenzorn* / Lions' Anger, Gemsberg 2-4: a tavern with Renaissance doorway c.1560 and trompe-l'œil facade. Part of roof is from the original timbered construction, c.1357; a restaurant since 1874. Gothic half-timbered houses around the inner courtyard are *Haus zum Weissenburg, Haus zum dürren Sod, Haus zum Gunach*.
- *Gemsberg* / the chamois hill: small Gothic houses once belonging to artisans; the fountain is 19th century.
- *Schönes Haus*, Nadelberg 6: built c.1271; recorded since 1294 as Schönes Haus, likely the oldest profane building in Switzerland. It has a medieval knight's hall and a magnificently painted 13th-century ceiling. The street

front rebuilt in late baroque period. It now houses the English Seminar of the university.

- *Zerkindenhof*, Nadelberg 10: 13th/14th centuries, named after the knight Nikolaus von Zerkinden. The deep parcel of land contains several buildings and courtyards, which end at the former inner and middle city wall on Petersgraben; renovated with baroque facade. Now houses the Theological Seminar of the university.

The Münsterplatz. One of Europe's most complete main squares, conveying an enclosed impression as all the streets leading into it curve before the square, leaving it unencumbered.

The best way to appreciate the square is to walk, look and listen. In the 1760s, Johann Jakob Fechter (1717-1797) and Samuel Werenfels (1720-1800) redesigned many buildings, including those once belonging to the canons until their allocation to the town councilors after the Reformation.

- *Schürhof* 19: main building contains 13th-century elements, additions in 1453/54, the 1560s and 18th century.
- *Rollerhof* 20: name originates from the 1574/78 resident, Gavin de Beaufort / von Rolle. Main building contains substantial 12th-century elements on the western wall; renovated 1583; in 1758/59 baroque remodeling after plans by Johann Jakob Fechter. Baroque room is open to the public; now a restaurant.
- *Zehntenkeller*/ Cellar of the Tithes: once owned by the bishop; houses the *Marionetten-Theater* and the *Allgemeine Lesegesellschaft,* and has its history to tell.

Several houses in the vicinity were associated with money lending and banking during the Church Council.

- *Haus zur Mücke* / House of the Gnat, Schlüsselberg 14: a tavern in the late Middle Ages; in 1439 its small dark rooms housed sessions of the Church

Council which elected the anti-pope Felix V in 1440; rebuilt in 1544/45. In the 1660s it was the venue for the Amerbach Art Collection and in the 19th century for the Faesch Art Collection (foundation of Basel's museums). To note: the Gothic doorway and the two Renaissance lions holding the Basel coat of arms.

- *Haus zum Venedig,* Schlüsselberg 3: Gothic facade with a winged lion; the symbol of Venice stands half in the water and half on the earth, symbolizing the power of Venice by land and sea. Earlier house was seat of Venetian merchants.

- *Haus zum Weissen Bären*, Schlüsselberg 5: Gothic facade, part of the Museum der Kulturen Basel; sold in 1441 by Bernard von Efringen to Florentine financiers. The Lombard bankers of Milan occupied a house on Streitgasse near Barfüsserplatz, now Café Huguenin.

- *Haus zum Schlüssel,* Schlüsselberg / Freie Strasse 25: originally built as a noble home in early 1400s; rebuilt in 1486/88 by Ruman Faesch. Facade and rear building altered in 1733; further changes in 1955 and 1985. It is the guild house of merchants and drapers, and a restaurant. Fresco (1985) by Samuel Buri in the now-covered courtyard.

- *Ringelhof,* Petersgasse 23: home of Cristoforo d'Annone, a forwarding agent, who fled religious persecution in Lombardy; portraits of owner and his wife in spandrels of portal arch.

Petersgasse deserves more attention.

Petersgasse by Niklaus Stoecklin

***Rathaus* / City Hall**, Marktplatz: early 16th, 17th and neo-Gothic of the late-19th and early-20th centuries; the building to the left of the archways and the tower to the right were added on the 400th anniversary of Basel's entrance into the Confederation.

When the city joined the Confederation in 1501, a larger and more appropriate building was necessary. The middle section built from 1504/14 to a design by Ruman Faesch (c.1476-1533) enlarging the existing building. The large clock (1510/11) on the facade by Hans Thur is evidence of the city's prosperity at the time. Surmounting the clock are figures of Justice, Emperor Heinrich II and Empress Kunigunde. In 1608 the original statue of the Virgin Mary was modified to that of Justice.

The northern addition built in 1606/08 is in conjunction with parts of the inner courtyard. Both inner courtyard and facade decorated with trompe-l'œil, Judaic and heroic themes by Hans Bock the Elder and his sons (1608/11). The mural in the courtyard gallery, which depicts the Last Judgment, probably done in 1510 by Hans Franck; later retouched by Bock in 1610. The vividly colored and charming small animals, figures and heraldic emblems on the facade add to its brilliance. A vigorous renovation took place in 1898/1904. Wall paintings by Wilhelm Balmer (1903) show the Swiss Federation marching into the city to welcome Basel into the Confederation; Heinrich II is depicted above the procession; facade refreshed at this time; Marktplatz also expanded. A renovation in 1977 brought it to its present glory.

The *Regierungsratsaal* / assembly room is a splendid example of late-Gothic artisanship with added baroque emphasis. Heraldic glass panels by Antoni Glaser (1519/20); an amusing sculpted ceiling frieze of wild men and women mounted on unicorns fighting among themselves; another of the world turned upside down with rabbits hunting the hunters and barbecuing them; the wooden-carved portal is by Franz Pergo (1595). The spiral staircase with the figure of Justice in the antechamber c.1581 is by Daniel Heintz (1530-1596).

In 1521 the *Grosse Rat* / cantonal parliament received its own room. Hans Holbein obtained the commission to paint several walls of the great council chamber; two undertaken in 1521 were completed the following year, the south wall was painted in 1530. With minor exceptions, all were lost during renovations in the 1820s; some fragments and some of the designs are at the Kunstmuseum Basel. In the remodeled room (1901), the ceiling, wall paintings and stained glass are by Emil Schill (1870-1958).

The courtyard is home to a Renaissance statue by Hans Michel, Strasbourg (1580) of the Roman General, Munatius Plancus, founder of a colony in the region (perhaps Basel or Augst) in 44 BC.

Editor's note: Tours in English are available and definitely recommended.

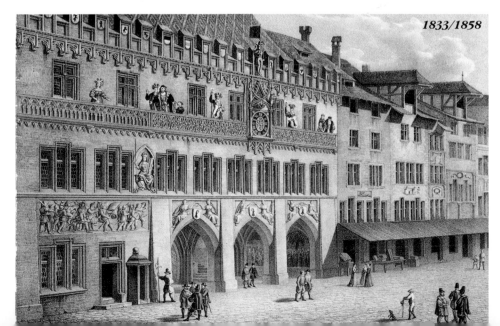

1833/1858

- *Stachelschützenhaus*, Petersplatz 10: 16th-century half-timbered assembly house, wings added in 18th century. Crossbow competitions took place during the 16th century. Today houses the Institute of Microbiology of the university. Adjoining the building are the botanical gardens of the university.

Stachelschützenhaus, 1878

- *Seidenhof*
  Blumenrain 34: formed a corner of the *Burkhard'sche* wall (1080/1100) and middle (1200/50) city walls; in 1577 became the property of the Pellizari silk merchants. Adorned with a Gothic tower and oriel; a statue of Rudolf von Habsburg is in the inner court.

High Renaissance

- *Spiesshof*, Heuberg 5-7: The manor has a checkered history of private owners and architects, starting in the 13th century and ending with a hat maker in 1844. Purchased in 1546 by David Joris. The Renaissance renovation begun c.1550 was completed in High Renaissance euphoria by Daniel Heintz c.1589; baroque wing added 1724. Since 1853, property of the Swiss Railway System.

- *Geltenzunft*, Marktplatz 13: the Vintners' Guild since 1377; rebuilt in 1578 by Daniel Heintz. Both buildings are thought to be inspired by designs by Vitruvius (1st century BC) and Andrea Palladio (1508-1580).

Editor's note: The City Hall, Spiesshof, Geltenzunft—and other buildings with painted facades—hint at how colorful Basel was with its brightly colored and elaborately decorated surfaces.

Following the Reformation and as wealthy Catholics departed for friendlier terrain, simpler and smaller Gothic-type houses became the fashion. During the 17th century, employing architects for design was a common practice. Clients, however, engaged their own builders, stonemasons and artisans. Eventually designs were influenced by Parisian town palaces built as *hôtel entre cour et jardin* / a main building with an enclosed courtyard on one side and garden access on the other, e.g., the unfinished *Markgräflerhof*, the *Ramsteinerhof*, *Blaues Haus* and *Weisses Haus* / The Blue House and the White House.

Baroque period of the 17ᵗʰ–18ᵗʰ century

- *Hebelstrasse 15*: the sole Dutch baroque house, it is best viewed from the garden side.
- *Holsteinerhof,* Hebelstrasse 32: c.1696 for the basement and 1743 onwards for the house; and the
- *Markgräflerhof*, Hebelstrasse 4: 1698/1705 both built for the Margrave of Baden-Durlach, Friedrich Magnus, and his wife, the Duchess of Holstein, in fashionable French style. The Markgräflerhof, considered the finest and largest baroque palace in Switzerland, duly influenced the city with its grandeur and luxurious tulip gardens. The Hebelstrasse wing is based on plans by Johann Carl Hemeling (1702-1737). The Holsteinerhof, rebuilt in 1752, was the residence of Peter Ochs.
- *Ramsteinerhof*, Rittergasse 17: (previously mentioned) built on the remains of the earlier building belonging to the Knights of Ramstein; renovated in 1727/32, designed by Johann Carl Hemeling for Samuel Burckhardt-Zäslin, financier.
- *Wendelstörferhof / Weisses Haus* / White House, Rheinsprung 18: built in 1762/68 after plans by Samuel Werenfels (1720-1800) for the brothers, Lucas and Jacob Sarasin, silk-ribbon manufacturers. According to the brothers' construction account book, Werenfels not only designed the architecture but also the portals, ironwork, stucco, fireplaces, etc.
- *Reichensteinerhof / Blaues Haus* / Blue House, Rheinsprung 16, belonged to Lucas and was a favored musical locale. Jacob entertained scholars and philosophers at the White House. The living quarters faced the Rhine and the family business opened on to Martinsgasse. The buildings, which are shown below, now house the Department of Justice.

Iron gate on Blue House, Martinsgasse

- Across the street: *Gelbes Haus,* Rheinsprung 11: location of the first university; permission granted by Pope Pius II / Aeneas Silvius Piccolomini in 1459; inaugurated in 1460. Remodeled and enlarged in mid-19th century by Johann Jakob Stehlin the Younger (1826-1894), now the location of the Institute of Zoology of the university.
- *Wenkenhof* / manor house and *Wenkenpark* at Hellring 41, Riehen: (Basel purchased the village in 1514). The main house, *Neuer Wenkenhof,* built in 1736 as the single-storied garden residence for Johann Heinrich Zäslin, at that time one of Basel's wealthiest citizens. In the early 20th century the entrepreneur Alexander Clavel purchased the property, at which time the upper story and the *Reithalle* / riding hall were added. Reminiscent of Versailles with French formal gardens, statuary and park in the Le Nôtre style (André Le Nôtre, 1613-1700, French landscape designer).
- The cathedral in Arlesheim is an ecclesiastical example of this period.

Wenkenhof

Rococo period at its best in the *Wildt'sche Haus*, Petersplatz 13: built in 1761/63 by Johann Jakob Fechter (1717-1797) for the financier, silk-ribbon merchant and eccentric Jeremias Wildt-Socin for entertaining; later used as a residence. Original painted landscape wall-coverings and furnishings; *sopra porte* painting; stucco ceilings and ceiling paintings; faience stove in each room. The Wildt family also owned and lived at the *Gyrengarten* (1740) at Hebelstrasse 7; the two houses shared one garden.

Jeremias (1753-1760)   *Ursula Wildt-Socin*   *Margarethlein*
                           (1729-1772)   *(1755-1810)*

Louis XVI period is best seen in the *Haus zum Kirschgarten*, Elisabethenstrasse 27, built 1775/80 by the Basel architect Ulrich Büchel for the silk merchant Johann Rudolf Burckhardt-de Bary. It is now part of the Historisches Museum Basel.

- *Stadthaus*, Stadthausgasse 13, former post house for the merchants association; later offices of *Bürgergemeinde & Bürgerrat* / Citizens' Council; the red sandstone building built 1771/75 after designs by Samuel Werenfels (1720-1800), who combined late baroque and neoclassical elements; originally had an open view onto Marktplatz.

During the 1830s, several architects led the way to an architectural explosion in Basel:

Melchior Berri (1801-1854), a classicist and the most important architect of this period in Switzerland. (He was married to the sister of art historian Jacob Burckhardt). A selection of his buildings:

- *Altes Gemeindehaus,* Baselstrasse 43, Riehen: built 1834/35 to plans by Berri, executed by Amadeus Merian. Facade recalls earlier classical building styles.
- *Haus zum Schwarzen Adler or 'Zahnlücke',* St. Alban-Vorstadt 25: built 1839/40. A city house, it is a mature representation of Berri's work. Unusual placement of house: the front overlooks the Rhine; the rear is set back from the street. Now houses the offices of the Health Department.

St. Alban-Vorstadt 25

- *Museum der Kulturen* / Museum of Ethnology, Augustinerstrasse 2: Melchior Berri's late classical design (1844/49) is the largest 19th-century construction in Basel. Built on the site of the 1276 Augustinian monastery; subsequently occupied by the university. A proposed addition by Herzog & de Meuron will provide further exhibition space and open the interior courtyard to the public.

- *Antikenmuseum Basel und Sammlung Ludwig*, St.Alban-Graben 5 and 7: No. 5 built for Isaac Iselin; No. 7 former residence of the elder Bachofen family. Executed in Berri's classical style with assistance from J. J. Stehlin-Hagenbach, 1826/28; renovated in 1965 and 2004.
- Also designed by Berri are the *Baslerdybli* / white dove mailbox, six of which are still in use, and the postage stamp introduced in 1845 with the same theme—the world's first three-color, embossed stamp.

Amadeus Merian (1808–1889), a romantic who was the city superintendent of building.
- *Café Spitz,* Greifengasse 2 at the Rhine in Kleinbasel: built 1838/41 for the three Honorable Societies of Kleinbasel.

Three Kings Hotel (1793) with salt tower

- *Hotel Drei Könige* / Three Kings Hotel, Blumenrain 8, completely rebuilt in neo-byzantine style, 1842/44. First mention of the building 'zer Blumen' or 'zur Blume' was in the 14th century. Whether it served as a public house or an inn is uncertain. (First reference to an innkeeper was in the early 1430s). Until 1681 it was known as the Gasthaus zur Blume, hence the street Blumenrain. There is no evidence of a Three Kings Hotel before 1681, or that a meeting of three kings during the 11th century ever took place at the inn; this most likely came about as a 'later embellishment' following a history of Basel written by Peter Ochs. The three figures perched over the entrance arrived in 1754 and represent the Three Magi. Several days before Fasnacht, they are dressed in traditional *Waggis* costume. The Hotel has been a meeting place for the cognoscenti, nobility and more since the 18th century. Renovated and enlarged (2004/06) to incorporate the adjoining building.

Christoph Riggenbach (1810-1863)

- *Bachofenhaus* / Zur St. Johanneskapelle, Münsterplatz 2: built 1839/41. J. J. Bachofen, historian and author, lived here with his wife Louise Burckhardt-Bachofen, 1870/87. In 2004 it was remodeled as a condominium.
- *Elisabethenkirche* (1857/65) *and surrounding houses* after plans by Ferdinand Stadler (1813–1870); completed after his death by Karl Wartner. The neo-Gothic church marks a transition from romantic classicism to pure historicism, which coincided with the razing of the city walls and the consequent building boom.
- *St. Alban-Kirchrain 10* designed by Christoph Riggenbach; built by Melchior Berri in 1851. Originally a passementerie (trimmings) factory; now the *Jugendherberge* / youth hostel; renovated in 1978/80.

Johann Jakob Stehlin, the Elder (1803-1879) and Johann Jakob Stehlin, the Younger (1826-1894).

- *St. Alban-Vorstadt 93–95*: built 1844 for the ribbon manufacturer Carl Sarasin; housed the Sarasin Bros. firm until late-20th century.
- *Schilthof*, corner of Steinenberg and Freie Strasse, begun by J. J. Stehlin the Elder, 1840/42, for the silk merchant Forcart; continued by the younger Stehlin and extended by Fritz Stehlin, 1899/1900.
- *Hauptpost* / the main post office, Rüdengasse / Freie Strasse / Gerbergasse. Design by J. J. Stehlin the Younger, built 1851/53 on site of merchants' hall (1376/78) incorporating the stone archway on Freie Strasse (originally on Gerbergasse) from Daniel Heintz's renovation in the mid-1550s; later expanded to reach Rüdengasse. The neo-Gothic interior wall paintings and stained-glass panels designed by Burkhard Mangold 1909/10.

In the mid-19th century Basel was linked to three railway systems—French in 1844 in the St. Johann area which lasted 15 years; German at the *Badischer Bahnhof* in 1854, which was located at today's Messeplatz; Swiss and French in 1859, integrating the former French railway. The construction of the Eisenbahn-brücke in 1873 connected the three systems and made Basel an important

French railway station at St. Johann (1845)

railway junction for north/south traffic. With the advent of a typical industrial revolution, more living space was needed. The city walls came down. There was a metamorphosis in the structure of the city. Architectural careers flourished. New neighborhoods developed, each with its own architectural, economic and social characteristics. Sections of the Gellert, Gundeli, St. Johann—and beyond—still maintain their architectural charm.

After the 'formal' birth of *Art Nouveau / Jugendstil* in the 1890s, new motifs appeared in Basel architecture; the new design was at times 'plastered' on to existing buildings. Neo-Gothic and less ornate styles also thrived.

Art Nouveau / Jugendstil as found in the city.

- *Zunfthaus zu Safran,* Gerbergasse 11: prior building was the guildhall of grocers and apothecaries. Since the mid-14th century the makers of *Leckerli*, the gingerbread biscuit, belonged to the guild. Present building with strong neo-Gothic flavor, designed by Rudolf Linder (1849-1929) and Gustav Adolf Visscher van Gaasbeek (1859-1911) completed in 1903. They built many houses during their brief collaboration (1896/1900): on Hirzbodenweg, Pilgerstrasse, Pelikanweg and Palmenstrasse.
- *Globus Department Store,* Marktplatz: built 1904/05 by Alfred Romang (1860-1919) and Wilhelm Bernoulli (1869-1909) a charming *Jugendstil* facade with contrasting sandstone and granite material.
- *Bundesbahnhof / SBB,* Centralbahnplatz: the new station built 1905/09, designed by Emil Faesch (1865-1915) and Emanuel La Roche (1863-1922).

Major renovations in early-21st century included a *Passerelle* (footbridge), which provides access to the tracks and connects the station to the Gundeldingerquartier.

- *Fischmarkt 1, Marktgasse 8, Falknerstrasse 31/33* and many more buildings in the inner city show and tell their stories of this new and decorative architecture.
- *Schützenmattstrasse 49–53,* 1905/06: designed by Karl Moser.
- *Arnold Böcklinstrasse, 40, 42 and 44:* built 1908 after plans by Wilhelm Bernoulli.
- *Badischer Bahnhof:* built 1912 by Karl Moser and Robert Curjel. (Moser, the most important Swiss architect of his time, also built houses and two churches in Basel, Pauluskirche and Antoniuskirche).

Badischer Bahnhof (1913)

With the 1920s came the *Art Deco style.*

- *Schweizerische Reederei,* Hafenstrasse 3-7: 1924 grain silo from which one has a marvellous panorama. Hans Bernoulli (1876-1959), architect, Oskar Brossard, engineer.
- *Wasserturm,* Reservoirstrasse on the Bruderholz: water reservoir constructed of brick, 1925/26 by Ernst and Paul Vischer.
- *Markthalle,* Viaduktstrasse 19: 1928, the first covered market in Switzerland; architect H. E. Ryhiner. Its cupola measures 60 meters in diameter.
- *Goetheanum,* Dornach: 1925/28, of reinforced concrete to plans by the founder of anthroposophy, Rudolf Steiner. Built to replace an earlier wooden building which was burned down. Ten buildings dating 1914/24 are among the 100 residences and functional buildings designed by Steiner.

Fischmarkt 1   *Wasserturm*

- *Messe Basel at Messeplatz* / Exhibition Square: Industrial fairground that
  reflects a change-as-needed philosophy of design. Architecture adapting
  to the demand for sophisticated exhibition space and its inherent infrastructure. *Kopfbau,* the main red brick building, 1925/26 by Herman
  Herter (1877-1945); *Rundhofhalle* (with clock) 1953/54 by Hans Hofmann (1897-1957); the glass hall (behind the Kopfbau), added 1999 by
  Theo Hotz (b.1928).

Goetheanum

Basel continues the tradition of leading innovation in concept and design with numerous well-known *local and international architects* enhancing the Basel architectural experience.

- *Bank for International Settlements (BIS)* with its 69.5-meter round tower, at the main railway station designed by Burckhardt Partner AG, Basel, 1972/77; and its *Botta Building,* Aeschenplatz 1: commissioned by *UBS AG* in 1995, designed by Mario Botta of Ticino; a gray and white-striped 'castle' building.
- *Museum für Gegenwartskunst,* St. Alban Rheinweg 60: designed by Wilfried and Katharina Steib, Basel, 1980; a converted 19th-century paper mill.
- *UBS AG Training and Conference Center,* Viaduktstrasse 33, designed by Diener & Diener, Basel, 1989/94.

UBS AG Training and Conference Center

- *The Tinguely Museum,* Grenzacherstrasse 210: near the Schwarzwaldbrücke and on the banks of the Rhine, designed by Mario Botta, 1996.
- *Fondation Beyeler,* Baselstrasse 101 Riehen / Basel: designed by Renzo Piano of Genoa, 1997; an elegantly restrained and harmoniously situated construction.
- *Euregio,* Viaduktstrasse and Margarethenstrasse: a finely structured semi-circular white office building designed by Richard Meier, American, 1998.
- *Peter Merian Haus,* Nauenstrasse and Peter Merian Strasse: a long, shimmering, emerald green glass-clad office building designed by Hans Zwimpfer, Basel; realized 1994/2000 in collaboration with American artist Donald Judd (1928/94).

- *Messeturm* at Messeplatz: designed by Basel architects Meinrad Morger and Heinrich Degelo and the Lucerne architect Daniele Marques, 2003. At 105 meters in height, it is one of the tallest buildings with hotel and office space in Switzerland. The top-floor café and bar offer a panorama of Basel and surrounding hills of France and Germany.

- *Jacob Burckhardt Haus* / Project Euroville, Nauenstrasse in the SBB area: concept by Hans Zwimpfer, project design won by Jakob Steib, Basel. A work combining art and architecture.

- *Novartis Campus Project,* St. Johann area: an innovative research campus; first phase designed by Diener & Diener, Basel, 2003/05. It will eventually include buildings by various architects.

Bahnhof Passerelle

A few buildings designed by the internationally acclaimed Basel-born architects, **Herzog & de Meuron:**

- *Karikatur & Cartoon Museum,* St.Alban-Vorstadt 28, 1996. A renovation of a late-Gothic townhouse.
- The *Zentrales Stellwerk Münchensteinerbrücke,* corner of Münchensteinerstrasse and the bridge: a copper-clad signal tower containing the electronic equipment for the switching lines of the Basel railway depot, 1997.

Zentrales Stellwerk

Its design is one reason the SBB received the Wakker Prize, awarded by the Swiss Heritage Society, in 2005.

- *Roche Pharma Research building,* Grenzacherstrasse, 2000.
- The *St. Jakob-Park* / football stadium, commercial center and seniors' residence, 2001.
- The *Schaulager,* Ruchfelderstrasse 19, Münchenstein: depository for the Emanuel Hoffmann Foundation, research center and art space for special exhibitions, 2003.
- The *Elsässertor complex* at the SBB, 2004; a glass marvel reflecting life. The sides are finished with red panels facing Basel and blue facing France.

Elsässertor

Vitra Design Museum in nearby Weil am Rhein is a combined work of world-famous architects: the Museum by the American Frank Gehry, the Fire Station by the Iraqi-British Zaha Hadid and the Conference Center by the Japanese Tadao Ando.

A new Stadtcasino designed by Zaha Hadid is in the planning stage.

222

This brief overview cannot do justice to Basel's varied and vibrant architecture. Around every corner there is a painted facade, a period window, a bas-relief, a wrought-iron gate, a historical date, a family coat-of-arms, commemorative signs, decorative elements and more, all confirming the city's rich innovative and architectural history. Buildings on Heuberg, Nadelberg, Petersgasse, Augustinergasse (and others) are all waiting to tell their stories. We need to stop, look and listen. *Remember that wise old bird.*

Rear view of Peter Merian Haus

Children admiring Markus Böhmer's The Giant, Kannenfeld Park

Outdoor Art

Presented below is a modest selection of art representative of the city's rich cultural heritage and ongoing involvement in supporting the arts. As you walk through the streets and squares of Basel, look and listen. Some pieces are identified by subject, others by artist. Art is all around us.

Sculpture and Installations

Abt, Otto: Basel, 1903-1982. *Sonnenaufgang* / Sunrise, 1934. Majolica panel over a fountain in the schoolyard next to Peterskirche.

Angel: Gothic statue at corner of Engelhof on Nadelberg.

Angel: Atop rear cathedral spire. Restored in 2002 to its original splendor after the 'room installation' by Japanese artist Tazro Niscino; a Klaus Littmann project.

Bänninger, Otto Charles: Zurich, 1897-1973. Janus. Sculpture in the small park facing the Predigerkirche; corner of Spitalstrasse and Totentanz.

Basilisk: 1879, one of the four original sculptures by Ferdinand Schlöth (1819-1898) for the Wettstein Bridge; located on right side of bridge, just beyond Kunstmuseum Basel. Basilisks are throughout the city, even on the roof of the main Basel railway station. It is also the theme for the city's sidewalk fountains, legends, and more.

Detail from Abt panel

One face of Janus, Totentanz

The Angel 'room installation' (2002)

Borofsky, Joseph: American, b.1942. The Hammering Man, 1989. Front of UBS office at Aeschenplatz 6. – Large Ruby, 1989. Entrance hall of same building.

Bourdelle, Antoine: French, 1861-1929. *Fruit,* 1907. Garden of Kunsthalle Restaurant, Steinenberg 7.

Burckhardt, Carl: Basel, 1878-1923; innovator of freestanding sculpture in Switzerland. *Amazone* / Girl Leading Horse, corner of Middle Bridge. – *Ritter George* / the Knight St. George, 1921/23. At top of the stairs on Kohlenberg above Barfüsserplatz.

Fruit, garden Kunsthalle Restaurant   *St. George, Kohlenberg*

Calder, Alexander: American, 1898–1976. The Big Spider. Courtyard of the Kunstmuseum Basel. – The Tree, 1966. Garden of Fondation Beyeler, Riehen/Basel.

Chillida, Eduardo: Spanish, 1924–2002. Around the World. Courtyard of Kunstmuseum Basel.

Cragg, Tony: British, b.1949. Realms and Neighbors, 1984. Merian Park Botanical Garden, Brüglingen.

Cucchi, Enzo: Italian, b.1949. Untitled, 1984. Merian Park Botanical Garden, Brüglingen.

Dog: sculpture perched on the wall behind the Sevogel / Warrior fountain and the corner of the Staatsarchiv building, Martinsgasse 2.

Dreiländereck: Missile-shaped pylon marker at the Rhine port where the three countries—France, Germany and Switzerland—meet.

Eggenschwiler, Franz: Swiss, b.1930. *Baumtorso* / Tree Trunk, 1980. Merian Park Botanical Garden, Brüglingen.

Eichin, Bettina: Swiss, b.1942. *Helvetia auf der Reise* / Helvetia on a Voyage, 1980. From the city on left side of the Middle Rhine Bridge, Kleinbasel side. – *Marktplatzbrunnen* / Two bronze tables for proposed Marketplace Fountain, Basel, 1990. Cloister of the Cathedral. – Memorial tablet to Peter Ochs. On the Totentanz street side of the Predigerkirche, Spitalstrasse. – *Neun Musen* / Nine Muses. University campus in Freiburg im Breisgau, Germany.

Bronze table in Cathedral cloister, Bettina Eichin

Fish, Solitude Promenade

Fabro, Luciano: Italian, b.1936. *Sinn für Geometrie, Sinn für Freiheit, Die Säule* / Spirit of Geometry, Spirit of Freedom, The Column. Merian Park Botanical Garden, Brüglingen. – *Giardino all' italiana,* 1994. Office building plaza of Diener & Diener near Picassoplatz.

Fish: A jumping fish by Willy Hege, Basel (1907-1976), at the entrance to the Solitude Park.

Flavin, Dan: American, b.1933. Untitled, 1975. In memory of Urs Graf. Neon-tube lighting in courtyard of Kunstmuseum Basel.

Grosserts, Michael: Basel, b.1927. *Lieu dit* at Heuwaage.

Hebel, Johann Peter: Basel, 1760 –1826; writer and poet. Statue in fore-court of St. Peter's Church, Petersgra-ben, by Max Leu, 1899.

Heussler, Valery: Swiss, b.1920. *Brot Teilen* / Share Bread *'Die Erde ist rund sie kennt keine Grenzen'* / the earth is round, it knows no borders, 23 June 2000. In the Wettsteingraben / Wettstein Park. – *Die Sinne des Men-schen: Sehen, Hören, Fühlen /* Aspirations of Mankind: To See, Hear and Feel, 23 June 2000.

Iselin, Isaak: Basel, 1728-1782; philosopher, writer and city clerk. Statue in Schmiedenhof courtyard, which is nestled between Gerbergasse and Rümelinsplatz; by Alfred Lanz, 1891.

Share Bread, Wettstein Park

Kabakov, Ilya: Ukrainian, b. 1933. Lives and works in New York. *Denkmal für einen verlorenen Handschuh* / Memorial to a Lost Glove. Red bronze glove surrounded by nine metal panels with text in four languages, 1998. An installation at St. Alban-Rheinweg in front of the Goldenen Sternen Restaurant.

Memorial to a Lost Glove, St. Alban-Rheinweg

Kelly, Ellsworth: American, b.1923. White Curves, 2001. Metal sculpture. Fondation Beyeler, Riehen / Basel.

Küng, René: Swiss, b.1934. Granite Sculpture, 1982/83. Front of Basler Versicherung building, Aeschengraben 21. – *Mondleiter* / Moon Ladder. Front of Basel Theater, near Richard Serra's Intersection.

Lällekönig: King sticking out his tongue. Original 17th-century 'king' is in Historisches Museum Basel. Copy is located at entrance to the Lällekönig Restaurant at Schifflände and at Restaurant Gifthüttli, Schneidergasse.

Luginbühl, Bernhard: Swiss, b.1929. *Grosser Stengel für La Roche* / Large Stem for La Roche. Outside La Roche complex at Grenzacherstrasse 124. – *Wyss Maa* / White Man. Courtyard of Kunstmuseum Basel.

Merian, Christoph: Basel, 1800-1858; philanthropist. Bust in Christoph Merian Park, garden of the Summer Casino at Münchensteinerstrasse / St. Jakob-Strasse, cast in 1958 after an 1899 model by Richard Kisslinger.

Murus Gallicus: Display designed in 1993 by Hannes and Petruschka Vogel, Swiss, (b.1938 / b.1943). Archaeology Park, Rittergasse 4. Vestiges of Celtic wall and fortification.

Dirk's Pod, Richard Serra

Granite Sculpture, Aeschengraben 21

Oekolampad, Johannes: German, 1482–1531; leader of the Reformation in Basel. Statue on Rittergasse, to the left of the Cathedral cloister, by Ludwig Keiser, 1862.

Plancus, Lucius Munatius: Roman general; founder of a Roman colony at Augst (or) Basel. Statue completed in 1580 by Hans Michel. Courtyard of the *Rathaus* / City Hall, Marketplace.

Picasso, Pablo: Spanish, 1881-1973. *Mann mit ausgebreiteten Armen* / Man with Extended Arms, 1961/1991. At Picassoplatz behind the Kunstmuseum Basel.

Probst, Jakob: Basel, 1880-1966. *Ohne Titel* / Without Title. Sculpture forms the top corner of the University Hospital, Spitalstrasse, opposite No. 6 Spital-gasse.

Raetz, Markus: Swiss, b.1941. *Kopf* / Head, 1984. Merian Park Botanical Garden, Brüglingen.

Riggenbach, Rudolf (nicknamed 'Dingedinge'): Basel, 1882–1961; art historian and conservator of historical monuments for the city. – Statue at Leonhardsplatz by Peter Moillet, 1921. – Prostrate figure, one of three metal

Man with Extended Arms, Picassoplatz   *Rudolf Riggenbach, Leonhardsplatz*

pieces over archway on Münsterberg, just after the Pfauen department store's employee entrance, and before Stoecklin's wall painting.

Rodin, Auguste: French, 1840-1917. *Die Bürger von Calais* / The Burghers of Calais, 1884/1886. Courtyard of Kunstmuseum Basel.

Serra, Richard: American, b.1939. Intersection. Basel Theater (near Küng's *Mondleiter*). – Dirk's Pod, a five-piece steel installation at the Novartis Campus Park.

Spescha, Matias: Swiss, b.1925. *Sans Titre.* Garden complex of the University Hospital.

Stocker, Ludwig: Swiss, b.1933. *Zeitwende.* Sandstone and marble sculpture. Garden of Basler Versicherung office complex, Aeschengraben 21.

Zaugg, Rémy: Swiss, 1943-2005. *Im Werden* / To Become. Metal words imbedded in concrete, 1999. On walkway to the Staastarchiv, Martinsgasse 2.

Zschokke, Alexander: Basel, 1894-1981. *Christophorus* / St. Christopher, 1955. Gartenstrasse. – *Drei lachende Mädchen* / Three Laughing Maidens,

White Curves, Ellsworth Kelly

St. Christopher, Gartenstrasse

1966. Behind gate descending to the Rhine on Rheinsprung, at location of the first university. Building now houses the Zoological Institute. – *Lehrer und Schüler* / Professor and Student, 1945. At the University, Petersgraben. – *Artisan*, 1962/66. Summer Casino, the youth center, at the Denkmal tram stop.

Wall Paintings

Altherr, Heinrich: Swiss, 1878-1947. In courtyard of Staatsarchiv, Martinsgasse 2. Theme: *Den Unentwegten* / to the stalwart, *Den Lichtbringer* / to the light-bearers, *Den Künder* / to the announcers, *Die Wanderer* / the travelers, 1942/46.

Bock, Hans: German, 1550-1624. Sections of the facade and the inner courtyard of the City Hall. Decorated by Bock and his sons; facade restored in 1977. Inner courtyard theme is the Last Judgment, c.1610/11, which includes the story of Susanna and Daniel.

Buri, Samuel: Bern, b.1935. *Gänse-Liesel* / Lisa and the Geese (the scaffold painting), 1978. Beginning of Rheinsprung near the Middle Bridge.

Detail, Haus zur Krähe

Detail, The Rescue

Lisa and the Geese

Coghuf, Ernst: Swiss, 1905-1976. An assumed name; he was born Ernst Stocker, brother of Hans Stocker, artist (1896-1983). *Le Chant de l'Occident*, 1944. Courtyard of the Gymnasium at Münsterplatz.

Neustück, Maximilian: German, 1756-1834. Facade painting on building at Holbeinplatz near the Holbein fountain; built in 1816 for the suburban society Zur Krähe. Painting depicts the story of the oath-taking on the Rütliwiese and Gessler's death. *See Swiss History.*

Pellegrini, Alfred: Basel, 1881-1958. Apollo and the Muses, 1941. Facade of the Stadtcasino, Barfüsserplatz. – Wall in Spiegelhof courtyard, Spiegelgasse 6. Originally part of the former Stock Exchange building.– Side wall of ÖKK building at Fischmarkt. – Facade of St. Jakobskapelle, St. Jakobsstrasse, 377. Behind the St. Jakob Wirtshaus (restaurant).

Stoecklin, Niklaus: Basel, 1896-1982. *Liebespaare* / The Lovers. At Civil Registry Office, Münsterberg, left-hand side just before the Cathedral. – *Die Rettung* / The Rescue. Above the inner gate of Lohnhof, Leonhardsplatz.

Monuments

Vreneli in front of Clarakirche

Clarakirche / **St. Clara's Church:** In front of the church; a monument with fountain (*Vreneli*) offered by the children of Baden-Württemberg in commemoration of Basel's humanitarian aid during World War II.

Kannenfeld Park: French War Memorial. Dedicated to the French soldiers who lived in Basel and surrounding area and who died defending their country during various wars. Also commemorates the French soldiers who died in Switzerland as a result of their internment by the Bourbaki Army, winter 1871. A memorial ceremony is held each year on 11 November.

Schützenmatt Park: French Monument. Sculpture donated by France in gratitude for Basel's humanitarian aid during WW II; by Georges Salendre, 1946/48.

St. Jakobs-Denkmal / **St. James Monument:** Erected on the site where the victims of the Battle of St. Jakob-on-the-Birs in 1444 were believed to have died. Present monument at Denkmal tram stop is allegorical and historical; by Ferdinand Schlöth, 1872.

Strassburger Denkmal / **Strasbourg Monument:** Elisabethenanlage, near the main railway station. Memorial donated by France to the Swiss Confederation for the humanitarian help given to Strasbourg during the Franco-Prussian War of 1870/71. By Frédéric-Auguste Bartholdi, designer of Statue of Liberty in New York. (A museum dedicated to Bartholdi is located in Colmar, France).

Details, St. James Monument

Okapi

Basel Zoo

The Basel Zoo is an oasis from the hustle and bustle of city life and only a short walk from the main railway station or from Barfüsserplatz. Beloved by Basel's residents, it also enjoys an international reputation among professionals, as well as amateur zoological enthusiasts.

The Zoo opened in 1874 with 94 animals, 416 birds and a restaurant. Expansion occurred ten years later; a fairground was built, which until 1932 served as a venue for exotic animals and tribal folklore events. The present restaurant opened in 1935.

Johannes Beck bequeathed a sizable legacy to the Zoo in 1901. On each 24 June *(Johannes Beck Tag)*, admission is free between four and ten p.m.

The founding of the Association of Friends of the Zoological Garden in 1919 rescued it from its then weakened financial state. Because of the continuing generosity of its supporters, the Zoo has witnessed a steady increase in its attractions, size and educational facilities. It plays a primary role in Basel's cultural life.

Rhinoceros with baby

After World War II several improvements took place, including the construction of a second entrance at Dorenbachviadukt, a viewing stand at the seal pool and further refinements. More animals were imported.

The Zoo began its successful breeding program in 1956 with the birth of the first Indian rhino, resulting in its acknowledged reputation in this field, due in no small part to over 30 rhinos born to date. The first flamingo to see the light of day in a European zoo did so at the 'Zolli' in 1958. In 1959 the female gorilla Goma, the first gorilla born in Europe, and the second born in captivity, achieved celebrity status, when, out of necessity, the staff of the Zoo became her 'ersatz' parents. Goma's child, Tamtam, is the world's first second-generation gorilla born in captivity.

Editor's note: 'Goma, the Gorilla Baby. The Illustrated Story of the First Gorilla Born in Europe' by E. Lang was published in 1961.

The okapi (a deer-like animal related to the giraffe) arrived in Basel in 1949; the first youngster was born in 1960. During the last ten years, nearly half the okapis born in Europe are from the Basel Zoo. A consequence of the Zoo's successful breeding program is that a large number of the animals act as ambassadors for the community.

A vivarium, an indoor monkey house, an aviary and a children's zoo, with a hands-on policy, have embellished the park-like surroundings and the philosophy of the Zoo.

Goma with Tamtam

A new addition that fosters this principle is the Etoscha project. Etoscha is the largest national park in Namibia, southwest Africa. Two buildings make up this exhibit, the Etoscha and the Gamgoas. Gamgoas is the bush peoples' word for 'where the lions live'; after several years' absence, lions are back in their 'natural' habitat. The project puts emphasis on the ecological food cycle of nutrition and decomposition. That is, plants grow and are devoured; the animals and insects that eat the plants are in turn eaten; with decomposition, the cycle is complete. From this decomposition, new plants germinate and the food cycle recommences—unless interrupted by man. This concept heralds a new approach in understanding the delicate ecological balance and interaction of animals with their natural environment, a paradigm for zoos of the future.

A favorite sight during the cooler months is the parade of the penguins as they waddle their way into visitors' hearts.

Some of the ambassadors or founders of famous breeding lines:

Condor	Hannes	male
Pygmy zebu	Charly	male
Bongo	Azuba	male
Chimpanzees	Eros	male
	Jacky	female
Lowland gorillas	Pepe	male
	Goma	female
Indian rhinoceros	Tanaya	female
Giraffe	Jelmo	male
Hippos	Helvetia	female
	Wilhelm	male
Lion	Tschibo	male
African elephants	Ruaha	female
	Calimero	male
Orangutans	Nico	male
	Kiki	female
Grouper	Fritz	male
Ostrich	Moro	male

Helvetia and Wilhelm

Kiki

Tschibo

Calimero

Jelmo

241

Exhibition Warbol to Tillmans, Kunstmuseum Basel, 2005

Museums

For ease of reference, we list some museums pertaining to Basel's culture as seen through the eyes of '*Basel: A Cultural Experience*'. On a per capita basis, the city has one of the most comprehensive concentrations of art galleries in the world. Brochures with information on the galleries and museums, including travel hints and telephone numbers, are available from the tourist office and elsewhere. Many of the museums offer lectures, some in English.

Anatomisches Museum Basel / Anatomy Museum

Pestalozzistrasse 20. All one needs to know about the human body, and more. Skeletons prepared by Vesalius are preserved in the museum.

Antikenmuseum Basel und Sammlung Ludwig / Museum of Ancient Art and the Ludwig Collection

St. Alban-Graben 5. Opened in 1966; housed in two classic town houses.

It is the only Swiss museum devoted exclusively to the ancient civilizations of the Mediterranean area. In the lower-floor passageway, remains of a Roman storage-cellar are visible. Special exhibitions—in 2004 the Tutankhamen treasures.

Architekturmuseum Basel / Architecture Museum, Steinenberg 7.

Located in the *Kunsthalle* building. Varied exhibitions on Swiss and international architecture are presented with accompanying publications. A series of tours, presented in different languages, of 20th- and 21st-century buildings are on offer.

Feuerwehrmuseum, Schweizerisches / Swiss Fire Fighting Museum
Spalenvorstadt 11
Display of fire-fighting equipment spanning the centuries.

Fondation Beyeler, Baselstrasse 101, Riehen / Basel
Home to over 200 works of 20th-century art collected by Hildy and Ernst
Beyeler; tribal art is interspersed among the paintings. Building designed by
Renzo Piano; restaurant in 19th-century villa in the park.

Fondation Herzog / Herzog Foundation, Oslostrasse 8/ E11, Dreispitz,
Zollfreilager, Tor / Gate 13 (entrance/exit Reinacherstrasse)
An extraordinary collection of more than 300,000 photographs in a building
converted by the architects Herzog & de Meuron.

Friedhof Hörnli, Sammlung / Hörnli Cemetery Collection,
Hörnliallee 70, Riehen / Basel
Objects pertaining to funerary culture.

Gegenwartskunst, Museum für / Museum of Contemporary Art,
St. Alban-Rheinweg 60
A division of the Kunstmuseum Basel housed in a renovated paper mill,
designed by Wilfried and Katharina Steib, Basel; it features works from the
Kunstmuseum and the Emanuel Hoffmann Foundation and mounts tempor-
ary exhibits.

Historisches Museum Basel / Historical Museum Basel,
Barfüsserplatz
An exceptional and important museum for the cultural history of the Upper
Rhine; impressive space in late-Gothic church. The Cathedral Treasury, treasures of the Basel guilds, medieval goldsmiths' art and ceremonial vessels,
outstanding collection of late-Gothic tapestries made in and around Basel,
comparable in quality to the Holbein paintings at the Kunstmuseum Basel.
Original figures from some of the old fountains, sculpture of Virgin and Child
from the Spalentor, fragments from the Dance of Death frescoes, coin cabinet,
historical rooms from former Basel houses, and more, including a video in
English on the Cathedral Treasury.

The four museums belonging to the Historisches Museum Basel are:
Barfüsserkirche, Haus zum Kirschgarten, Musikmuseum and *Kutschen-
museum.*

Jüdisches Museum der Schweiz / The Jewish Museum of Switzerland
Kornhausgasse 8

Displays on Jewish daily life, law and history in Basel, supplemented with an explanatory video in English. Tombstones of the medieval communities are exhibited; periodic new shows on special themes.

Karikatur und Cartoon Museum Basel / Caricature and Cartoon Museum
St. Alban-Vorstadt 28

A collection of over 3,000 cartoons housed in a late-Gothic town house renovated by Herzog & de Meuron to incorporate the openness and lightness of modern architecture.

Kirschgarten, Haus zum
Elisabethenstrasse 27

Built 1775/1780 as residence and office for the silk-ribbon manufacturer, Johann Rudolf Burckhardt, father of Sheik Ibrahim Burckhardt. Historical rooms of domestic life in Basel from 18th to 19th centuries. Houses the Pauls-Eisenbeiss collection of German porcelain and the Nathan-Rupp and Gschwind clock and watch collections.

Kleines Klingental, Museum / Museum in the former Klingental Dominican Convent
Unterer Rheinweg 26, Kleinbasel

Preserves and exhibits the original medieval and Gothic sculptures of the Cathedral. Contains a number of historical rooms from 14th and 16th centuries —two Gothic dining rooms, former kitchen, two cells and an anteroom with wall paintings. Flower and herb garden at the entrance. The museum is administered by the *Basler Denkmalpflege* / Basel Authority for the Conservation of Ancient Monuments, housed in the same building.
See Churches and Monasteries.

Kulturen, Museum der / Museum of Ethnology
Augustinergasse 2

Exhibits of the cultural life in Europe, the South Seas, Ancient America, Tibet and Bali. It houses the most important collection of Tibetan art and cult objects in Europe; a world-famous textile collection is part of the exhibition. The same building houses the **Naturhistorisches Museum** / **Museum of Natural History** with a dinosaur hall, fossils, minerals, live animals in terrariums, and more.

Kunsthalle Basel
Steinenberg 7
The first exhibition space of its kind to open in Switzerland (1872).
Temporary shows of local and international contemporary art.

Kunstmuseum Basel / Museum of Fine Arts
St. Alban Graben 16
Established in 1662 with the Amerbach Collection, Faesch Collection added in 1823. Upper Rhine and Flemish works from 1400s to 1600s and 19th-and 20th-century art. The world's largest collection of works by Konrad Witz and the Holbein family; works by Arnold Böcklin; paintings discarded from German museums during the Nazi period, collectively known as *Entartete Kunst /* Degenerate Art; Picasso paintings, two of which were purchased with donations from the citizens of Basel, and two donated by the artist. In 1959 the then radical donation of four post-war American abstract expressionist paintings entered the museum. Numerous private gifts contribute to the impressive collection. Also houses the significant *Kupferstichkabinett /* **Drawings and Engraving Cabinet.**

Kutschenmuseum / Coach and Sleigh Museum located in Merian Park
Botanical Garden, Brüglingen
Historical coaches and sleighs of the 19th and 20th centuries from Basel families.

Mühlemuseum / Water Mill Museum
Merian Park Botanical Garden, Brüglingen
Former water mill contains exhibition on the history of the water mill and daily life of the miller from the Bronze Age to 20th century.

Musikmuseum / Musical Instrument Museum
Im Lohnhof 9, above Barfüsserplatz
Musical instruments from five centuries, including the oldest surviving trumpets in stirrup form (1578), are on display in former prison cells. Visitors can hear the instruments; for each theme, information is available, via an interactive display, in three languages (German, English and French).

Papiermühle / Swiss Museum of Paper, Writing and Printing
St. Alban-Tal 37
In the restored medieval 15th-century Gallician Mill. A working museum producing goods for sale; a hands-on environment for visitors who are encouraged to make paper and then to print on it; the history of paper, writing, printing

and bookbinding. A restaurant is located in the former Stegreif Mill, next to a functioning waterwheel between the two former mills. A definite must in order to appreciate Basel's history of paper making and printing.

Pharmazie-Historisches Museum der Universität Basel / **Museum of Pharmaceutical History**
Totengässlein 3
An 'eye of newt and toe of frog' institution. The origins of the pharmaceutical industry, superstitions, old-wives' tales and ancient remedies are reflected in the exhibition. History of the apothecary's art from the Middle Ages to the 19th century.

Puppenhausmuseum / **Doll House Museum**
Steinenvorstadt 1
More than 6,000 exhibits charmingly presented on four floors. An interactive information system offers background details; restaurant on the premises.

Römerstadt Augusta Raurica / **Roman town of August Raurica**
Giebenacherstrasse 17, Augst
Roman ruins, Roman farm-animal park, a reconstructed Roman villa and a museum. The museum houses the Kaiseraugst Silver Treasure, 58 kilos of pure silver wrought into magnificent objects. Walk into Roman times; explore the continuing excavations. And more.

Salzkammer / **Salt Room**
in the Villa Glenck, Pratteln
History of the regional salt industry, including technology, science, geology, chemistry, literature and religion; by appointment.

Schaulager
Ruchfeldstrasse 19, Münchenstein
Depository for the Emanuel Hoffmann Foundation. A research and warehouse concept intended for specialists. Special yearly exhibition is open to the public, otherwise by appointment. Building designed by Herzog & de Meuron.

Skulpturhalle
Mittlere Strasse 17
Collection of plaster casts of ancient sculpture. Known worldwide for its unique reconstruction of the sculptural work from the Parthenon. Special exhibits; renovated in 2005.

Spielzeugmuseum, Dorf und Rebbaumuseum / Toy, Village and Wine Growing Museum

Baselstrasse 34, Riehen

Three branches of the museum housed in a 17th-century villa, former residence of Johann Rudolf Wettstein. Collection of European toys, displays of village life around 1900 and, in the wine cellar, an exhibit explaining the importance of wine growing in the area.

Sportmuseum Schweiz

Missionsstrasse 28

The history of physical culture.

Tinguely Museum

Paul Sacher-Anlage 1

Dedicated to the life and work of Jean Tinguely, with sculptures, some mechanical, made of scrap metal and odds and ends. Special exhibitions are held of Tinguely's artist friends and other contemporary artists. The building bordering the Rhine, designed by the Ticino architect Mario Botta, was a donation to the city by F. Hoffmann-La Roche AG to mark the company's centenary; restaurant on the premises.

Verkehrsdrehscheibe Schweiz und unser Weg zum Meer / Swiss Shipping Museum

Westquaistrasse 2, Kleinhüningen

Take a fascinating journey into the history and actualities of Rhine shipping and transportation. Explanations of the various means of transporting merchandise to and from Basel are attractively presented; explanatory video in French and German. Models of ships. And more.

Vitra Design Museum

Outlying Museums

Burghofmuseum
Basler Strasse 143, Lörrach, Germany
The permanent exhibition *ExpoTriRhena* explains the history of the confluence of the three countries: France, Germany and Switzerland. Interactive terminals make the presentation a unique experience.

Delémont, Musée jurassien d'art et d'histoire
52, rue du 23 juin, Delémont
Located in the former palace of the bishops of Basel. An eclectic collection ranging from pre-historic artifacts to contemporary art.

Heimatmuseen, Ortsmuseen / **Village and local museums**
Most villages in the region have a collection of local history and memorabilia.

Kantonsmuseum Baselland: Museum im alten Zeughaus
Zeughausplatz 28, Liestal
Permanent exhibition on the history of the silk-ribbon industry in the region; an open forum for issues related to the environment

Kloster Schönthal
4438 Langenbruck
An excursion to this former Romanesque monastery (1140) and the permanent installation of sculpture set in a natural habitat, is to experience art, history and nature in perfect harmony.

Museum für Musikautomaten
Seewen, Solothurn
A musical journey through time; a fairground organ, music boxes and highly intricate automata. And more.

Vitra Design Museum
Charles-Eames Strasse 1, Weil am Rhein, Germany
Founded by the Basel entrepreneur Rolf Fehlbaum. Industrial furniture design and architecture; known for its collection and production of contemporary chairs. Housed in building designed by the Californian architect Frank O. Gehry. The complex includes the Firehouse designed by the Iraqi-British architect Zaha Hadid and the cement Conference Center by the Japanese architect Tadao Ando.

"Have you heard...?"

Glossary

Anabaptist: member of a Protestant sect in 16th-century northwest Europe. Its rampant growth and appeal turned friend to foe; the carnage at Munster, Germany (1535) resulted in a heretical reputation. Advocate of adult baptism.

Archivolt: the inner contour of an arch; the moldings and ornaments decorating this area.

Armagnacs: mercenaries from an ancient province of France, the duchy of Gascony; they fought for Louis XI.

Bishopric: the diocese or office of a bishop.

Circle 48: an artists' group founded by Max Kämpf in 1948; its members painted principally in gray and blue tones.

Dance of Death: a motif which appeared in the early 15th century in France before spreading to Germany, Italy, the Swiss cantons and Spain. Theme originated as wall paintings in a church or on the walls of a churchyard, and depicted figures, dead or alive, in a procession. Possibly a dance of the dead and not a dance of death.

Group of 33: a group of Swiss artists who in 1933 split off from the existing society of artists, sculptors and architects in opposition to its policy concerning the arts.

Hallstatt: the archaeological term used to designate the Early Iron Age (750-450 BC) in central and western Europe; its name is derived from the prehistoric cemetery and salt mine at Hallstatt in upper Austria.

Holy Roman Empire: the designation commonly given to the various complexes of lands ruled over first by the Carolingian / Frankish and then the German kings for ten centuries, from the coronation of Charlemagne in 800 until its dissolution in 1806. It could be said that it was not holy, nor Roman, nor an empire; it endured, however, for more than 1000 years.

Hussite: follower of John Huss (c.1370-1415) a Bohemian religious reformer convicted of heresy by the Council of Constance and burnt alive. During the Church Council (1431/48), 300 Hussites marched into Basel to present their case.

Iconoclasm: the breaking of images, generally religious objects; an attack or disregard of established opinions.

Kaufhaus: a customs and warehouse; wholesalers paid the obligatory tax and stored their merchandise until distribution for retail sale. Basel had three such establishments: the first at Gerbergasse; the second at Freie Strasse (1400s); the third on Steinenberg between the Stadtcasino and Barfüsserkirche, demolished 1873.

Kunsthalle: exhibition space without a permanent collection which allows for art that does not yet hang on museum walls or appear in mainstream galleries, to be shown.

La Tène: the archaeological term used to designate the Late Iron Age (c. 450-15 BC) based on the pottery and metalwork found at this site near the Lake of Neuchâtel.

Markgräflerland: area situated in southwestern Germany; Müllheim is generally accepted as the geographical center.

Metope: stone panel inserted between pairs of triglyphs in a Doric frieze.

Minnesinger: a German lyric poet of the 12th-14th centuries. In German, *minne* means love.

Misericord: a projection on underside of hinged seat in choir stall, serving when the seat is turned up to support the person standing. Elaborately and amusingly carved during the Middle Ages.

Nabataeans: an Arab nomadic people (c.168 BC-106 AD) who established a kingdom centered at Petra in today's Jordan, which in 106 AD was annexed by Emperor Trajan, creating the Roman province of Arabia.

Nazarene: member of a group of German romantic painters in the early 19th century; their aspiration was to revive religious art.

Oppidum: an ancient fortified town serving as a provincial strongpoint and not necessarily inhabited.

Parler School: referring to a German family of master stonemasons active in the 1300s.

Philology: the science of language.

Rappenkrieg: a conflict (1591/94) which arose among some country villages when the city tried to impose 'Rappen' / penny taxes.

Triglyph: an ornament on a Doric frieze consisting of a tablet with three vertical grooves.

Vitruvius: a Roman writer, architect and engineer active in the 1st century BC; author of *De Architectura,* known today as 'The Ten Books of Architecture'.

University Library

A Basel Time Line

150/80 BC	Celtic settlements on the left bank of the Rhine, today's Voltaplatz / Nordtangente
c. 80	Migration of Rauraci and Helvetii to the southwest (into France)
58	Celts return from defeat at Bibracte and build fortification on the Cathedral Hill—the Murus Gallicus
44	Munatius Plancus establishes Roman colony (perhaps at Basel)
27	Under Augustus (27BC-14 AD) building at Augst begins
260 AD	Beginning of Alemannic incursions over the Rhine
c.290	New Roman strongholds in Augst and Basel
346	First mention of a bishop in region
374	First mention of the name *Basilia* and of a nearby stronghold during visit of Emperor Valentinian I
c.500	Alemannic presence near Basel changes customs and language
c.600	Enters into Frankish possession
740	Final transfer of bishopric to Basel; Haito (805/23) named bishop by Charlemagne; first Cathedral erected
c.912	Passes to Burgundian ownership
917	Sacking of city by Hungarians; destruction of Cathedral; Bishop Rudolph II killed
1006	King Heinrich II receives the city from his uncle, King Rudolph III
1019	Consecration of Cathedral in presence of King Heinrich II
1025	Becomes part of the Holy Roman Empire
1080/1100	Bishop Burkhard von Fenis (1072-1107) mandates first wall (Burkhard'sche Wall) around the city and in 1083 first monastery built at St. Alban-Tal
1200/50	Construction of second (inner or middle) city wall
1225	Construction of first permanent bridge over the Rhine, Middle Rhine Bridge
1220s	Decline of episcopal power, rise of burghers' power with foundation of the guilds; development of Kleinbasel
c.1270	Completion of Kleinbasel's fortifications
1347	Heinrich II becomes patron saint of Basel, joining the Virgin and St. Pantalus
1348/9	Bubonic plague kills one-third of the city's population Massacre of Jews; end of their first community
1356	18 October devastating earthquake and fire
1362/98	Construction of third (outer) city wall
1386	Purchase of imperial jurisdiction from German king shortly after Confederate victory in Battle of Sempach
1392	Purchase of Kleinbasel from bishop, uniting Grossbasel and Kleinbasel
1397	Jews banned from Basel for 400 years; end of second community
1401	Founding of last monastery in Basel (Carthusian)
1417	Great fire
1418	Population: 11,800
1430s	First paper mill and beginning of paper manufacturing
1431/48	Pope Martin V selects Basel to host the Church Council; Pope is deposed; election of antipope Felix V (1440); Aeneas Silvius Piccolomini (later Pope Pius II) attends as a secretary
1440s	Dance of Death wall paintings at Predigerkirche cemetery wall

1444	Battle of St. Jakob-on-the-Birs
1460	Founding of University of Basel under the patronage of Pope Pius II
1460s	Introduction of letterpress printing
1471	Privilege given by Emperor Frederick III for city to hold two fairs yearly
1492	Dürer visits Basel
1494	Publication of Ship of Fools by Sebastian Brant
1498	Population: 9,200
1499	City remains neutral during Swabian War. In March a skirmish on the Bruderholz; in July the Battle of Dornach
1500s	Basel flourishes as important center for study, trade, printing and the arts
1500	Completion of Cathedral
1501	Basel joins the Confederation on 13 July, feast day of Heinrich II
1504	First public bank established (closed in 1744)
1504/15	Rebuilding and extension of *Rathaus* / city hall
1512	Urs Graf arrives
1514	Erasmus arrives
1515	Hans Holbein the Younger arrives
1516	Election of first mayor from the merchant class, Mayor Jacob Meyer zum Hasen.
1521	City renounces secular rule of bishop
1522	Oekolampad arrives
1522	Purchase of the village of Riehen
1525	First Farmers' Revolt
1528	First iconoclastic demonstration on Easter Day
1529	*Bildersturm* / iconoclasm in city; Reformation triumphs
1530/31	Persecution of Anabaptists in the countryside
1544	Joris arrives
1544/78	Thomas Platter principal of the Cathedral High School
1550s	Arrival of refugees fleeing religious persecution
1585	Freedom from bishop bought for 200,000 florins/guldens
1591/94	*Rappenkrieg:* conflict over 'penny' taxes among some country villages settled through the diplomatic persuasion of Andreas Ryff
1618/48	Thirty Years' War results in arrival of refugees
1648	Mayor Johann Rudolph Wettstein secures tax relief for Basel; establishes independence from Holy Roman Empire (German kings) for the Confederation
1653	Peasants' War: demand to city for cheaper salt and reasonable taxes
1661	Wettstein saves the Amerbach Kabinett for Basel
1662	Amerbach Kabinett—the first public museum—opens
1670s	Silk-ribbon industry expands
1685	Louis XIV revokes the Edict of Nantes; 200,000 Protestants (Huguenots) flee France
1700s	Further development of the silk and silk-ribbon industries
1758	Founding of trading house of Johann Rudolf Geigy; dye production begins
1777	Isaak Iselin creates a non-profit association for public welfare, the *Gesellschaft zur Förderung des Guten und Gemeinnützigen (GGG)*.
1790	Official abolishment of serfdom
1795	Signing of The Peace of Basel ends war between France, Spain and Prussia

1798/1803	Napoleonic troops occupy most of Switzerland; Peter Ochs helps draw up constitution; Basel is part of the Helvetic Republic with a centralized system
1803/14	Mediation, country is a French satellite
1805	Third Jewish community
1814/30	Restoration based on new constitution of 1814, restoring earlier cantonal system, while adhering to the Napoleonic Code
1815	Congress of Vienna recognizes Switzerland's 'eternal armed neutrality.'
1817	Economic crisis, famine
1832	First steamship arrives
1833	Separation of canton into two half cantons: Basel-Stadt and Basel-Landschaft
1836	Discovery of salt deposits in Muttenz
1838	Introduction of compulsory school attendance for all children
1844	First railway reaches city (Strasbourg-Basel)
1848	Adoption of Swiss Federal Constitution
1860s	Razing of city walls; St. Albantor, St. Johannstor and Spalentor (3 gates) are spared; expansion of city
1874	Basel Zoo opens
1875	Adoption of new cantonal constitution
1881	Installation of first telephone lines
1894/96	Founding of F. Hoffmann-LaRoche & Co. as pharmaceutical firm
1897	First Zionist Conference
1900	Basel's streets electrically illuminated
	Population: 110,000
1904	First commercial shipment from the north arrives in Basel due to the farsightedness of Rudolf Gelpke; this proved that large vessels could travel the Rhine to Basel
1905	Replacement of first Middle Rhine Bridge (1225)
1911	Landing of first airplane at St. Jakob
1911	Separation of church and state
1914/18	Swiss armies stationed on borders during WWI; industrial unrest
1917	Opening of first Swiss Industries Fair (present-day MUBA)
1919	Carl Spitteler wins Nobel Prize for literature
	General strike in city
1925/27	Construction of first raw reinforced cement church in Switzerland, St. Anthony's, designed by K. Moser
1930	Central banks choose Basel as home for the Bank for International Settlements
1939/45	W W II; cross-border trade declines; city hit by allied bombers
1946	Construction of Basel-Mulhouse Airport, today (EuroAirport)
1963	Creation of *Regio Basiliensis:* a cooperative undertaking for planning and promotion of the economic, political and cultural development of France (Alsace), Germany (southwest corner) and Switzerland (northwest corner)
1966	Jewish Museum of Switzerland and The Museum of Ancient Art open
	Women receive the right to vote at the cantonal level
1969	Population: 236,000
1971	Swiss women receive right to vote at the federal level
1974	Both half cantons introduce a partnership clause in their constitutions
1980	Population: 204,000

1990s	Waves of mergers: Ciba-Geigy and Sandoz form Novartis; Swiss Bank Corporation and Union Bank of Switzerland form UBS AG; spin-offs; increase in biotechnology; new and renovated museums, office buildings and hospitals add to the architectural cityscape
1995	Creation of Regio *TriRhena* by the three regional associations of Switzerland, France and Germany
2000	Renovation of main railway station (SBB) begins
2004	Population including Riehen: 182,800
2005	Acceptance of the new citizens' constitution
	FCB (Football Club of Basel) wins National Championship again, after 2002 and 2004; Roger Federer retains number 1 ranking in World Tennis

A city in transition, comparable to the 1860s—a building boom

Afterword

One often hears the term Golden Age when comparing one period of development in a city or country to another. Basel has experienced many such ages. From the Celts to the Romans; from the growth during the early Middle Ages to the Church Council and Humanism; from the reforms brought about by the Reformation and the influx of refugees bringing new ideas, skills, capital, etc; from the expansion and modernization during the late 1800s, up to 2005. Will the current growth of the city, the changes in demographics, ethnicity, languages, culture, and religion now underway, usher in another Golden Age?

If our experiences of Basel's varied Ages are shared; if interests and appetites to see and listen are opened, then one of our goals is achieved and the second will follow. We wish you further discoveries. It's a Wonderful Town—experience it for yourself.

Acknowledgments

We owe our sincere gratitude to the long list of those who gave their time, effort and knowledge to our project:

Dr. Hans Christoph Ackermann, Former Director, Historisches Museum Basel

Catherine Aitken, Römerstadt Augst

Dr. Ulrich Barth, Basel

Dr. Hans-Anton Drewes, Karl Barth Archiv, Basel

Diane Eaton, Basel Symphony Orchestra

Bettina Eichin, Sculptress

Dr. Markus Fürstenberger

Dr. Katia Guth-Dreyfus, Curator, Jüdisches Museum der Schweiz

Prof. Dr. Heiko Haumann, Historisches Seminar, Universität Basel

Dr. h.c. Jörg Hess, Basel Zoo

Historisches Museum Basel: Dr. Marie-Claire Berkemeier, Dr. Franz Egger,
   Johanna Stammler, lic. phil.

Dominik Hunger, Universitätsbibliothek, Basel

Dr. Martin Kirnbauer, Curator, Musikmuseum Basel

Kleines Klingental Museum: Barbara Fiedler, Vera Stehlin, lic.phil

Katrin Kusmierz, Theologian, Evangelisch-reformierte Kirche Basel-Stadt

Jürg Lieberherr, Director, Vereinigte Schweizerische Rheinsalinen AG, Schweizerhalle

Werner Maier, General Manager, Kraftwerk Birsfelden AG

Heinz H. Merzweiler, President, Verein Verkehrsdrehscheibe Schweiz

Werner Mundschin, Architect, Evangelisch-reformierte Kirche Basel-Stadt

Dr. h.c. Maja Oeri, Emanuel Hoffmann-Stiftung, Münchenstein

Oliver Plüss, WWZ-Bibliothek und Schweiz. Wirtschaftsarchiv, Universität Basel

Dr. Andreas Riggenbach

Dr. Martin Sallmann, Theologian and Lecturer in Church History,
   Theologisches Seminar, Universität Basel

René Schraner, Curator, Sammlung des Kunstkredits Basel-Stadt

Dr. Georges B. Ségal, Art historian and antique dealer

Norbert Spichtig, lic. phil, Archäologische Bodenforschung Basel-Stadt

Dr. Peter Studer, former Director, Zoologischer Garten Basel

Dr. Maximilian Triet, Historian

Friedrich Weibel, Basel

Daniel Wimmer-Davison, Industrielle Werke Basel

Dr. Therese Wollmann, Art Historian

Our thanks also go to our contacts at the Antikenmuseum Basel und Sammlung Ludwig; Architekturmuseum, Basel; Kunstmuseum Basel; Kunstmuseum Solothurn; Hotel Drei Könige am Rhein, Basel; Clariant AG, Muttenz; F. Hoffmann-La Roche AG, Basel; Lonza AG, Basel; Novartis AG, Basel; Schweizerisches Institut für Kunstwissenschaft, Zurich; Schweizerisches Bundesarchiv, Bern; Staatsarchiv, Basel.

Index

Bibliography

Archaeology

Matt, C.H.: Rund um den Lohnhof: die archäologischen Informationsstellen: Lohnhof, Leonhardskirchturm, Teufelhof, Leonhardsgraben 43. Basel, 2002 (Archäologische Denkmäler in Basel, 2)

Stadt der Kelten: Geschichten aus dem Untergrund. Basel, 2002 (Schriften des Historischen Museums Basel, 13)

Art Catalogues

Art in Basel, Edited by Denys Sutton: Apollo, No. 178, December, 1976

Degenerate art: The fate of the avant-garde in Nazi Germany. Los Angeles, 1991

Hans Holbein der Jüngere (1497-1543). Berlin, 1939

Hans Holbein d.J., Zeichnungen aus dem Kupferstichkabinett der Öffentlichen Kunstsammlung Basel by Christian Müller. Basel, 1988

Jenny, C: Von Böcklin bis Tinguely, Internationale Kunst auf Basels Strassen, Wiese Verlag, 1993 Schmidt, Georg: Konrad Witz. Königstein am Taunus, [1982]

Kunstdenkmäler des Kantons Basel Stadt, Band VI: Die Altstadt von Kleinbasel by Thomas Lutz. Bern, 2004

Kunstdenkmäler des Kantons Basel Stadt, Band I: Vorgeschichtliche, römische und fränkische Zeit. Geschichte und Stadtbild. Befestigungen, Areal und Rheinbrücke. Rathaus und Staatsarchiv von C. H. Baer. Basel, 1932

Kunstdenkmäler des Kantons Basel Stadt, Band II: Der Basler Münsterschatz von Rudolf F. Burckhardt. Basel, 1933

Kunstdenkmäler des Kantons Basel Stadt, Band III-V: Die Kirchen, Klöster und Kapellen. Basel 1941, 1961, 1966

Kunstdenkmäler des Kantons Baselland, Band I: Der Bezirk Arlesheim von Hans-Rudolf Heyer. Basel, 1969

Kunstführer durch die Schweiz: Basel Stadt (François Maurer) und Basel Land (Hans-Rudolf Heyer). Bern, 1982

Rowlands, J.: Holbein, The Paintings of Hans Holbein the Younger, Complete Edition. Oxford, 1985

1000 Years of Swiss Art, Edited by H. Horat. New York, 1992

Basel General

Basel, Editions Générales S.A. Genève for Sandoz, 1967

Basel, die schöne Altstadt. Basel, 1973

Basel Seen Through the Eyes of an English Friend. Basel

Basel, Past and Present. Basel, 1954

Basel Lexikon, von Fränzi Jenny und Chris Gugger. Basel, 2001

Das Basler Rathaus, Hrsg. Staatskanzlei Basel-Stadt. Basel, 1983

Fasnacht in Basel, Basel Fasnachts-Comité. Basel, 2003

Föllmi, T. and Brodhage, K: Basel und seine Kultur. Basel, 2002

Fürstenberger, M.: Basel. Basel, 1982

Habicht, P.: Lifting the Mask, your guide to Basel Fasnacht. Basel, 2001

Kearney, S.: Basel: A Cultural Experience. FAWCO, 1986

Leuzinger, V.: Trachsler, B. : Die 5 Altstadtrundgänge/ The 5 strolls through the old city.
Basel, 1990
Maier, J. (text) Heman, Peter (photos): Basel. Basel, 1988
Meier, E.A.: z'Basel an mym Rhy, von Fähren und Fischergalgen. Basel, 1970
Trachsler, B.: A Trace of Art Nouveau. Basel, 1996
Trachsler, B.: A Trace of Gothic Art. Basel, 1999
Trachsler, B.: Basler Brunnen aus alter und neuer Zeit, Band 1. Basel, 1998
Rudolf Riggenbach gesehen von Freunden, Photographen und Fachgenossen. Basel, 1965
Seidenbande. Die Familie De Bary & die Basler Seidenbandproduktion von 1600 bis 2000,
von I. Amstutz, S. Strebel. Baden, 2002

Basel History
Ansichtssache, Neun Frauenstadtrundgänge durch Basel: Kämpferische Nonnen,
Limmat Verlag, 2001
Barth, Ulrich: Zünftiges Basel. Basel, 1997
Basel Paper Mill, Swiss Museum of Paper, Writing and Printing. Basel, 2002
Basler Stadtgeschichte 2, Historisches Museum. Basel, 1981
Basel 1501 – 2001. Basel, 2001 (179. Neujahrsblatt der GGG)
Berchtold, A.: Bâle et l'Europe. Lausanne, 1990/91 (2 volumes)
Bruckner, A.: Wirtschaftsgeschichte Basel. Basel, 1947
Burckhardt, J.: Reflections on History / Weltgeschichtliche Betrachtungen, Introduction by
G. Dietze. Indianapolis, 1979
Burckhardt, P.: David Joris und seine Gemeinde in Basel. In: Basler Zeitschrift für Geschichte
und Altertumskunde 1949, p. 5-106
INSA: Inventar der neueren Schweizer Architektur 1850-1920, 2: Basel, Bellinzona, Bern.
Bern, 1986
Gossman, L.: Basel in the Age of Burckhardt. Chicago, 2000
Gruner, G.: Die Basler Gewerbekanäle und Ihre Geschichte.
In: Basler Stadtbuch 99, 1978, p. 23-42
First Zionist Congress in 1897, edited by Heiko Haumann. Basel, 1997
Schaffendes Basel. Basel, 1957
Teuteberg, R.: Basler Geschichte. Basel, 1986
Teuteberg, R.: 7 Biographien: Berühmte Basler und ihre Zeit. Basel, 1976
The anabaptist writings of David Joris, edited by G. Waite. Waterloo, 1994
Wanner, G.A. and Tschudin, P.: The Basler Paper Mill, Off-prints Sandoz Bulletin No. 54
Wanner, G.A.: Rund um Basels Denkmäler, photos by Peter Armbruster. Basel, 1975
Weis-Müller, R.: Die Reform des Klosters Klingental und ihr Personenkreis. Basel, 1956

Church, Museum Brochures and Guides
Arlesheim Cathedral by Claus Detjen. Regensburg, 2000
Das Basler Münster, von Toni Arnet. Basel, 2000
The Cathedral of Basel by François Maurer. Bern, 1977
The Basel Cathedral Treasury, Timothy B. Husband and Julien Chapuis, Metropolitan Museum
of Art. New York, 2001
Heiliggeistkirche Basel, von Alfred Wyss. Bern, 1999
Kartause - Das Bürgerliche Waisenhaus in Basel, von Ernst Murbach. Bern, 1974

Kloster Klingental in Basel by Dorothea Schwinn Schürmann. Basel, 2002

St. Leonard's Church in Basel by Rudolf Suter. Basel, 1970

St. Leonhard in Basel by François Maurer-Kuhn. Bern, 1981

Pauluskirche: 1901-2001 by Hans-Adam Ritter. Basel, 2001

Predigerkirche Basel, von François Maurer-Kuhn. Basel, 1979

Theodorskirche in Basel – Ein kurzer Rundgang für schnelle Besucher, von K. Hammer, 1997

50 Jahre St. Anton, Basel 1927–1977. Basel, 1977

Guides

Abramson, S. and Postal, B.: The Travelers' Guide to Jewish Landmarks of Europe.
New York, 1971

Basel, Pendo Stadtführer für Basler and Nichtbasler. Basel, 1979

Basel, Culture Unlimited: The Guide to the City for Visitors and Residents. Basel, 2004

Basle for Visitors, Pendo City Guide. Basel, 1980

Bertschi, H.: Basel Getting to Know the City - Basel City Guide. Basel, 2001

Liebendörfer, H.: Spaziergänge zu Malern, Dichtern und Musikern in Basel. Basel, 2000

Liebendörfer, H.: Spaziergänge zu Frauen und Kindern in Basel. Basel, 2003

Robertson, I.: Blue Guide: Switzerland. London, 1997

History: Swiss and General

Bradford, B.: Pocket Book of Switzerland. Zürich, 1963

Cunliffe, B.: The Celtic World. New York, 1979

Guerber, H.A.: Legends of Switzerland. New York, 1899

Heer, F.: The Medieval World. New York, 1961

Rosier, W. and Savary, E.: Histoire illustrée de la Suisse. Lausanne, 1933

Sorell, W.: The Swiss. New York, 1972

Wandel, L. P.: Voracious Idols and Violent Hands: Iconoclasm in Reformation Zurich,
Strasbourg and Basel. Cambridge, 1994

Weninger, B.: Der Basilisk. Gossau, 2001

Houses and Parks

Botanical Gardens Brüglingen, Christoph Merian Stiftung, von Hans Rudolf Heyer. Bern, 1977

Public Parks and Gardens in Basle. Basel, 1973

Das Wildt'sche Haus am Petersplatz zu Basel: Denkschrift. Basel, 1955

Museum Catalogues

Butts, B. and Hendrix, L.: Painting on Light, Drawings and Stained Glass in the Age of Dürer
and Holbein, J. Paul Getty Museum in collaboration with The Saint Louis Art Museum.
Los Angeles, 2000.

Der Dom zu Bamberg by W. Zeissner. Strasbourg, 1997

Historical Museum Basel: Guide to the Collections. 1994

Historical Museum Basel. Basel, 1990

Kunstmuseum Basel by Christian Geelhaar. Zurich; Basel, 1992

Others

Bank for International Settlements 1930-1980, published on the occasion of the 50th anniversary of the BIS. Basel, 1980

Basler Zeitung, Various articles

Brönnimann, R.: Basler Bauten 1860-1910. Basel, 1973

Brönnimann, R.: Villen des Historismus in Basel. Basel, 1982

Brönnimann, R.: Industriebauten 1850-1930. Basel, 1990

Columbia Encyclopedia, 6th edition. New York, 2001

Cundall, J: Hans Holbein, (from "Holbein und seine Zeit" by A. Woltmann). London, 1892

Encyclopedia Britannica, 1973

Holbein, H.: The Dance of Death. New York, 1971

INSA, Inventar der neueren Schweizer Architektur 1850–1920. Band. 2: Basel, Bellinzona, Bern. Bern 1986

McPhee, J.: La Place de la Concorde Suisse. New York, 1983/84

Platter, The Beggar and the Professor: a 16th century family saga, by Le Roy Ladurie, Emmanuel, translated by Arthur Goldhammer. Chicago and London, 1998

Photo Credits

We express our gratitude to all individuals, firms and institutions who have granted permission and reproduction rights for the images which appear in *Basel: A Cultural Experience*. We have jointly undertaken, in the words of G.B. Shaw, to "give credit where credit is due" and in as accurate and complete a manner as possible. We apologize for any oversights.

5 Staatssiegel von Basel
Historisches Museum Basel,
Photo: HMB Maurice Babey

6 Basilisk at the City Hall
Photo: Christian Lienhard

8 Wilde Leute auf dem 'Flachsland-
teppich', Basel um 1468
Historisches Museum Basel
Photo: HMB Maurice Babey

13 Illustration: Cornelia Ziegler
after a map from 'Verein Verkehrsdrehscheibe Schweiz'

15 Wandbild 'Das alte Kaufhaus' von
Burkhard Mangold, 1910,
Hauptpost, Freie Strasse 12
Basler Denkmalpflege
Photo: Eric Schmidt
Lauertanne
Verein Verkehrsdrehscheibe Schweiz

16 Emigrants departing from Schifflände,
1805; Daniel Burckhardt-Werthemann:
'Vom alten Basel und seinen Gästen'
Friedrich Reinhardt AG, Basel
Schiff 'Dom van Utrecht'
Verein Verkehrsdrehscheibe Schweiz

18 The Old Middle Bridge as seen from
Rheinsprung, 1858, Louis Dubois,
Water Color, 1858, private collection

21 Image of hydro-electric plant and
locks, Kraftwerk Birsfelden AG

22 Photo: Christian Lienhard

23 Swimming in the Rhine, detail,
Staatsarchiv Basel-Stadt, Bild 1/1060
Photo: Franco Meneghetti

25 Former Spalengraben with deer
Daniel Burckhardt-Werthemann
'Vom alten Basel und seinen Gästen'
Friedrich Reinhardt AG, Basel
Schloss Wildenstein

Photo: Christian Lienhard

26 The former open Birsig River
J.J. Schneider in 'Das Alte Basel'
by courtesy of Ségal Antiquités

30 Wettstein Bridge, Postcard, c.1900

32 Photos: Christian Lienhard

38 Basilisk mit dem Wappen der Stadt
Meister D.S. (tätig um 1501/1511
in Basel), Kunstmuseum Basel,
Kupferstichkabinett
Photo: Kunstmuseum Basel

39 Illustration: Cornelia Ziegler
Adaptation of 'Celtic Feast'
by Mark Adrian

41 Kugelflasche
2. Hälfte 2. Jh bis 1. Hälfte 1. Jh v. Chr.
Fundort: Gasfabrik Basel
Historisches Museum Basel
Photo: HMB Peter Portner

46 Underground well house
Kaiseraugst Silver Treasure
Römerstadt Augusta Raurica, Augst

47 Roman Road, Photo: Shirley Kearney

48 Zwiebelknopffibel mit breitem Fuss
und Bügel, Aeschenvorstadt, Grab 379
4/5. Jh., Historisches Museum Basel
Photo: HMB Maurice Babey

49 Büstenreliquiar der Hl. Ursula aus dem
Basler Münsterschatz, 14. Jh.
Historisches Museum Basel
Photo: HMB Maurice Babey

50 Photo: Christian Lienhard

51 Arnold Böcklin, Die Pest, 1898
Inv. Nr. 114, Gefirnisste Tempera auf
Tannenholz, 149,5 x 104,5 cm
Kunstmuseum Basel, Depositum der
Gottfried Keller-Stiftung
Kunstmuseum Basel
Photo: Martin Bühler

Photo: Franco Meneghetti

206 Niklaus Stoecklin,
private collection, Basel
Photo: Maria Gambino

207 Das Rathaus in Basel
gezeichnet von C. Guise, Lithographie
von R. Rey, Hasler & Cie, Basel,
1833/1858
Universitätsbibliothek Basel

208 Photo: Christian Lienhard

209 Stachelschützenhaus
J.J. Schneider: 'Das alte Basel'

211 Photo: Christian Lienhard

213 Stiftung Wildt'sches Haus, Basel

214: Photo: Christian Lienhard

215 Three Kings Hotel
J.J. Schneider: 'Das alte Basel'

217 French railway station at St. Johann
J.J. Schneider: 'Das alte Basel'

218 Postcard, 1913

219 Goetheanum, Dornach

223 Photo: Christian Lienhard

225 Angel, Photo: Kevin J. Kearney

230 Dirk's Pod

Courtesy of Novartis
Granite Sculpture
Courtesy Basler Versicherungs-
gesellschaft

232 Ellsworth Kelly, White Curves, 2001
Welded aluminium and stainless steel
plate. 234 x 131 7/8 x 49 1/2 inches
(594.4 x 335 x 125.7 cm)
Weight: 6250 lbs, EK 903
© Ellsworth Kelly
Fondation Beyeler Riehen/Basel

235 Photo: Christian Lienhard

236 Photo: Dr. Jörg Hess, Basel

237 Photo: Joseph Zimmermann, Basel

238 Photos: Dr. Jörg Hess, Basel

240 Photos: Dr. Jörg Hess, Basel

241 Photos: Dr. Jörg Hess, Basel

252 Photo: Christian Lienhard

265 Basler Fahne
Historisches Museum Basel

All original artwork: Cornelia Ziegler
All other photos: Klaus Brodhage

271